Lecture Notes in Computer Science 4396

Commenced Publication in 1973
Founding and Former Series Editors:
Gerhard Goos, Juris Hartmanis, and Jan van Leeuwen

Jorge García-Vidal
Llorenç Cerdà-Alabern (Eds.)

Wireless Systems and Mobility in Next Generation Internet

Third International Workshop
of the EURO-NGI Network of Excellence
Sitges, Spain, June 6-9, 2006
Revised Selected Papers

 Springer

Volume Editors

Jorge García-Vidal
Llorenç Cerdà-Alabern
Polytechnic University of Catalonia
Computer Architecture Department
Jordi Girona 1-3, 08034 Barcelona, Spain
E-mail: {jorge, llorenc}@ac.upc.edu

Library of Congress Control Number: 2007920934

CR Subject Classification (1998): C.2, H.4, H.3

LNCS Sublibrary: SL 5 – Computer Communication Networks and
Telecommunications

ISSN   0302-9743
ISBN-10   3-540-70968-1 Springer Berlin Heidelberg New York
ISBN-13   978-3-540-70968-8 Springer Berlin Heidelberg New York

Springer is a part of Springer Science+Business Media

springer.com

© Springer-Verlag Berlin Heidelberg 2007

Typesetting: Camera-ready by author, data conversion by Scientific Publishing Services, Chennai, India
Printed on acid-free paper   SPIN: 12022311   06/3142   5 4 3 2 1 0

Preface

The Network of Excellence on Next-Generation Internet (EuroNGI) is a European project funded by the European Union within the IST Sixth Framework Program. The target of the EuroNGI network is to put together European research centers in the networking field, focusing on next-generation Internet design and engineering. Sixty partners from technical universities and research centers in Europe participated in EuroNGI.

One of the *integration activities* inside EuroNGI consists of the organization of an annual workshop on "Wireless and Mobility." The workshop intends to bring together leading researchers from the Network of Excellence in this field of research in order to identify the fundamental challenges and future perspective of this important area.

This post-proceedings volume contains a selection of 19 research contributions presented at the third edition of the Workshop on Wireless and Mobility. The workshop was held during June 6-9, 2006 in the village of Sitges, Spain, organized by CompNet Research Group from the Technical University of Catalonia (http://research.ac.upc.edu/CompNet). The previous editions of the workshop were organized by Aachen University in Dagstuhl (Germany) and by Politechnico di Milano in Lago di Como (Italy).

To participate in the workshop, the authors submitted an extended abstract of their ongoing work in the field of wireless and mobility. Twenty-six papers were presented and discussed in the workshop. Following the discussions and suggestions made in the workshop, the authors submitted a full paper that was carefully reviewed by experts in the field. Finally, accepted papers incorporated the numerous referee comments producing the final version published in this book.

The papers contained in this book provide a general view of the ongoing research on wireless and mobility in the European Union, and address many of the problems currently investigated in this area.

December 2006

Llorenç Cerdà-Alabern
Jorge García-Vidal

Organization

Reviewers

Andrés-Colás, Jorge
Bruneel, Herwig
Casares-Giner, Vicente
Casetti, Claudio
Cesana, Matteo
De Meer, Hermann
De Turck, Koen
Deepak, Sarath
Fiedler, Markus
Fratta, Luigi
Helvik, Bjarne E.
Ibrahim, Ismail Khalil
Jensen, Terje
Laevens, Koenraad

Menth, Michael
Mäder, Andreas
Norros, Ilkka
Núñez-Queija, Rudesindo
Pries, Rastin
Tan, Hwee Pink
Tran-Gia, Phuoc
Tutschku, Kurt
Van De Velde, Erwin
Villen-Altamirano, Manuel
Voorhaen, Michael
Welzl, Michael
Wüchner, Patrick

Table of Contents

WLAN Characterization

Vehicular Networks

WLAN and Sensor Networks Protocols

QoS and Routing in Ad-Hoc Networks

Heterogeneous Networks

Resource Management in Cellular Networks

TCP in Wireless

Mobility Agents

Performance Analysis of Wireless Multihop Data Networks

Nidhi Hegde[1] and Alexandre Proutiere[2]

[1] France Telecom R&D
38-40 rue du Général Leclerc, 92794 Issy-les-Moulineaux, France
[2] Royal Institute of Technology
Electrum 418, SE-164 40 Kista, Sweden
nidhi.hegde@rd.francetelecom.com, Alexandre.Proutiere@ens.fr

Abstract. We consider wireless multihop data networks with random multi-access mechanisms at the MAC layer. In general, our aim is to study the performance as perceived by users in a dynamic setting where data flows are generated randomly by users and cease upon completion. This task comprises two major difficulties: first, the behavior of random multi-access algorithms at slot-level in a multi-hop network is even more complex than in the case of a single hop hotspot. Second, in order to study user-level performance accounting for a dynamic population of flows, one has to first characterize the so-called rate region when the population is fixed. The rate region is defined by the set of rates at which the various active users can generate packets without inducing any instabilities in the network. Since links interact with each other through interference, characterizing the rate region is as difficult as studying the behavior of a set of interacting queues. In addition, the behavior of the congestion control algorithm must be taken into account since it impacts the set of active links and thus the interference. We propose a model, based on the so-called mean field approach, that circumvents both difficulties and allows the derivation of explicit expressions for the rate region.

1   Introduction

An emerging solution to expand network access to poorly-served or highly-loaded areas is to extend WLAN coverage. The additional WLAN access points are then connected to wired Internet gateways through wireless links to other access points or relays, creating wireless multi-hop networks with increasingly decentralized architectures. A fundamental problem is characterizing the performance of such networks, with an aim of creating decentralized algorithms that optimize performance.

We consider wireless multihop data networks with some random access mechanism at the MAC layer. Our focus is the performance as perceived by users, for example the time to transfer a data flow in a dynamic setting, where users begin finite-sized data transfers and cease transfers upon completion. A basic requirement is that the transfer times remain finite, meaning that the network should

J. García-Vidal and L. Cerdà-Alabern (Eds.): Wireless and Mobility, LNCS 4396, pp. 1–11, 2007.

be stable, that is, buffers should not overflow. We characterize the rate region, that is, the set of rates at which the active users can generate packets, such that the network is stable. In the case of wired networks or wireless networks with scheduling coordination, the performance has been extensively studied both at packet (i.e., when the number of active users is fixed) and at flow levels, see [1], [2] and references therein. Characterizing the performance of wireless networks with random multi-access algorithms presents additional challenges due to the interaction of several protocol layers. Slot-level contentions determine channel access, these transmission opportunities in turn determine packet-level rates, and this has an impact on the flow completion times.

At the slot-level, the set of active links, those with packets to transmit in the corresponding buffer, is fixed. The aim is to determine the instantaneous capacity of each link depending on the scheduling algorithm. There are two broad classes of algorithms: scheduling with coordination, and scheduling without coordination. With coordination, nodes are scheduled in a way that only non-interfering transmissions are allowed at any time. Without coordination, each node uses a random access mechanism, such as Aloha-type and IEEE 802.11 CSMA-based mechanism, to determine its transmission times. When all links interfere with each other, slot-level performance is well understood, see for example Bianchi's analysis [3] of the CSMA/CA algorithm. For the case where all links do not interfere with each other, there are few works on slot-level performance.

Previous literature on random-access multihop networks focus on slotted or unslotted Aloha and seek channel attempt probabilities that satisfy certain constraints. For Aloha-type schemes Kar et al [4] and Gupta and Stolyar [5] derive the attempt probabilities corresponding to proportional fairness, i.e., the probabilities such that the sum of the log of link throughputs is maximized. They also present distributed algorithms to achieve these probabilities. In [6] Wang and Kar identify attempt probabilities that realize max-min fairness. Furthermore, previous work considered saturated conditions where users always have a packet to transmit. Here we propose a general model for the analysis of the slot-level behavior for various types of random multi-access algorithms including those mentioned above. In addition, we do not consider saturated conditions and characterize the proportion of time a user may be active, which may depend on the congestion control mechanism implemented.

At the packet level the aim is to characterize the rate region when the number of active flows on each route is fixed. The rate region is defined by the set of feasible rates of the various flow classes - by feasible we mean that all buffers in the network must remain stable. The rate region strongly depends on the slot-level scheduling policy. When node transmissions are coordinated by a central scheduler, characterizing the rate region is fairly straightforward because the scheduler avoids interference. Scheduling coordination leads to the largest rate region possible, however is difficult to realize in a distributed way. An interesting approach is maximal scheduling, which has a distributed implementation. However, it may imply a large reduction of the rate region [7]. Without scheduling coordination, interfering nodes may attempt the channel simultaneously. In this case, characterizing the rate region is not trivial because the transmission rate of a link depends on the probabilities that the interfering links are active. At the packet level the network behaves as a set of interacting queues whose stability is largely unknown [8], [9], [10]. An additional difficulty in characterizing the rate region is that the behavior of the congestion control algorithm must be taken into consideration. Indeed, since the link capacities depend on the buffer contents of interfering links, the congestion control algorithm has a strong impact on the rate region. The greedy behavior of congestion control algorithms implies that along each route there is always one saturated buffer. We will show that this tends to reduce the rate region. The main contributions of this paper is to provide approximate expressions for the rate region, based on the mean field approach, and evaluate the impact of congestion control algorithms.

In the next section we present our model and discuss the impact of congestion control in wired networks. We describe the slot-level dynamics and the rate region at the packet level for centralized algorithms in Section 3 and for distributed algorithms in Section 4. In Section 5 we characterize the rate regions for some examples and we conclude in Section 6.

2   Model

2.1   Network Topology and Interference

We consider a network consisting of a set of nodes $\mathcal{N}$ and a set of links $\mathcal{L}$. We assume each node has a single outgoing link. This is a valid assumption for linear networks and networks based on a tree structure where traffic is aggregated at each point and there is a single path to a gateway node. A link may be present only between nodes that are within each other's transmission range. For a transmission on a given link l, another link k is an interfering link if link k's simultaneous transmission would 'collide' with link l's transmission and thus cancel it. Link k then interferes with link l if the source node of link k and the destination node of link l are within transmission range of each other. Furthermore a node cannot receive and transmit at the same time. We denote by $\mathcal{L}_l$ the set of links that interfere with a transmission on link l, more specifically, links that interfere with reception at the destination node of link l. This model of interference is often referred to as the exclusion model in the literature; it simplifies the analysis and the design of efficient distributed scheduling algorithms.

Remark 1. *The set of interfering links will in general depend not only on physical distances between nodes, but also to some extent on the random access mechanism in use. For example, the RTS/CTS virtual reservation scheme in IEEE 802.11 access mechanisms aims to avoid collisions due to so-called 'hidden nodes'. In doing so, it requires a larger set of nodes to be silent for a given transmission and thus increases the set of interfering links for a given link.*

2.2 Scheduling Algorithms

We assume that time is slotted, and for the sake of simplicity, that the duration of packet transmission is equal to the slot length. At each time slot, a scheduler decides which links are going to be activated. This decision can be done in a centralized manner, or in a distributed manner as in WLANs, mesh, and ad-hoc networks. Important examples of distributed scheduling schemes are random multi-access algorithms, such as Aloha or CSMA. We are particularly interested here in distributed algorithms since we believe that a distributed solution ensures the scalability and rapid growth of a network. However, we will present performance results with centralized scheduling for the sake of comparison.

2.3 The Rate Region

In the present paper we restrict the analysis to packet-level performance. We assume that packets are categorized into K classes according to their route in the network. The routes are further assumed to be fixed. We denote by r_k the route of packets of class k, i.e., the set of links traversed by class-k flows. In general we are interested in deriving the rate region of the network, i.e., the set of vectors representing the rates at which the packets of the various classes can be generated without inducing instability in the network. In the following we denote by ϕ_k the rate in bit/s generated by packets of class k.

2.4 The Impact of Congestion Control

In addition to scheduling decisions, the transfers of data packets are operated under the control of TCP that defines the packet rates of sources, i.e., it defines the rates ϕ_k. This protocol adapts the source rates only through the experienced packet losses in the network. In wired networks where it can be assumed that packet losses occur only because of buffer overflow, TCP exhibits what we call a *greedy behavior*. This means that there is always at least one saturated link along each route r_k (because otherwise TCP would increase the corresponding source rate). In the wireless networks we consider, we also assume that packet losses are mainly due to buffer overflow. The greedy behavior of TCP must then be taken into account in deriving the rate region.

We now present a simple network example to illustrate the impact of the greedy behavior of TCP on the rate region. Consider the wired network depicted in Figure 1. When we do not account for the greedy behavior of TCP the rate region is the set of $\phi = (\phi_1, \phi_2)$ such that $\phi_1 + \phi_2 \leq C_1$ and $\phi_2 \leq C_2$. Note that we should take strict inequalities to ensure buffer stability. However as explained below, it is more convenient to define the rate region as the closure of the set of achievable vectors ϕ. When accounting for the greedy behavior of TCP, there must be at least one saturated buffer along each route, which means in our example that both buffers are saturated. In this case, the rate region reduces to the set of vectors ϕ such that $\phi_1 + \phi_2 = C_1$ and $\phi_2 = C_2$.

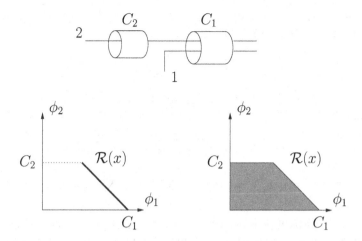

Fig. 1. A wired tree network and the corresponding rate regions accounting (left) or not (right) for the greedy behavior of TCP

In wired networks in general, without the greedy behavior of TCP, the rate region is the smallest coordinate convex[1] set containing the rate region obtained with the greedy behavior of TCP. As a consequence, this behavior does not really impact the user-level performance as explained in [2]. On the contrary, in the case of wireless networks with distributed scheduling, we will show that this may have a strong impact on the performance as perceived by users.

To summarize we give the definition of the rate region: it is the set of achievable rate vectors $\phi = (\phi_1, \ldots, \phi_K)$, where achievable means that ϕ is such that under the considered scheduling algorithm:

(i) All buffers are stable or at the stability limit;
(ii) ϕ is greedy in the sense that at least one buffer on each route is saturated.

3 Rate Region: Centralized Scheduling

Assume here that there is a central scheduler choosing at each slot the set of links that should transmit. The chosen set should always be optimal in the sense that it is not possible to add a new link that has packets in its buffer to this set without adding interference to one of the links already in the set. Denote by $\mathcal{P}$ the set of optimal link sets and by P its cardinality. A link l may belong to different optimal link sets, we denote by $\mathcal{P}_l$ this set of optimal sets. Further denote by $\mathcal{T}$ the set of vectors $\tau = (\tau_1, \ldots, \tau_P)$ such that $\tau_p \geq 0$, and $\sum_{p=1}^{P} \tau_p = 1$. Here τ_p may be interpreted as the fraction of time the link set p is scheduled. Note finally that in this setting, a link may be scheduled even if the corresponding

---

[1] A set $\mathcal{Y} \subset \mathbb{R}_+^K$ is coordinate convex iff $\forall y = (y_1, \ldots, y_K) \in \mathcal{Y}$ then $(z_1, \ldots, z_K) \in \mathcal{Y}$ for all $z_i \leq y_i$.

buffer is empty. Then the scheduling $\tau \in \mathcal{T}$ is compatible with the packet-level traffic $\phi = (\phi_1, \ldots, \phi_K)$ only if for any link l, we have:

$$\sum_{k:l\in r_k} \phi_k \leq \sum_{p\in \mathcal{P}_l} \tau_p.$$

Now the rate regions considering the greedy behavior of TCP or not are given by the following:

$$\mathcal{R}^{TCP} = \{\phi : \exists \tau \in \mathcal{T} : \forall l, \sum_{k:l\in r_k} \phi_k = \sum_{p\in \mathcal{P}_l} \tau_p\},$$

$$\mathcal{R} = \{\phi : \exists \tau \in \mathcal{T} : \forall l, \sum_{k:l\in r_k} \phi_k \leq \sum_{p\in \mathcal{P}_l} \tau_p\}.$$

The above result was first proved by Tassiulas and Ephremides [11] in a much more general context. Note that the rate regions are in general convex, and that $\mathcal{R}$ is obtained as the smallest convex and coordinate convex set containing $\mathcal{R}^{TCP}$. In case of centralized scheduling, the situation is very close to that of wired networks.

4   Rate Region: Distributed Scheduling

In the absence of scheduling coordination, it is impossible in general to exactly characterize the packet-level stability condition, and then to derive the rate region. As mentioned above, this is due to the fact that the capacity of a particular link depends on buffer contents of interfering links. We now present a heuristic based on mean field asymptotics that allow us to circumvent this problem.

4.1   Slot-Level Dynamics

Consider a random multi-access algorithm such as Aloha or CSMA. In order to determine the traffic that link l can handle, we must infer the stationary probability p_l that link l attempts to use the channel. To do so, we apply the mean field approach, first implicitly introduced by Bianchi [3] and recently theoretically justified [12]. This approach assumes that in order to compute the probability p_l, we can consider that the behavior of link l depends on that of the interfering links only through a constant stationary collision probability c_l. This assumption then provides a formula relating p_l and c_l:

$$p_l = F_l(c_l). \tag{1}$$

For Aloha-type multi-access algorithms, the functions F_l are constants. For IEEE 802.11 algorithms, Bianchi identified this function for all links l as follows:

$$F_l(c) = \frac{2(1-2c)}{(CW+1)(1-2c) + CW \times c(1-(2c)^m)},$$

where CW and m are parameters of the 802.11 backoff mechanism.

Remark 2. *Note that in the latter case, the assumption that the time to transmit a packet is one slot, is crucial. Indeed, Bianchi's analysis consists in modelling the behavior of one link via a Markov chain representing the corresponding backoff at the instants of a point process. These instants correspond to the end of empty slots, packet transmissions, and collisions. For the analysis to be valid, all links must share the same point process. This implies that either all links interfere with each other, which is not necessarily true here, or that the duration of a packet transmission or of a collision are equal to that of an empty slot.*

For any link m, let a_m denote the proportion of time link m is active, that is, has a packet to transmit. Then the collision probability for link l is given by:

$$c_l = 1 - \prod_{m \in \mathcal{L}(x) \cap \mathcal{L}_l} (1 - a_m p_m). \tag{2}$$

Remark 3. *Our model differs from that of Bianchi in how the interference set $\mathcal{L}_l$ is defined. We have defined this set in Section 2.1 from the perspective of the destination node of link l. Thus, this set includes all links k such that the destination node of link l is in the transmission range of the source node of link k. The set then includes so-called* hidden nodes *that are sensed by the receiver but not by the transmitter. Therefore, while the form of (2) is similar to Bianchi's analysis, the collision probability here is calculated over a set of links defined appropriately for a mesh network.*

4.2 Packet-Level Dynamics

To complete the model, we now must infer the proportion of time each link is active, i.e., we compute the a_l's. Assume here that packets of class k are emitted at rate ϕ_k. Then when the rate vector ϕ is achievable, the quantities (a_l, p_l, c_l) are determined using (1), (2), and following conservation laws, for all $l \in \mathcal{L}(x)$ we have the following:

$$\sum_{k: l \in r_k} \phi_k = a_l p_l (1 - c_l). \tag{3}$$

In the above model, under the packet-level traffic $\phi = (\phi_1, \ldots, \phi_K)$ the network is stable only if the system of equations (1)-(2)-(3) has a unique solution such that for all links l, $a_l, p_l, c_l \in [0, 1]$. Note that the mean field approach alleviates the two main difficulties in evaluating the performance of mesh networks, namely the interaction between the backoff processes at the various links and the impact of buffer contents of interfering links on the capacity of a given link.

Finally, using the mean field heuristic, we are able to characterize the rate region. The conditions (i) and (ii) are (see Section 2):

$$\forall l \in \mathcal{L}(x), \exists p_l, c_l, a_l \in [0:1] \text{ satisfying (1), (2), and (3),} \tag{4}$$

$$\forall k, \exists l \in r_k : a_l = 1. \tag{5}$$

Now the rate regions with or without the greedy behavior of TCP are given by:

$$\mathcal{R}^{TCP} = \{\phi : (4),(5) \text{ are satisfied}\}. \tag{6}$$

$$\mathcal{R} = \{\phi : (4) \text{ is satisfied}\}. \tag{7}$$

5   Examples

5.1   Impact of the Greedy Behavior of the Congestion Control Algorithm

In wireless networks with no scheduling coordination, the greedy behavior of TCP can result in a significant reduction in the rate region. To illustrate this, consider a simple network composed of two interfering links depicted in Figure 2. There are 2 classes of flows, class-1 (resp. class-2) flows use link 1 (resp. 2) only.

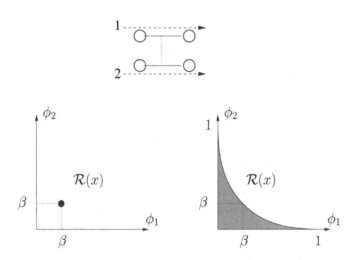

Fig. 2. The two-link network and the corresponding rate region when $x_1, x_2 > 0$ accounting (left) or not (right) for the greedy behavior of TCP - $\beta \approx 0.24$. When representing networks, links are solid lines, a dotted line between two links indicates interfering links.

Let us investigate the rate region when $x_1, x_2 > 0$. If the congestion control algorithm is greedy, then we know that both buffers will be saturated and as a consequence, the rate region reduces to a single point $\phi = (p_1(1-p_2), p_2(1-p_1))$ where p_1, p_2 satisfies $p_1 = F_1(p_2)$ and $p_2 = F_2(p_1)$. Now if the congestion control is not greedy, the buffers may not always be saturated, and the set of rates at which the network can operate is then given by:

$$\mathcal{R}(x) = \{\phi : \exists p_1, p_2, a_1, a_2 \in [0 : 1],$$
$$\phi_1 = a_1 p_1(1 - a_2 p_2), \phi_2 = a_2 p_2(1 - a_1 p_1),$$
$$p_1 = F_1(a_2 p_2), p_2 = F_2(a_1 p_1)\}.$$

The rate region for both cases is shown in Figure 2 for the MAC algorithm DCF used in IEEE 802.11. The reduction of the rate region due to the greedy behavior of TCP is much more important here than in the case of wired networks. In this example, the rate region is reduced to a single point.

5.2 Further Examples

We now present numerical examples of rate regions, accounting for greedy congestion control, for simple networks running the IEEE 802.11 DCF algorithm with $CW = 4$. If the network reduces to a single link and a single flow class, the achievable rate is then $r_0 = 0.4$. When the network has two links with a single class going

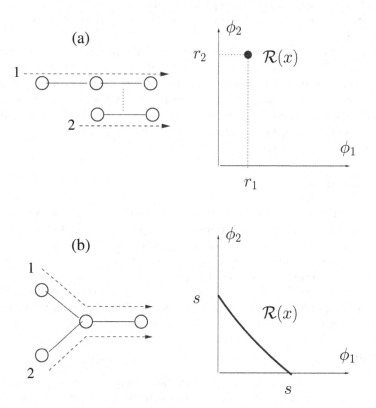

Fig. 3. Left: network topologies. Right: the corresponding rate regions when $x_1, x_2 > 0$; $r_1 \approx 0.08$, $r_2 \approx 0.29$, and $s \approx 0.2$.

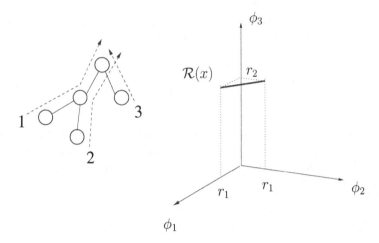

Fig. 4. A tree network and the corresponding rate region when $x_1, x_2, x_3 > 0$

through both links, the achievable rate is s around 0.2. In Figure 3, two networks with two flow classes and the corresponding rate regions are presented.

In Figure 4 a tree network with 3 flow classes and its rate region when $x_1, x_2, x_3 > 0$ is given.

Having characterized the rate regions of such networks, we are able to study the flow-level performance. Note that unlike wired networks where the rate regions are convex, the rate regions for wireless networks with distributed scheduling may be arbitrary. This has important implications on the flow-level performance, as shown in [13]. We leave the study of flow-level performance for the networks considered here for future work, but note that for the case of two flow-classes, this is characterized explicitly in [13].

6   Conclusion

We have presented an integrated slot and packet-level model based on the mean field approach that allows explicit approximate expressions for the rate region of wireless multi-hop data networks. These expressions may then used to evaluate the flow-level performance of the network. The analysis demonstrates that for networks with random access algorithms, the rate region can in general have an arbitrary shape and that may in particular be non-convex. Furthermore, this region may be significantly reduced due to the greedy behavior of the congestion control algorithm.

References

1. Georgiadis, L., Neely, M., Tassiulas, L.: Resource allocation and cross-layer control in wireless networks. Foundations and Trends in Networking **1**(1) (2006) 1–144
2. Bonald, T., Massoulie, L., Proutiere, A., Virtamo, J.: A queueing analysis of max-min fairness, proportional fairness and balanced fairness. Queueing Systems (2006)

3. Bianchi, G.: Performance analysis of the IEEE 802.11 distributed coordination function. IEEE Journal on Selected Areas in Communications **18**(3) (2000) 535–547
4. Kar, K., Sarkar, S., Tassiulas, L.: Achieving proportionally fair rates using local information in aloha networks. IEEE Transactions on Automatic Control **49**(10) (2004) 1858–1862
5. Gupta, P., Stolyar, A.: Optimal throughput allocation in general random-access networks. In: Proceedings of the Conference on Information Systems and Sciences (CISS). (2006)
6. Wang, X., Kar, K.: Distributed algorithms for max-min fair rate allocation in aloha networks. In: Proceedings of the 42nd Annual Allerton Conference. (2004)
7. Chaporkar, P., Kar, K., Sarkar, S.: Throughput guarantees through maximal scheduling in wireless networks. In: proceedings of the 43nd Annual Allerton Conference. (2005)
8. Luo, W., Ephremides, A.: Stability of n interacting queues in random-access systems. IEEE trans. on Information Theory **45**(5) (1999) 1579–1587
9. Szpankowski, W.: Stability conditions for some multiqueue distributed systems: Buffered random access systems. Advances in Applied Probability **26** (1994) 498–515
10. Bonald, T., Borst, S., Hegde, N., Proutiere, A.: Wireless data performance in multi-cell scenarios. In: Proceedings of ACM Sigmetrics. (2004)
11. Tassiulas, L., Ephremides, A.: Stability properties of constrained queueing systems and scheduling policies for maximum throughput in multi-hop radio networks. IEEE Transactions on Automatic Control (1992) 1936–1948
12. Bordenave, C., McDonald, D., Proutière, A.: Random multi-access algorithms: A mean field analysis. In: Proceedings of Allerton conference. (2005)
13. Bonald, T., Proutiere, A.: Flow-level stability of utility-based allocations on non-convex rate region. In: Proceedings of the Conference on Information Systems and Sciences (CISS). (2006)

On the Shaping Introduced by IEEE 802.11 Nodes in Long-Range Dependent Traffic

David Rincón[1], David Remondo[1], and Cristina Cano[2]

[1] Technical University of Catalonia (UPC)
Av. Canal Olímpic s/n, Castelldefels - 08860 Barcelona, Spain
drincon@entel.upc.edu, remondo@mat.upc.edu
[2] Pompeu Fabra University (UPF)
Pg. de Circumval·lació, 8 - 08003 Barcelona, Spain
cristina.cano@upf.edu

Abstract. Fractal or scaling phenomena, such as self-similarity and long-range dependence, have been detected in network traffic, with important implications for network performance. This paper describes how the characteristics of traffic change when it traverses IEEE 802.11 networks. First, a simple, unidirectional traffic scenario with two nodes has been simulated. This scenario and two more general situations that include the hidden node situation and the effect of relaying (which appears in multihop communications) have been replicated in a real testbed. The most significant results are the smoothing effect of the MAC mechanisms on the traffic at the highest frequencies, while at the lowest frequencies a mitigation of fractality seems to be caused by packet loss induced by propagation impairments, with an overall effect of mitigation of the scaling characteristics on the output traffic. On the other hand, the scenarios with traffic aggregation show an increase of fractality.

1 Introduction

Network traffic exhibits some fractal or scaling properties, such as self-similarity, long-range dependence (LRD) or multifractality [1,2]. Roughly speaking, this means that network traffic presents similar behavior at different time scales. The scaling properties of traffic have important implications on network performance, such as an increase of buffer overflow probability when compared with traditional traffic models such as Poisson arrival processes [3]. This paper addresses the influence of medium access control (MAC) mechanisms and propagation impairments on the traffic characteristics when long-range dependent traffic traverses IEEE 802.11 links. This is relevant not only by itself, but also because the traffic shaping performed by 802.11 access nodes may influence the performance of backbone networks, given the general evolution towards a heterogeneous network scenario.

In a previous study [4,5] the authors attacked the problem with a simulation-based approach, using the `ns-2` simulator [6]. Though the results were coherent with those obtained by other authors, the inherent limitations of the simulator

J. García-Vidal and L. Cerdà-Alabern (Eds.): Wireless and Mobility, LNCS 4396, pp. 12–28, 2007.

encouraged us to deploy real scenarios with IEEE 802.11 nodes working in different physical environments. For these experiments, a real traffic generator with LRD properties has been used. The results have been analyzed at the application layer in order to determine the influence of all the mechanisms involved. In each scenario we compare the statistical properties of input traffic with those found at intermediate nodes and at the output.

The paper is organized as follows: Section 2 introduces the topic of LRD in network traffic and its estimation. Section 3 describes the work done by other authors related to the fractal features present in Wireless Local Area Networks (WLANs). Section 4 contains an overview of IEEE 802.11, with special emphasis on the delays introduced by MAC mechanisms. Section 5 describes the scenarios, whose results are presented in Section 6. Section 7 concludes the paper and describes future research topics.

2   LRD in Network Traffic

2.1   Long-Range Dependence

A stationary stochastic process is considered long-range dependent (LRD) if its autocorrelation function decays at a rate slower than a negative exponential [2]. In the frequency domain, an LRD process $x(n)$ follows a $1/f$-like spectrum around the origin:

$$S_x(f) \sim \frac{c_f}{|f|^\alpha} \quad \text{when} \quad |f| \to 0 \tag{1}$$

The parameters of LRD are α and c_f. The scaling parameter α is related to the intensity of the LRD phenomenon (a qualitative measure) and is usually expressed as the Hurst parameter $H = (1 + \alpha)/2$, while c_f has dimensions of variance and can be interpreted as a quantitative measure of LRD [7]. H ranges from 0.5, which corresponds to a non-correlated process (such as the memoryless Poisson process) to 1.0 (a highly-correlated process).

2.2   LRD in Network Traffic

The LRD property has been found in several traffic measurements, both at the single source and aggregated (backbone) levels. For example, single sources of variable bit rate (VBR) video usually show a high degree of LRD, whereas on-off sources with Pareto-distributed sojourn times are LRD only when several sources are aggregated [2]. LRD is related to the well known traffic burstiness (long bursts of packets followed by long silences). The novelty is that bursts appear at some range of time scales instead of just at a certain characteristic scale. This property makes LRD sources to have a higher buffer loss probability than classical models (such as Poisson processes) for the same traffic load [3].

2.3   Estimating LRD with the Discrete Wavelet Transform

The Discrete Wavelet Transform (DWT) is a powerful tool for a fast, efficient and precise estimation of LRD parameters. For a discrete-time signal $x(n)$, we denote the coefficients of the DWT by the inner product of $x(n)$ and $\psi_{j,k}$,

$$d_x(j,k) = \langle x, \psi_{j,k} \rangle \tag{2}$$

where $\psi_{j,k}$ is a function (usually with finite support), and j and k are the scale and the location where the analysis is performed, respectively. The basis of the decomposition is a family of translated and dilated versions of the *mother wavelet* ψ_0,

$$\psi_{j,k}(n) = 2^{-j/2}\psi_0(2^{-j}n - k) \quad \text{for} \quad j = 1 \ldots J, \quad k \in \mathcal{Z} \tag{3}$$

An intuitive interpretation of the DWT is a cascade of quadrature-mirror low-pass and high-pass filters ($h(n)$ and $g(n)$, respectively), where the output of the high-pass filter (the details of the signal) are the coefficients of the DWT at scale j, while the output of the low-pass filter (the approximation of the signal) is filtered iteratively (see Figure 1). Downsampling maintains orthogonality by halving the coefficients at the output of each filter. The output of the DWT can be understood as a multiresolution analysis (MRA) in which the original signal is decomposed into a low-pass approximation at scale J, $a_x(J,k)$, and a set of high-pass details $d_x(j,k)$ for each scale $j = 1 \ldots J$.

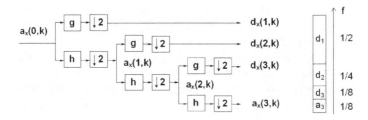

Fig. 1. *Left*: The DWT as filter bank for a level 3 decomposition. *Right*: The subbands of the normalized spectrum, with the approximation a_3 and details $d_{1\ldots3}$.

2.4   Wavelet-Based Analysis of LRD Signals

Abry and Veitch developed the LogScale diagram (LD) [7], an unbiased and efficient estimator of the LRD parameters. It consists on the computation of the sample variance of the coefficients at each subband of the DWT decomposition, μ_j, as an estimation of the power of the original signal at those subbands. Since the signal follows the power-law, μ_j verifies the following expression:

$$\mu_j = E[d_x^2(j,k)] = 2^{j\alpha}c_f C(\alpha, \psi_0) \tag{4}$$

Taking logarithms at both sides, $\log_2(\mu_j) = j\alpha + \log_2(c_f C) + g_j$, where g_j is a bias-correction term that depends only on n_j, the number of wavelet coefficients at scale j. Parameters α and $c_f C$ can be estimated from expression (4) performing a weighted linear regression on μ_j, in which the weight is related to the number of coefficients available at the corresponding scale (decreasing by 2 for each increase in the scale). Assuming μ_j follows a Gaussian distribution, confidence intervals for the estimation can be derived. Figure 2 shows the LogScale diagrams of two processes with $H = 0.5$ and $H = 0.9$.

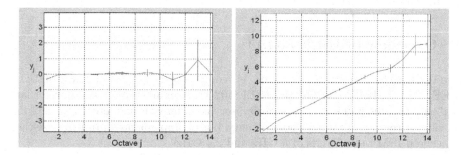

Fig. 2. *Left*: LogScale diagram of a Poisson, uncorrelated process ($H = 0.5$). *Right*: LogScale diagram of a highly correlated LRD process with $H = 0.9$.

3   Related Work

To our knowledge, a rather small number of contributions have studied fractal traffic in WLAN networks. Liang [8] exploited the self-similar properties found in a real ad-hoc network for traffic forecasting. Yu and Petropolu [9] studied the propagation of self-similar traffic through wireless, energy-conserving gateways and showed that fractality can disappear if the gateway's buffer is large as compared to the channel capacity. In a study that is closer to the present work, Tickoo and Sikdar [10] developed an analytical model of the interarrival time distribution in IEEE 802.11 networks, detecting a clustering effect of the interarrival times around some values. Their study is completed with simulations where fractal traffic is used and they argue that aggregated traffic at the output of the IEEE 802.11 nodes seems to follow a multifractal model, but it is not corroborated with an analytical study. To our knowledge, this is so far the most comprehensive effort related fractal traffic in IEEE 802.11 WLAN networks.

In [4,5] we performed a simulation-based study with the intention of confirming the results obtained by Tickoo and Sikdar and expanding them to more complex scenarios, with up to four terminals. We identified MAC and packet losses as potential pacers of traffic at the shorter and longer time scales, respectively. When combined, a global decrease in the LRD properties of traffic is clearly seen in our simulations. We corroborated the simulation-based study with a real test bed, in which we found the same effect. Our findings confirm and in some aspects expand the results described by Tickoo and Sikdar. We found traffic pacing but only at the highest frequencies (shorter time scales), and identified the propagation losses as responsible for the behaviour of the lowest frequencies (longer time scales). Tickoo and Sikdar did not single out these two effects. Furthermore, their work was an analytical-based interarrival time study and the simulations were far too complex to determine exactly the influence of each parameter or feature, while our approach was more systematic and allowed us to identify the role of each parameter. Last but not least, we reproduced the simplest simulation scenario in a real environment and confirmed the goodness of our results.

4   Overview of IEEE 802.11

The IEEE 802.11 family of standards [11] comprises the standards IEEE 802.11, IEEE 802.11b, IEEE 802.11g and IEEE 802.11a, amongst other standards that deal with specific issues such as security, service differentiation, etc. IEEE 802.11 provides wireless and infrared connectivity, but all implemented products use the unlicensed ISM radio bands of 5 GHz and 2.4 GHz.

The physical layer offers a number of channels. A set of terminals that use the same channel and are within the communication range of (some of) the other terminals of the set is called Basic Service Set (BSS). The number of physical channels depends on whether BSSs are multiplexed by using FHSS, Direct Sequence Spread Spectrum (DSSS) or Orthogonal Frequency Division Multiplexing (OFDM) techniques. Also, the gross communication rates per channel range from 1 Mb/s to 54 Mb/s.

IEEE 802.11 contemplates two operating modes: infrastructure mode and ad hoc mode. The infrastructure mode implies the participation of a node called the Access Point (AP), which is in charge of the synchronization and management of power saving mechanisms in the rest of the terminals within the BSS. The ad hoc mode is more general, since responsibilities are evenly distributed among all terminals in the BSS. Therefore, in this paper we consider the ad hoc mode.

In the ad hoc mode, users belonging to the same BSS share the medium by means of a distributed random access mechanism called Distributed Coordination Function (DCF), basically a Carrier-Sense Medium Access with Collision Avoidance (CSMA/CA) technique [12]. When a Mobile Station (MS) gets a frame from upper layers to transmit, it first senses the channel to determine whether another MS is transmitting. If the MS has sensed the channel to be idle for a period of time equal to the DCF Inter Frame Space (DIFS), which is a quantity equal for all stations, then it starts transmitting the frame. Otherwise, as soon at it senses the channel to be busy, it will defer the transmission. When deferring, the station will continue sensing the channel. At the point in time when the medium becomes idle again, the station will continue sensing and it will wait for the period DIFS to elapse again. If the medium becomes busy during this period, the station will go back to the deferring state again. However, if the medium remains idle for this DIFS period, the station will go to the back-off state. When entering the back-off state, the MS selects a Back-off Interval (BI) randomly between zero and a Contention Window period (CW). The quantity CW is an integer number of basic time slots. When a station attempts to transmit a frame for the first time, CW is equal to the CWmin value. If the medium remains idle for the duration of BI, then the station transmits the frame. However, if the medium becomes busy before the BI elapses, then the MS stores the remaining BI time (that is, the value of the chosen BI minus the elapsed time since entering the backoff state). A collision will occur if two or more MSs select the same BI (provided the condition stated above, that the frames coexist spatially at one or more of the receiving stations). When a collision occurs, the stations that have caused the collision sense the medium again for DIFS and go again to the back-off state, selecting a new BI randomly with the value of CW doubled. The other contending stations, which stored their remaining BI times, also wait for DIFS and then go to the back-off state with BI equal to the stored value (this is done to increase fairness). The value of CW is doubled every time that a station tries to transmit a given frame and a collision occurs, until a maximum CW (CWmax) is reached. When this maximum value is reached, the BI will be randomly selected out of the interval $[0, CWmax]$. There is a maximum number of retransmission attempts: if the station has tried to transmit the frame this number of times and a collision has always occurred, then the station gives up trying to transmit the frame. Figure 3 illustrates the basic functioning of DCF. There, we see how three stations behave as a function of time if they are all within reach of each other.

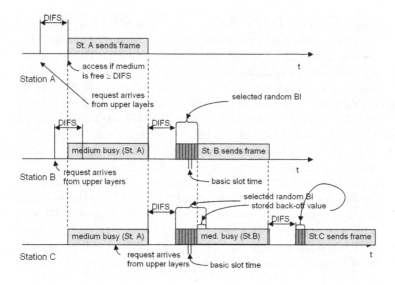

Fig. 3. Basic functioning of DCF

The radio transmission channel is relatively unreliable and the probability of transmitting a frame successfully is highly variable, even if there is no competition from other stations. Therefore, in IEEE 802.11 DCF, frames that have a single destination (which will be the case we will concentrate on) have a corresponding reception acknowledgement. This is illustrated in Figure 4, where we find the behavior of one transmitting station, the corresponding station (receiver) and a third station that has received a request to transmit from upper layers after the first station. After a station has received the data frame correctly, it will send back an acknowledge frame (ACK) after a time period SIFS (Short IFS). The size of SIFS is unique for all stations and is smaller than DIFS. In this way, we guarantee that the first frame that is transmitted after the data frame is the acknowledgement of that frame and not any other data frame (unless the transmission medium fails temporarily).

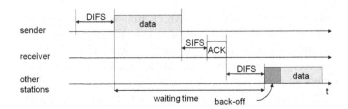

Fig. 4. Acknowledgements for DCF

An optional feature of DCF is the Request-To-Send / Clear-To-Send (RTS / CTS) extension, common in commercial implementations. This option prevents many collisions induced by the hidden-terminal problem. This problem, which is of major relevance in multihop wireless networks, consists in the following. Assume that Station A intends to send a frame to Station B. Station A will be able to hear only some but not necessarily all transmissions from other stations affecting Station B, thereby A could assume that the medium is free even if it is busy at its intended destination node. To mitigate this problem, a station first transmits an RTS message and waits for a CTS message from the recipient before beginning data transmission. RTS and CTS frames also include the size of the data to be sent, so that a station hearing an RTS/CTS frame granting access to a different station refrains from sending an RTS to the medium for the duration of the indicated transmission time. Upon reception of an RTS, a station must wait for a time period SIFS before replying with a CTS; upon reception of a positive CTS, a station has to wait for an SIFS before sending the data frame.

Since in all scenarios we consider the contention of at most two stations, the probability that a frame causes a collision is very small. This implies a high probability that a frame is transmitted either at once (after the DIFS and, if enabled, the RTS/CTS exchange), or after an additional single backoff, or after an additional single backoff plus a frame transmission time (the time it takes for the other station to transmit a frame). Due to the fairness mechanism, the

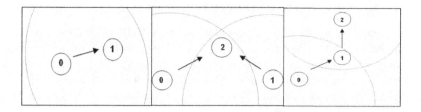

Fig. 5. Testbed scenarios 1, 2 and 3

probability of getting longer delays with only two contending stations is rather small. This implies that the delay incurred by a frame will depend on the time it has to wait in the output queue rather than on the medium contention time.

5   Scenarios

In our testbeds, traffic with known characteristics is injected into IEEE 802.11 networks in scenarios composed of 2 or 3 static nodes in ad-hoc mode. We analyze the characteristics of traffic at the destination node in order to determine the effects of MAC mechanisms and propagation impairments. Although the number of nodes is small, the chosen scenarios are representative of common situations in larger networks. Therefore, the experiments will be useful in order to draw conclusions on the behavior of systems with more nodes.

For each simulated or real source and receiver a statistical analysis has been performed, including interarrival time distribution, aggregated bitrate series, losses, and Hurst parameter estimation with the LogScale diagram.

5.1   Topology Scenarios

Figure 5 shows the topology scenarios. The first scenario includes two nodes and a unidirectional data flow between them. This simple scenario had been exhaustively simulated in [4,5]. This helped us determining the significant parameters. The hidden node situation is studied in the second scenario, where two nodes communicate with a third one, but they cannot detect the transmissions of each other. Finally, the third scenario is a relaying situation with an intermediate node between sender and receiver and a unidirectional data flow. This scenario is of interest because of the cumulative traffic pacing effect.

5.2   Configuration

All the scenarios employ IEEE 802.11 DCF (Distributed Control Function), DropTail queue, queue length of 50 packets (for the simulations) or 1000 packets (for the real testbeds) and link rate of 11 Mbit/s. The packet length was set at 1000 bytes of payload, increased to 1042 bytes by the protocol headers. Other parameters The parameters are set by default and follow the High Rate - Direct Sequence Standard Spectrum (HR/DSSS) specification [11].

5.3   Traffic Sources and Transport Protocols

The traffic generators used in the simulations were CBR (Constant Bit Rate), Poisson, and an LRD generator based on the aggregation of Pareto-distributed on-off sources. UDP has been used as transport protocol. TCP was not considered at this stage since its dynamics (retransmissions, congestion control) would make the analysis more difficult. Therefore retransmissions occur only at MAC level and not at the transport layer.

The generation of LRD real traffic is done by means of a UDP traffic generator, `flashudp` [13] and the `fft-fgn` synthesizer [14].

5.4   Propagation Models

Three different propagation models are considered. The TwoRayGround model, which is included in `ns-2`, predicts the power received by modeling the communication range as an ideal circle and thus no packet loss related with the propagation model will happen if the nodes are close enough. The Shadowing model extends the approach to a richer statistic model that incorporates a loss probability dependent on the distance between nodes, though it lacks the time correlation present in real situations. Finally, the Ricean/Rayleigh fast fading model [15,16], which includes time correlation properties through the addition of reflections on a circle around the transmitter plus the line-of-sight component.

Regarding the real testbeds, we wanted to perform the test in an environment with a known propagation model in order to analyze the effect produced by packet loss on the scaling behavior. Two scenarios have been used: the first one has been carried out in an indoor environment (our laboratory) where the model was found to be Shadowing with $4 < \beta < 6$, while the second test has been developed in an outdoor environment (Castelldefels' beach), whose propagation model was measured in a previous study [17] and was found to fit the Shadowing model with $\beta = 2.7$. Both environments were relatively controlled, which was helpful to avoid interferences from nearby IEEE 802.11 or Bluetooth emissions.

5.5   Maximum Throughput in IEEE 802.11

It is well-known that the effective attainable throughput is lower than the nominal 11 Mbits/s. To begin with, ACKs and long PLCP Preambles are used, and they are both transmitted at 1 Mbit/s. The effective throughput is also reduced when the RTS/CTS mechanism is used. Besides, efficiency is further reduced by the time dedicated to contention resolution, namely IFS and backoff. These facts have been considered for the selection of the offered traffic load in the simulations and experiments.

5.6   Packet Error Ratio (PER) and Bit Error Ratio (BER)

In simulations where packet losses are present, typical PERs of radio environments are assumed. In our simulations PER will range from 1% to 4%, which corresponds to typical BERs of 10^{-6} to 10^{-4} (accounting for the improvement of the error correction mechanisms). In the real scenarios we tried to maintain these values.

6   Results and Analysis

6.1   Scenario 1 - Simulation

This subsection describes only the most relevant simulation results for Scenario 1. A complete description of the simulation-based study can be found in [4].

For a Poisson source ($H = 0.5$), interarrival time distributions at the destination node are clearly exponential at lower traffic loads (10% of the maximum effective throughput). However, at higher loads (50% and 90%) the distributions are not exponential at all: packets with very small intergeneration time are grouped in the sender queue, causing interarrival times to concentrate around multiples of the packet transmission time (see Figure 6), as shown by Tickoo and Sikdar.

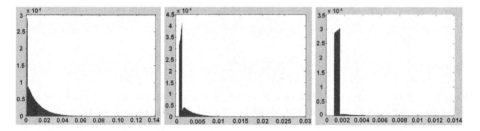

Fig. 6. Interarrival time distributions (in seconds) when Poisson traffic is generated in Scenario 1 for 10%, 50% and 90% loads

At lower rates, the scaling behavior of traffic at the destination node does not differ from that at the source node, and no modification in the traffic fractality is perceived. At higher rates the highest frequency components of the process (the shorter time scales) decrease noticeably, as shown in Figure 7. Packets with smaller interarrival times have to wait in the queue or are dropped. The effect is that high frequencies are mitigated and, therefore, the lowest scales decrease.

When packet loss (caused either by collisions or propagation problems) is introduced in the simulation, the interarrival time distributions change considerably. We can observe high interarrival values produced by retransmission delays, and important amounts of small interarrival values produced by packets waiting in queue due to retransmission delay and therefore sent back-to-back. This increases the high frequency components of the traffic process. In the LogScale diagram this effect is shown as an increase of short time scales, as shown in Figure 8. Notice the mitigation of LRD: at the source, H is estimated to be 0.682

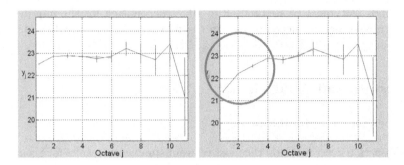

Fig. 7. LogScale diagrams of the bitrate series for scenario 1 at source (left) and destination (right) with 90% load Poisson traffic

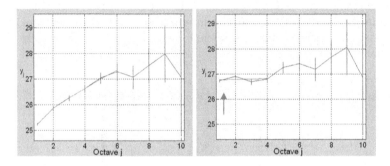

Fig. 8. LogScale diagrams of the bitrate series, scenario 1 at source (left) and destination (right) with LRD traffic at the input ($H \approx 0.7$) and Rayleigh/Rice channel

with 95% confidence intervals $[0.637, 0.727]$, whereas at the destination H drops to 0.508 $[0.486, 0.530]$.

When the Shadowing propagation model is used, large scales decrease noticeably, as shown in Figure 9. This propagation model lacks time correlation properties and this feature seems to be the cause for the destruction of the lower frequencies of traffic; in other words, this model is mitigating the original long range dependence of the process. As a result, the LogScale diagram at the destination is more similar to a Poisson process ($H = 0.528$ $[0.489, 0.566]$) than a self-similar one ($H = 0.784$ $[0.725, 0.843]$ at the source). When collisions and propagation impairments are combined, the shorter scales suffer a more noticeable increase. The combined impact superposes both effects.

6.2   Scenario 1 - Testbed

We present now the results obtained at the beach of Castelldefels. The load was the 50% of the maximum capacity. Though we tried to keep the scenario as ideal as possible by avoiding interferences coming from objects or people, the

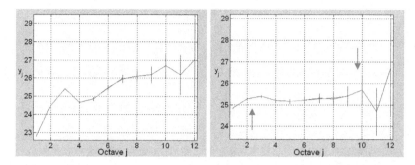

Fig. 9. LogScale diagrams of the bitrate series, scenario 1 at source (left) and destination (right) with LRD at the input ($H \approx 0.8$) and Shadowing propagation model

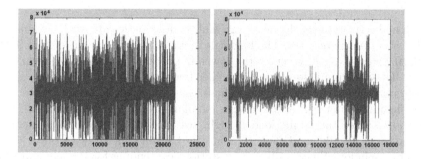

Fig. 10. Instantaneous bitrate series (bytes arrived per 10 ms slot) of traffic received in an environment with high variability (left) and moderate variability (right). The figure on the right has a stable zone in the center (samples 2000-12000).

results show a high variability introduced by the channel. This produces a high variability in the characteristics of the traffic at the destination and it is reflected by packet bursts, as shown in Figure 10. We discarded the trace segments with clear non-stationarities and focused only on the stable zones. The results of this analysis show the same scaling behavior found in the simulations: a mitigation of Long Range Dependence. As shown in Figure 11, the source has an H parameter of 0.742 [0.727, 0.757], while at the destination a value of 0.554 [0.543, 0.564] is measured. In this case, we only find mitigation of the lower frequencies of the traffic process, which implies a mitigation of the LRD phenomenon, consistent with the simulation results above and the results of Tickoo and Sikdar [10].

6.3 Scenario 2 - Testbed

In this case the experiments were carried out in the premises of our laboratory (indoor channel). Since this scenario represents a typical hidden terminal situation and the data packets are relatively large, the RTS/CTS option was enabled. An LRD traffic flow created from a trace with $H = 0.7$ was sent from the two

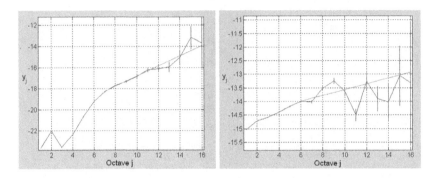

Fig. 11. LogScale diagrams of the interarrival time series in emission (left, H=0.742) and reception after non-stationarity filtering (left H=0.554)

hidden nodes (working each one at a 25% of the maximum rate, with a combined load of 50%) to the receiver. The LogScale diagram returns a value of $H = 0.899$ [0.869, 0.928] for the receiver at the lower frequencies ($j = 7 \dots 14$), while an almost flat spectrum is found at the higher frequencies (see Figure 12).

We interpret this dual regime as follows. Some transmission errors flatten the LogScale diagram at higher frequencies, similarly to the effects we have seen in Scenario 1. Since the traffic load is high, stations will often find the medium busy and will usually send their RTS after a backoff time drawn from a [0, 15] contention window. Since we have two stations contending for the medium, this implies that the probability that two RTS frames collide is rather small. In any case, the occurrence of a collision will only contribute to the slope reduction at lower scales. On the other hand, we recall that the transmission of a frame by one station will often discourage the other station from transmitting at once through the RTS/CTS mechanism. Once the medium becomes free again, there will be a nonzero probability that the former station transmits a new frame rather than the latter station transmits the frame that was already contending, despite the fairness mechanism (see Section 4). This implies that, given the relatively high load, both transmitters will build relatively long queues and thus introduce long memory components in the traffic process, making the overall system memory higher than in the single LRD source case[1]. The effect is an increase in the low frequency components of the LogScale diagram of the interarrival time series. This is consistent with the theoretical results presented in [18], where it is stated that the concurring aggregation of self-similar traffic tends to increase the LRD.

6.4   Scenario 3 - Testbed

This was also an indoor test carried out in our laboratory. The RTS/CTS option was disabled, since the only contending nodes are the source (Node 0) and the

---

[1] The buffer size is 1000 packets, and we consider the buffer overflow probability to be approximately 0.

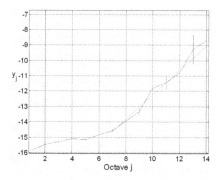

Fig. 12. LogScale diagram of the interarrival time series in reception, for Scenario 2

relay (Node 1) and they are within transmission range of each other. This relay node case was studied by comparing the reception at the destination node and the reception at the relay node with the input at the source node, which is an $H = 0.7$ LRD traffic series with a load of 40%.

Figure 13 shows the LogScale diagrams for the scenario. The measured traffic at the reception stage of the relay node shows an LRD parameter $H = 0.611$ [0.598, 0.624]. On the contrary, the LRD characteristics of the traffic received by the destination node have been found to have $H = 0.758$ [0.713, 0.804]. At the MAC level, the competition between nodes is very similar to that of Scenario 2, the main difference is that every frame transmission does not need to wait for the RTS/CTS exchange. The probability of collision is also very low.

The main difference between Scenario 2 and Scenario 3 lays on the output queues. The relay node will try to transmit every frame that it has received from the source node after some processing time. If the relay node gets access to the medium for several consecutive frames, the source node will not have supplied frames to the relay node for some time and then the relay node will have no frames to transmit. This implies that the output queue of the source node will be rather empty with a high probability, rendering a lower memory than in the case of Scenario 2. This is the reason behind the low LRD at the receiver.

The relay node will perceive the source node's contention very similarly to any of the sources of Scenario 2: if the source node wins the contention for several consecutive times, the output queue of the relay node will contain many frames, thereby suffering memory effects and thus an increased LRD. However, the amount of accumulated frames will still be lower than in Scenario 2, so the components of the Log-Scale diagram that increase are not the highest scales, but also the intermediate. We also made experiments with a lower load (25% for each transmitter), finding that the mitigation of LRD at the first node ($H = 0.674$ [0.657, 0.692]) and the increase of correlation at the receiver ($H = 0.719$ [0.710, 0.727]) are lower when compared with the higher load case 40%.

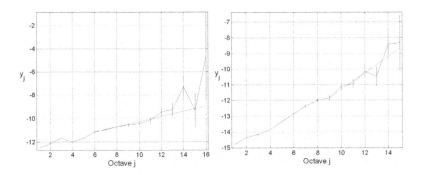

Fig. 13. LogScale diagrams of the interarrival time series at the reception stage of the relay node (left) and the receiver (right), for Scenario 3, with 40% load

7   Conclusions

This paper studies the influence of IEEE 802.11 DCF MAC and transmission impairments on the characteristics of traffic when long-range dependent features are present at the traffic sources. For a unidirectional data flow between two nodes without disturbances from other nodes, the results extracted from both the simulations and the testbed experiments agree with the results found in literature: the Hurst parameter H increases with growing traffic loads and transmission losses.

The experiments carried out in a hidden-node scenario show that, for relatively high traffic loads, output queues can be filled considerably, thereby introducing memory and an important increase of H at high scales, while for low scales the main influence comes from the transmission impairments.

The experiments done in a two hop scenario had interesting outcomes. The characteristics of the frame arrival times at the second link resemble the results of the previous scenario, also due to the accumulation of frames at the output queue of the relay node; however, the frame arrival process at the first link shows lower H because the accumulation effect at the output queue of the source node cannot be as strong as in the relay node. From the presented results, we argue that for routers with large number of nodes attached the memory effect will be more noticeable and the Hurst parameter of the aggregated traffic will be higher.

The results provide a detailed study of traffic characteristics in wireless networks that can be used to develop accurate models, Quality of Service and admission control policies as well as network performance prediction. In particular, our findings can be applied to the dimensioning of buffers in Access Points and wired networks nodes receiving traffic from IEEE 802.11 networks.

This study can be further expanded with more complex scenarios, including more nodes, interfering nodes and node mobility. Other, more realistic traffic models than the relatively simply LRD generators we have used could provide more information, possibly incorporating traffic from real applications, such as Voice over IP, P2P applications or web browsing. The extension of the simulations and real testbeds to the case of TCP would incorporate the shaping effects of the error and congestion control mechanisms.

Acknowledgments

This work has been partially supported by the Spanish Government and FEDER (TSI2005-06092), the Spanish Ramón y Cajal Programme, and by the European Commission (EuroNGI Network of Excellence, contract 507613). The authors wish to thank E. García, A. Ibáñez, O. López, M. Oliveras, M. C. Sánchez, D. Ruíz and R. Vidal for their help and comments.

References

1. Leland, W., Taqqu, M., Willinger, W., Wilson, D.: On the self-similar nature of Ethernet traffic. IEEE/ACM Transactions on Networking **2** (February 1994) 1–15
2. Park, K., Willinger, W., eds.: Self-similar traffic and network performance. John Wiley & Sons (2000)
3. Norros, I.: A storage model with self-similar input. Queueing systems **16** (1994) 387–396
4. Cano, C.: Study of traffic fractality in ad-hoc WLAN networks (in Spanish). Master's thesis, Technical School of Castelldefels (EPSC), Technical University of Catalonia (UPC), Barcelona, Spain (March 2006)
5. Cano, C., Rincón, D., Remondo, D.: On the mitigation of long-range dependence in IEEE 802.11 networks. Proceedings of the IEEE International Symposyum on Personal, Indoor and Mobile Radio Communications PIMRC 2006 (to be published). (September 2006)
6. ns-2 simulator website. http://www.isi.edu/nsnam/ns
7. Veitch, D., Abry, P.: A wavelet-based joint estimator of the parameters of long-range dependence. IEEE Transactions on Information Theory **45**(3) (April 1999) 878–897
8. Liang, Q.: Ad hoc wireless network traffic - self-similarity and forecasting. IEEE Communications Letters **6**(7) (July 2002) 297–299
9. Yu, J., Petropolu, A.: On propagation of self-similar traffic through an energy-conserving wireless gateway. Proceedings of IEEE ICASSP 2005. Volume IV. (2005) 285–288
10. Tickoo, O., Sikdar, B.: On the impact of IEEE 802.11 MAC on traffic characteristics. IEEE Journal on Selected Areas in Communications **21**(2) (February 2003) 189–203
11. IEEE standard 802.11, wireless LAN medium access control (MAC) and physical layer (PHY) specifications (1999)
12. Remondo, D.: Tutorial on wireless ad hoc networks (invited paper). Proceedings of HET-NETs'04: Performance Modelling and Evaluation of Heterogeneous Networks. (July 2004)
13. Saka, F.: FlashUDP. http://www.hep.ucl.ac.uk/ fs/
14. Paxson, V.: Fast approximation of self-similar network traffic. LBL-36750/UC-405. http://ita.ee.lbl.gov/html/contrib/fft-fgn.html. Technical report (April 1995)

15. Punnoose, R.J., Niktin, P., Stancil, D.: Efficient simulation of Ricean fading within a packet simulator. http://www-ece.rice.edu/ jingpu/moar/ricean-sim.pdf. Technical report (September 2000)
16. CMU Antenna and Radio Comm. Group. Additions to the ns-2 network simulator to handle Ricean and Rayleigh fading, http://www.ece.cmu.edu/wireless/
17. Ruíz, D., Oliveras, M.: Open source 802.11 access points-based mesh networks (III) (in Spanish). Master's thesis, Technical School of Castelldefels (EPSC), Technical University of Catalonia (UPC), Barcelona, Spain (March 2006)
18. Fan, Y., Georganas, N.: On merging and splitting of self-similar traffic in highspeed networks. Proceedings of ICCC'95. (July 1995) 8A.1.1–6

Measurements of IEEE 802.11g-Based Ad-Hoc Networks in Motion

Karin A. Hummel, Alexander C. Adrowitzer, and Helmut Hlavacs

Institute of Distributed and Multimedia Systems,
University of Vienna, Lenaugasse 2/8, A-1080 Vienna
{karin.hummel,alexander.adrowitzer,helmut.hlavacs}@univie.ac.at
http://www.informatik.univie.ac.at/

Abstract. Vehicular ad-hoc networks (VANETs) are promising means for distributed automotive applications. In addition to developing new communication protocols for VANETs, the widespread use of general purpose wireless network standards like WLAN IEEE 802.11a/b/g raises the need to investigate whether these networks are suitable for VANETs. The results from such experimental studies allow to introduce better simulation models and to evaluate the appropriateness of analytical models for wireless networks.

This work proposes a structured, scenario-based approach for measuring wireless networks in motion, which can easily be exploited by simulations. By applying the approach to IEEE 802.11g ad-hoc networks, experiments and results are described. The signal strength has been investigated for all mobility scenarios and is presented for the most significant cases as well as compared to the free space loss formula of electromagnetic waves. Furthermore, the throughput and packet loss are studied for traffic bursts while moving.

Keywords: VANETs, IEEE 802.11g, Measurements.

1 Introduction

The widespread use of mobile devices and wireless networks allows communication spontaneously in ad-hoc manner. In particular in moving vehicles, energy supply is provided and multiple purpose mobile devices can be supported without the limitations caused by battery lifetime. Hence, vehicular ad-hoc networks (VANETs) are promising means for customer information distribution and decentralized coordination, for example, to avoid traffic jams.

Only few research studies have been carried out to measure ad-hoc wireless LANs in motion. On the other hand, multiple different research studies have been carried out to simulate mobile ad-hoc networks (MANETs). In this work, we contribute by measuring the behavior of IEEE 802.11g. We propose a scenario-based measurement framework which allows to easily carry out the measurements using a measurement tool and to support self-descriptiveness of scenarios by means of meta-data.

J. García-Vidal and L. Cerdà-Alabern (Eds.): Wireless and Mobility, LNCS 4396, pp. 29–42, 2007.
© Springer-Verlag Berlin Heidelberg 2007

The scenarios used are derived from typical street traffic scenarios, that are, moving towards each other, crossing, taking over, roundabouts, and getting out of range. We describe the major parameters of these scenarios and carry out measurements in motion using two standard notebooks with external antennas. We describe the signal strength of IEEE 802.11g in all scenarios and, in addition, the throughput of traffic bursts while being mobile.

The paper is structured as follows: Section 2 describes related work on wireless LAN measurement with particular focus on mobility. In Section 3 we detail the scenarios of interest. In Section 4 we describe how these scenarios can be specified by means of meta-data. Finally, we describe the experiments and results in Section 5, and conclude our work in Section 6.

2   Related Work

Measuring wireless networks in a realistic setup is often impaired by influencing and disturbing factors, like attenuation, multipath fading, refraction, reflection, and interference with other wireless networks. Various studies have investigated these phenomenas and the impact of co-channel interference. For IEEE 802.11 b/g in managed mode, Formisano et al. [1] describe some observed phenomena in outdoor scenarios, but on the other hand do not consider movement. One of the main results of their study on link quality and delivery errors states that IEEE 802.11b is more robust than IEEE 802.11g, which encourages our work to investigate in particular IEEE 802.11g in motion.

For networks in motion, Gass et al. [2] conducted motion experiments for investigating the UDP and TCP throughput. The experiments were carried out in the Californian desert to avoid as many disturbing factors as possible. IEEE 802.11b was used in managed mode without external antennas. Similarly, Singh et al. [3] carried out experiments with IEEE 802.11b under different environmental and speed conditions to investigate the signal to noise ratio (SNR) and the UDP throughput.

Bergamo et al. [4] investigated WLAN IEEE 802.11b managed mode in motion in three scenarios: free space, highways, and semi-free space propagation (parking lot). In this study, the vehicles moved with high speed (up to 240 km/h). The results in terms of packet loss and jitter were promising, saying that even at high speeds, WLAN IEEE 802.11b can be used for telemetry, but TCP-based applications might suffer from the packet losses. Similar to our approach, they defined movement scenarios.

Considering both IEEE 802.11 g/b, Ott et al. [5,6] investigated data transfer rates of UDP and TCP traffic for vehicles communicating via access points. This *drive-thru* system architecture assumes nearby hot-spots for vehicles on the move which allow not seamless, but intermittent connectivity.

IEEE 802.11b ad-hoc networks have been investigated by Singh et al. [7] for enhancements of Optimized Link State Routing (OLSR) in terms of signal quality and UDP throughput in different realistic traffic scenarios, like freeways or suburbian districts (which determines speed and movement behavior). The velocity and location measurements are derived from GPS data. The work of Dhoutaut et al. [8] investigate the UDP throughput using one moving device in IEEE 802.11b ad-hoc mode. In this work, the asymmetry of throughput measurements and the importance of the orientation of the device (and the WLAN card) is emphasized.

Our work contributes to this research field by investigating the signal behavior and UDP packet throughput for IEEE 802.11g in ad-hoc mode (using external antennas). The experiments are derived from typical urban traffic scenarios which and carried out in an environment with only minor interferences.

3   Scenarios

We propose a scenario-based approach for structured measurement derived from real-world automotive traffic scenarios. The most important situations which inspired our scenarios are: *moving towards* each other or a stationary vehicle, *crossing*, *taking over*, and *roundabouts*. Additionally, in order to investigate explicitly situations where vehicles move out of the ad-hoc communication range, we included another scenario termed *out of range*. These scenarios are described by a *name* which determines the movement path and the attribute types *speed*, *timestamp*, and *distance*. The latter attributes are different for different parts of the path. For example, consider a crossing, where the vehicle has to halt and wait before moving on again. The speed parameter is used to determine the average speed on a sub-path, distance describes the distance of this sub-path the moving vehicle has to cover, and the timestamps are used to determine the start and end time of such a sub-path (some of the timestamps serve for plausibility checks only). Table 1 lists the attributes for each of the scenarios in the simplest version. Fig. 1 and Fig.2 visualize the scenarios.

In addition to the parameters related to movement, parameters describing the simulated traffic can be specified depending on the application that should be investigated.

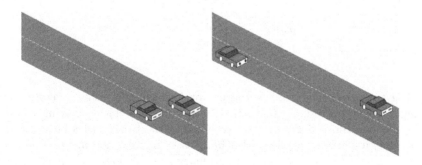

Fig. 1. Left: Taking over. Right: Moving towards.

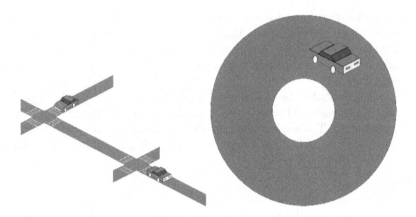

Fig. 2. Left: Crossing. Right: Roundabout.

Table 1. Description of traffic scenarios

Name	Average speed [km/h]	Timestamp [hh:mm:ss]	Distance [m]
Moving towards	$S1_{Vehicle1}$	$TS1_{Vehicle1}$, $TE1_{Vehicle1}$	$D1_{Vehicle1}$
Crossing (non-stop and stop)	$S1_{Vehicle1}$	$TS1_{Vehicle1}$, $TE1_{Vehicle1}$	$D1_{Vehicle1}$
	$S2_{Vehicle1}$	$TS2_{Vehicle1}$, $TE2_{Vehicle1}$	$D2_{Vehicle1}$
Taking over	$S1_{Vehicle1}$	$TS1_{Vehicle1}$, $TE1_{Vehicle1}$	$D1_{Vehicle1}$
	$S1_{Vehicle2}$	$TS1_{Vehicle2}$, $TE1_{Vehicle2}$	$D1_{Vehicle2}$
Roundabout	$S1_{Vehicle1}$	$TS1_{Vehicle1}$, $TE1_{Vehicle1}$	$D1_{Vehicle1}$
Out of range	$S1_{Vehicle1}$	$TS1_{Vehicle1}$, $TE1_{Vehicle1}$	$D1_{Vehicle1}$
	$S2_{Vehicle1}$	$TS2_{Vehicle1}$, $TE2_{Vehicle1}$	$D2_{Vehicle1}$

Moving towards: The traffic scenario envisioned here is either a vehicle moving straight towards a stationary vehicle or two vehicles moving towards each other. Since only the relative speed of the two vehicles between each other is important, we deal with both cases in the same manner as if one moving vehicle is approaching a stationary one. While moving towards each other, the devices carried by the vehicles are communicating with each other in WLAN ad-hoc mode (as in all other scenarios). The parameters determining this scenario are, thus, the average speed of the moving vehicle and the distance between the mobile and the stationary vehicle at the start time ($S1_{Vehicle1}$, $D1_{Vehicle1}$ $TS1_{Vehicle1}$ in Table 1).

Crossing: The crossing scenario applies for two real-world traffic cases. The first one describes the situation of a crossing with traffic light, which is currently red, the second one a crossing without traffic lights or green traffic light. In each scenario we assume one vehicle approaching straight and passing the crossing and another vehicle halting at the crossing as long as the experiment run lasts. We term the first scenario *crossing stop* and the second one *crossing non-stop*. In scenario *crossing stop*, the moving vehicle halts at the crossing and waits a configurable period of time. Table 1 details the parameters necessary to determine the average speed used, the starting time and the distance for the sub-path before the crossing and the distance after the crossing.

Taking over: This scenario is typical in many traffic situations, like urban traffic or freeways. In our experiments, both vehicles start at the same location and move straight forwards, but at a different time. The first vehicle starts moving with a low speed ($S1_{Vehicle1}$), then the second vehicle starts moving with a higher speed ($S1_{Vehicle2}$) and overtakes the first one, the experiment ends when the specified distance (for each) has been reached.

Roundabout: Here, the traffic scenario envisioned is a roundabout with some spot (communicating device) placed in the middle. In addition to modeling a real-world traffic situation, this scenario allows to investigate how motion influences the signal strength, since the distance of the vehicle to the device in the middle remains constant throughout the experiment. Each round determines one test case (see Table 1).

Out of range: The parameters of the out of range scenario are similar to the parameters of the crossing scenario. Here the moving vehicle moves out of the communication range of the stationary one. In our scenarios, we consider a straight movement towards a distant location where the ad-hoc connection is definitely lost. Then the vehicle turns around and returns to the starting point (thus, $D1_{Vehicle1} = D2_{Vehicle1}$).

4 Meta-data Based Approach

In order to make best use of the measurement results during evaluation but also to enable the easy input of these data for simulations, the experimental data is extended by a self-descriptive part. This part describes the main properties of the experiment as introduced in Section 3 and is stored for every experimental run. In the current approach only simple meta-data are proposed in XML format (and specified with XSD[1]), an extension to ontologies can be provided, if necessary.

Fig. 3 shows parts of an example XML file for the *out of range* scenario. The file consists of two parts: the first part describes the mobility configuration and the second part describes the characteristics of the traffic used. Our approach

---

[1] http://www.w3.org/XML/Schema

supports the simulation of audio and video streaming, and file bursts. Additionally, similar to the *ping* command, packets can be sent on a round trip to allow the calculation of the *round trip time (RTT)*. In the out of range scenario described, the experiment starts with both vehicles being stationary at zero distance, at the start time, one vehicle starts to accelerate up to a constant speed (20 km/h) and moves until a distance of 800 m is reached where the vehicle is out of range. Then, it immediately turns, accelerates again up to 20 km/h and moves back to the starting point. Similae parameter values have been used for the experiments.

```xml
<?xml version="1.0" encoding="ISO-8859-1" standalone="yes"?>
<!-- Dateiname: outOfRange.xml -->
<Scenario>
...
    <ScenarioName> Out of range </ScenarioName>
    <Speed>
        <SpeedVal1> 20 </SpeedVal1>
        <SpeedVal2> 20 </SpeedVal2>
        <SpeedUnit> km/h </SpeedUnit>
    </Speed>
    <TS>
        <StartVal1> 00:00:00 </StartVal1>
        <EndVal1> ... </EndVal1>
        <StartVal2> 00:02:30 </StartVal2>
        <EndVal2> ... </EndVal2>
        <TSUnit> hh:mm:ss </TSUnit>
    </TS>
    <Distance>
        <DistanceVal1> 800 </DistanceVal1>
        <DistanceVal2> 800 </DistanceVal2>
        <DistanceUnit> m </DistanceUnit>
    </Distance>
    <Traffic>
        <TrafficType> File Transfer </TrafficType>
        <FileSize> 10 000 000 </FileSize>
        <FileSizeUnit> bytes </FileSizeUnit>
        <Rate> 20 </Rate>
        <RateUnit> MBit per sec </RateUnit>
    </Traffic>
...
</Scenario>
```

Fig. 3. Example scenario meta-data: out of range

5   Experiments

We conducted experiments both with cars and bicycles in all the described scenarios. In this section, all experiments refer to movement by bicycle conducted in a Viennese recreation area with minor disturbances. For all experiments we used our own measurement toolbox (Java and C++ code).

5.1 Toolbox

The measurement toolbox developed is implemented in Java 1.5 in order to measure simultaneously the signal level [dBm], bitrate [Bit/s], remaining capacity [Ah], and present voltage [V]. Additionally, it is possible to select measuring the round trip time (RTT) or another traffic type (audio or video streaming, burst traffic to simulate file transfer). The RTT is measured in the time in milliseconds between monitoring and receiving small UDP packets in the Java program. The signal level and bitrate values were derived from the Linux Wireless Tools.[2] The present rate, remaining capacity and present voltage were directly read from /proc/acpi/battery/BATX/state.

The user can select via a GUI whether to monitor all of these metrics in real-time or to log them to a file (or both). Furthermore, the user can specify a measurement ID and a measurement description (Fig. 4). Further input parameters are the specification of the parameters for RTT measurement (the size of the UDP packets and the interval between two UDP packets),the IP address of the supporting node and its MAC address to simplify ad-hoc connection setup. The current implementation is dedicated to ad-hoc mode for two participants only.

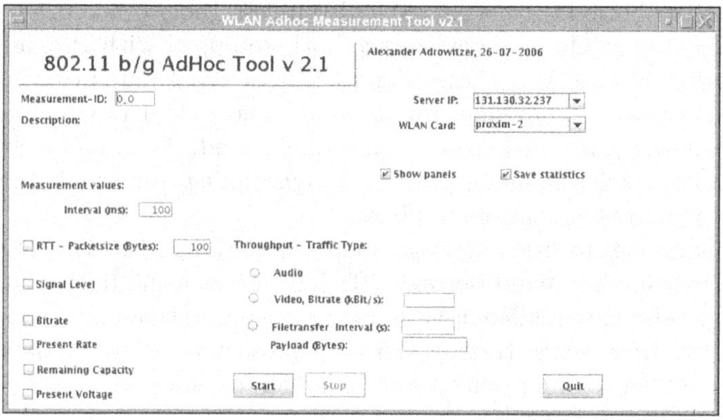

Fig. 4. GUI of our measurement tool

The toolbox supports the generation of different traffic types, namely audio streaming, video streaming, and file transfer (burst traffic). For audio streaming, the bitrate is fixed to 64 Kbit/s, while for video streaming the streaming rate can be specified via the GUI. For the burst traffic, the burst size and the transmission rate can be configured via the tool's GUI. While this toolbox is

---

[2] http://www.hpl.hp.com/personal/Jean_Tourrilhes/Linux/Tools.html

executed on the monitoring node, for RTT and the other traffic measurements, a small tool has been installed also on the supporting node. This application is mainly written in Java 1.5. For the burst traffic, the application on the supporting node is responsible for continuously creating traffic bursts according to the specified burst size and transmission rate. The time critical parts of each of the applications (both on the monitoring and on the supporting node) are written in C++ and called via the Java Native Interface (JNI).

In all experiments except the out of range setting, we measured all parameters. However, we will present only the results for the signal strength. The local system parameters have not been significantly influenced during our experiments, and since we only used small packets to measure RTT, the results are not interesting. For the out of range case, we measured throughput for different burst sizes which show best how a decreased link quality influences UDP traffic.

5.2   Experimental Setup

The experimental setup consists of two notebooks using external antennas. All experiments have been conducted under similar conditions with minimal external interferences. Each experiment has been carried out five times for reasons of reproducibility and outlier detection. All of the experiments have been carried out with cars and bicycles and produced similar results. We will present only experiments carried out by bicycle here.

We used two Dell Latitude D610 notebooks with the SUSE Linux 10.0 Operating System Distribution (kernel 2.6.13) and Wireless Tools Version 28 with Wireless Extensions v18. The notebooks were both equipped with Proxim Orinoco Gold 8470-WD b/g PCMCIA cards and 5 dBi external antennas. In the scenarios moving towards, crossing, round-about, and out of range, one antenna was placed at the side of the road on a 50 cm tripod. The other antenna was mounted on the carrier of one bicycle. In the overtaking scenario, both antennas were mounted on the carrier of each bike.

While conducting the first four experiments (experiment 1 to 4), a UDP packet of size 1300 bytes every 10 milliseconds (RTT measurement). In the out of range experiment we simulated different types of traffic: audio streaming, video streaming and file transfer (burst traffic). Here, we present burst traffic only because it shows the influence of movement and link degradation best.

5.3   Experiments and Results

We will now describe the experiments and results for five different experiments. The monitoring notebook was - except the overtaking scenario - always stationary while the supporting notebook was carried on the bike.

Experiment 1: Moving Towards

Each measurement started when the supporting notebook passed the 0 m mark on the road and ended when it passed the monitoring notebook at the end mark

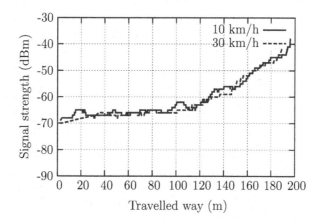

Fig. 5. Experiment 1: Moving towards with 10 km/h and 30 km/h speed. The distance is measured from the beginning mark (200 m away from the receiver).

in 200 m distance. The speed of the bicycle was held constant at $v = 10$ km/h in the first five runs and at $v = 30$ km/h in the second five ones. The measured signal strengths for the two situations are shown in Fig. 5. The experiments showed that there is no significant difference between the two different velocities.

Experiment 2: Crossing

We used two different settings for the crossing experiment. In both cases the total distance of the track was 400 m. The monitoring notebook was placed at half way of our track (200 m). The first setting (*crossing non-stop*) simulates a green-light traffic situation. The measurement started when the supporting notebook passed the 0 m mark with 10 km/h and ended when the 400 m mark was reached. The speed was constant the whole time.

In the second setting (*crossing stop*) we simulated a red-light traffic situation, typical for urban traffic. The measurement started when the bicycle with the supporting notebook started at the 0 m mark. It first accelerated to 20 km/h and then stopped at 200 m. After 20 seconds, it started again accelerating up to 20 km/h and finally stopped at 400 m. The signal strengths are shown for both cases in Fig. 6 and Fig. 7.

In this scenario, we can further show that the measured behavior approximates the free space loss formula (see, for example, Stallings [9]) considering antenna gains [10]:

$$L = 20 \log_{10} f + 20 \log_{10} d - 10 \log_{10} G_t - 10 \log_{10} G_r + 32.44 (dB), \quad (1)$$

where f is the frequency (in GHz) and d the propagation distance between the antennas (in m). Since we are using IEEE 802.11g WLAN, $f = 2.4$ GHz.

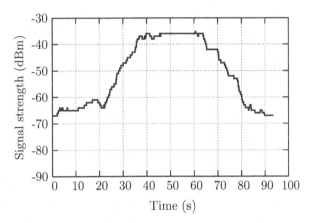

Fig. 6. Experiment 2: Crossing with stop (red light scenario). Between $t = 40$ s and $t = 60$ s the vehicle was waiting 20 seconds at the simulated red-light crossing.

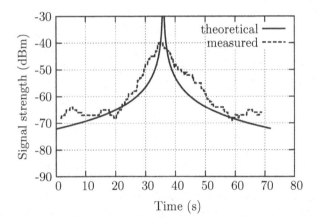

Fig. 7. Comparison measured and theoretical loss for crossing non-stop , v=20 km/h

G_t and G_r are the antenna gains for the transmitting and receiving antennas respectively. In our case, $G_t = G_r = 5$ dBi.

Experiment 3: Taking over

The supporting and the monitoring notebook were each placed on a bicycle. At the beginning of the experiment the first bicycle started to move. After it accelerated to 10 km/h it kept the speed and moved into one direction. When it passed the 200 m mark, the second bicycle started to accelerate to 30 km/h and chased the first bicycle. The two bicycles met approximately at the 300 m mark. The experiment ended when the first bicycle reached the 600 m mark. The signal strength for this scenario is shown in Fig. 8.

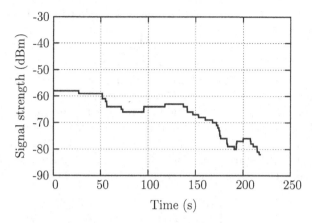

Fig. 8. Taking over: One vehicle is moving with the constant speed of 10 km/h, the overtaking vehicle with the speed of 30 km/h

Experiment 4: Roundabout

The supporting device was placed in the middle of a circle with radius 10 m. The monitoring notebook was mounted on the bicycle. The bicycle went around the circle 5 times at 10 km/h and 5 times at 20 km/h. As expected for the round-about scenario, the signal strength was constant for all runs.

Experiment 5: Out of Range

The supporting notebook was placed onto a bicycle which moved 800 m into one direction, then turned around and came back. The monitoring notebook was left at the starting point of the bike. The timing of the experiment was as follows: first, the bicycle waited for 10 s, then within approximately $dt = 5$ s it accelerated to $v = 20$ km/h and stopped after reaching 800 m to turn around. The turn of the bicycle took approximately 7 s. Then the bicycle again accelerated within $dt = 5$ s to a speed of $v = 20$ km/h and ran back to the start point. The experiment was stopped at the time the bicycle passed by the start point.

Unfortunately, it turned out that it was impossible to ride at exactly 20 km/h, and even small deviations from this target speed resulted in large deviations of the overall time each experiment lasted (between 288 and 320 seconds). In order to be able to relate the sending time to the distance between the notebooks, we therefore used the measurement data from the logfiles to compute an estimate $\hat{v}$ for v. Since the logfiles exactly determine the overall time T each experiment lasted, we set $a = \frac{20/3.6}{5}$ m/s^2 to be the acceleration at the start point and at the turning point when riding back, and $s = \frac{a}{2}dt^2$ to be the distance it approximately took to reach the target speed. The fixed times needed for waiting for the bicycle to accelerate (10 s), acceleration (2×5 s= 10 s), and turning (7 s), add up to 27 s. When assuming that the speed v for both directions was the same, we get

$$\hat{v} = \frac{800 - s}{(T - 27)/2}.$$

Furthermore we define the following time points as $t_0 = 10$ to be the start of acceleration, and $t_1 = t_0 + dt = 15$ to be the start of the phase with constant speed. At $t_2 = t_1 + (800 - s)/v$ the bike reaches the turning point, and turning is finished at time $t_3 = t_2 + 7$. At this time the bicycle enters an acceleration phase, and at $t_4 = t_3 + 5$ reaches again a speed of v. Finally, at time T the bicycle reaches the start point. In order to relate any time point $0 \leq t \leq T$ to the distance $d(t)$ between the bicycle and the starting point at this time, we compute

$$d(t) = \begin{cases} 0 & \text{if } t \leq t_0 \\ \frac{a}{2}(t - t_0)^2 & \text{if } t_0 < t \leq t_1 \\ s + \hat{v}(t - t_1) & \text{if } t_1 < t \leq t_2 \\ 800 & \text{if } t_2 < t \leq t_3 \\ 800 - \frac{a}{2}(t - t_3)^2 & \text{if } t_3 < t \leq t_4 \\ 800 - s - \hat{v}(t - t_4) & \text{if } t_4 < t \leq T \end{cases} \tag{2}$$

During each experiment, the supporting notebook continuously sent data bursts of a fixed size (1 MB, 5 MB, or 10 MB) to the monitoring notebook, each burst being sent at a target bitrate of 20 Mbit/s. As transport protocol we used UDP, the data was split into packets of size 1000 bytes, and each packet was filled with random data. The monitoring notebook ran a receiver application which recorded the arrival process of the packets.

Since we wanted to measure the available bitrate between sender and receiver depending on the distance between them, we adapted the sending bitrate to avoid packet loss. The Linux filesystem offers a file called /proc/net/udp, which shows the length of the used UDP transmission queues. It turned out that this is a good indicator for telling whether a UDP packet is still waiting to be sent, because the network might be unavailable. For every second packet, before sending, the sender therefore read the size of the UDP transmission queue. If the number of packets waiting in the queue was at least three packets, then the sender waited for 1 ms and tried again. This way, the sender adapted its sending bitrate depending on the current network condition, while the receiver recorded the currently available bandwidth (up to 20 Mbit/s).

Fig. 9 shows the arrival process of six bursts at the receiver, the burst size in this case was 10 MB. It can be clearly seen how the network becomes unavailable once the sender is out or range. We then computed the first derivative of the recorded arrival curves to get the bitrate available at the observed time t, and further used (equation (2)) to get the distance $d(t)$ between the bicycle and the start point. This yields a mapping between distance and available bandwidth.

We computed such a mapping for all experiments, and divided the distance of 800 m into 800 bins of length 1 m. For each such bin we computed the average

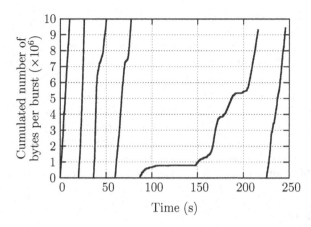

Fig. 9. Experiment 5: Arrival curves for bursts of size 10 MB when moving out of range (800 m) and back (800 m) at a specified constant speed of 20 km/h

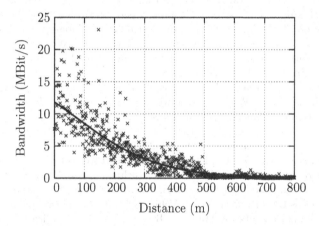

Fig. 10. Experiment 5: Average observed bitrate depending on the distance between sender and receiver. The solid line is a fitted analytical model.

observed bitrate. The result can be seen in Fig. 10. As one result it can be seen that the sender actually reduced its sending rate due to the unreliable network. On the other hand it must be noted that this procedure also dramatically reduced the observed packet loss rate (not shown here).

The figure also shows an analytical model we fitted to the data. The model relates the available average bitrate $\hat{b}$ as a function of distance d and is given by

$$\hat{b}(d) = 13 \, e^{-0.0002(d+60)^{1.51}}.$$

This model can be used, for instance, to represent the available bitrate for WLANs when simulating a mobile scenario.

6   Conclusions

In this paper we presented our measurements of 802.11g ad-hoc networks in motion. We defined different traffic situations and measured network parameters like round-trip time, signal strength, and available bandwidth at different speeds with cars and bicycles (here, presenting only the results for bicycles). We conducted all the measurements with our own measurement toolbox and stored the data (setting and results) in a metadata format. This enables one to use our results as input parameters for simulations. We showed that our measured signal strength is in good correlation to the theoretical loss model. We also calculated the available bandwidth as a function of distance between sender and receiver.

References

1. Formisano, F., Giustiniano, D., Bianchi, G.: 802.11b/g Link Level Measurements for an Outdoor Wireless Campus Network. In: 2006 International Symposium on a World of Wireless, Mobile and Multimedia Networks. (2006) 525–530
2. Gass, R., Scott, J., Diot, C.: Measurements of In-Motion 802.11 Networking. Technical Report IRC-TR-05-050, (Intel Research and Thomson R& D)
3. Singh, J., Bambos, N., Srinivasan, B., Clawin, D.: Wireless LAN Performance Under Varied Stress Conditions in Vehicular Traffic Scenarios. In: 2nd ACM Int. Workshop on VANETs. (2002) 83–84
4. Maniezzo, D., Bergamo, P., Cesana, M., Pau, G., Yao, K., Gerla, M., Whiteman, D.: IEEE 802.11 Wireless Networks under Aggressive Mobility Scenarios. In: International Telemetering Conference ITC 2003. (2003)
5. Ott, J., Kutscher, D.: Drive-thru Internet: IEEE 802.11b for Automobile Users. In: IEEE INFOCOM 2004. (2004) 362–373
6. Ott, J., Kutscher, D.: The Drive-thru Architecture: WLAN-based Internet Access on the Road. In: 59th IEEE Vehicular Technology Conference. (2004) 2615–2622
7. Singh, J., Bambos, N., Srinivasan, B., Clawin, D., Yan, Y.: Empirical Observations on Wireless LAN Performance in Vehicular Traffic Scenarios and Link Connectivity based Enhancements for Multihop Routing. In: IEEE Wireless Communications and Networking Conference. (2005)
8. Dhotaut, D., Guerin-Lassous, I.: Experiments with 802.11b in Ad Hoc Configurations. In: 14th IEEE Personal, Indoor and Mobile Radio Communications. (2003) 1618–1622
9. Stallings, W.: Wireless Communications & Networks. Prentice Hall (2005)
10. Prasad, A., Prasad, N., Kamerman, A., Moelard, H., Eikelenboom, A.: Performance Evaluation, System Design and Network Deployment of IEEE 802.11. Wireless Personal Communications 19(1) (2001) 57–79

TrafficNet: A L2 Network Architecture for Road-to-Vehicle Communication

David Fusté-Vilella, Jose-Miguel Pulido, Jorge García-Vidal,
and Steluţa Gheorghiu

Computer Architecture Department
Technical University of Catalonia, Barcelona, Spain
{dfuste, jorge, steluta}@ac.upc.edu, jpulido@stanfordalumni.org

Abstract. Information Technologies are called to play an important role in the world of transport services. One example is the combination between mobile Internet and automotive industry. This research is focused on the design of a new automotive network architecture called TrafficNet which, using IEEE 802.3 and 802.11 technologies, intends to support not only wireless communications to any type of vehicle driving along a circulatory route but also traffic management and road security services to the people in charge of the circulatory route. Results show that wired and wireless LAN technologies, together with new automotion-related protocols for optimization, can be used for high mobility applications in this type of network architecture.

1 Introduction

Information Technologies are called to play an important role in the world of transport services. An example of this is the combination of mobile Internet and automotive industry. There is a worldwide consensus among the main players of IT, Automotive and Transport industries that huge synergies exist among these three industries. In this paper we address the problem of road-to-vehicle communications in urban or densely populated suburban areas. We are not focused on any particular application, although we are interested in supporting communication of short messages between vehicles and fixed equipment or vehicle to vehicle through the fixed infrastructure, or even file downloads from the fixed infrastructure to the vehicles.

One of the key points in this design is the choice of either cellular networking or short range technology ([10], [3], etc) as wireless access technology in TrafficNet. Cellular networks are a good choice in terms of mobility support since they had been designed to support high-reliability mobility. However, they have high cost of deployment and they do not support high data rate services for applications such as telematics or traffic surveillance. On the other hand, short range technologies supply all limitations which cellular network technology lacks. Nevertheless, they do not have native support to user mobility and they have scalability problems to cover large areas like vehicular environments. In spite of

J. García-Vidal and L. Cerdà-Alabern (Eds.): Wireless and Mobility, LNCS 4396, pp. 43–61, 2007.

these lacks, they are a good choice to provide TrafficNet with wireless connectivity. Their high data rates, their low cost of deployment, their license-free use and their multicast/broadcast support are enough reasons to choose them as wireless access technology. Obviously, there are two important aspects we need to solve; it will be necessary to improve mobility and scalability support because of the nature of automotive networks (thousands of vehicular users in vehicular or metropolitan environments).

A layer-three (L3) network could be a good solution in terms of scalability support. However, due to the lack of satisfactory L3 solutions for supporting highly mobile users, we have developed a layer-two (L2) system which solves some of the problems arising of a flat L2 architecture, without losing the simplicity appeal of a pure L2 network. [12] is a solution for the lack of scalability of large L2 networks but they do not have native support for mobility management. On the other hand, [11] is a solution to achieve scalability in large L2 networks with mobility support but it is not optimized for vehicular environments in particular. So, we propose another solution: to divide the L2 network into different broadcast domains, maintaining the concept of a pure L2 network, in order to improve scalability support, and to implement new automotive-related protocols in order to reduce handover latencies and to improve mobility support.

The architecture has been designed as a three-tier system: a L2 wired backbone, a second tier base on a medium to large range wireless technology, and a shorter range wireless link which provides the road-to-vehicle communication. A key piece of this architecture is the MobiSwitch, a node which manages highly mobile vehicular users, optimizing the use of network resources. We have developed a prototype of this system. Results show that wireless LAN technology, together with new automotion-related protocols for optimization, can be used for high mobility applications in this type of network architecture.

In this paper we focus our interest in both scalability and mobility management mechanisms used in a pure L2 network architecture in vehicular environments. We don't have any application in mind for our architecture and this is left for future work. However, under this consideration, we will also take into account the security issues that emerge in vehicular networks for specific applications, such as cooperative driving, collision avoidance, toll collection, etc. In order to participate in a vehicular network, vehicles should be able to authenticate themselves and be traceable by law enforcement organisms (e.g. police has to find drivers who flee from an accident). At the same time, driver privacy should also be kept secret and not revealed, unless necessary. For traffic information applications, mechanisms that will ensure data authenticity and integrity must be provided. A malevolent user can inject false messages in the network and cause traffic disruption or even accidents. Therefore, nodes in a vehicular network should have the possibility to detect attackers and ignore messages they send. A short overview of what has been done by now in vehicular networks security will be given in the next section.

2   Related Work

Recently, the concept of transparent routing has been introduced to mitigate the problems of the Spanning Tree Protocol [1], and to adjust 802.3 networks to metropolitan environments. Transparent routing consists in the use of a link state protocol to route packets among switches, and the use of transparent learning by means of observation of traffic to know both the location of nodes and the distribution of the information through the routing protocol [12]. Limitations of transparent routing as for mobility management consist in that the supported speed depends on the frequency of update messages of the link state protocol, and that any update is distributed to all nodes through broadcast flooding, which affects network scalability.

Another alternative to mobility management in L2 metropolitan networks is [11], where switches of the network are divided into data groups and control groups. Every switch transmits the relevant information in multicast inside its group, e.g., data packets inside data groups and location messages as ARP Requests inside control groups. By means of an appropriate distribution of switches in data and control groups, i.e., where each data group has at least one representative in every control group and vice versa, the location of a user can be guaranteed confining broadcast messages to multicast groups. MobiLANe improves network scalability thanks to contain broadcast messages to the corresponding group. Its limitations consist in that scalability depends on the size of the group, which has to be defined a priori and in a static way.

Finally, TrafficNet architecture exploits the concepts of proximity and spatial locality inherent in vehicular environments to improve scalability. TrafficNet is formed by a set of switches named MobiSwitches (MS), interconnected each other, which divide the network into several network segments. Every MS learns in a transparent way the nodes which are located in its network segment. When a node moves from one segment to another, the new MS only notifies to its neighbors MSs of the new location of the node. TrafficNet guarantees that the old MS is located among the neighbors, and then mobility management traffic is limited only to near MSs. Each MS has one group of neighbors, the FROM group, which is used to notify the new location of a node. This group is implemented as a multicast group and is kept in a dynamic way.

The main advantage of TrafficNet, unlike transparent routing or MobiLANe, is that the information of location is not communicated to the rest of switches of the network (or of the multicast group), but only to the near ones. Moreover, and unlike MobiLANe, TrafficNet allows updating the multicast groups in a dynamic way, so that control and data traffic is sent only to interested switches.

When it comes to security in vehicular networks, many ideas have been taken from securing other wired and wireless networks, but in this environment additional challenges are faced due to high mobility of nodes, real-time constraints, short time of connection between nodes, low tolerance for errors, etc. One of the proposals was to use digital signatures ([17]) and a Public Key Infrastructure ([15], [16]). The factors that should be considered when electing a public key cryptosystem are the time to generate and verify a signature and the sizes of the certificates, the keys and signatures ([19]). The PKI relies on a Certification Authority (CA) to be in charge with key management. The problems are finding a CA which is available anytime, anywhere and finding the right entity to represent it (governmental authorities or vehicle manufacturers). Certification revocation is discussed only in [18], where three protocols that can be used in vehicular context are proposed.

Electronic License Plates (ELPs) are proposed in [14] to identify vehicles and they can be used in toll collection, for example. The problem is they are vulnerable to attacks as impersonation (a vehicle pretends to be another) and must not disclose personal information about the driver. One solution to allow authentication of vehicles and maintain drivers' privacy is an anonymization service [15]. The idea is that a driver authenticates with his or her permanent identity to an anonymization service and then receives a temporary identification that cannot be traced back to the owner. In order to enhance this service, the implementation of reanonymizers positioned at regular intervals by the roadside is also suggested. Another mechanism that can aid security is to equip vehicles with tamper-proof hardware, which can store cryptographic material, such as ELPs and PKI and can perform cryptographic operations. The integrity of this hardware can be verified through regular inspections at an authorized organism.

As vehicular networks have come to attention in the last years, there are a lot of aspects that need further investigations. A general security architecture has to be deployed to support nodes and messages authentication, data integrity verification, but specific solutions have to be designed for specific applications, to meet their requirements. Moreover, there could be more threats to discover.

3   The TrafficNet Architecture

TrafficNet has to cover a large geographical area, about tens of kilometers with thousands of simultaneous users with high data rates around Mbps. The complexity of the configuration required by the users has to be minimal. Users have to connect in the same way they connect to an 802.11b [5] conventional network. Moreover, administration, configuration and maintenance of the network have to be simple to reduce the price of cost.

TrafficNet has two differentiated parts: the Wireless Domain (WD) and the Backbone (see Fig. 1). These two parts are linked by the key node of this automotive network architecture, the MobiSwitch. The Wireless Domain is further divided in two subparts: the User Wireless Domain (UWD) and the Wireless Distribution System (WDS). The UWD is responsible for allowing vehicular users to connect to TrafficNet. The chosen wireless technology is the IEEE 802.11b/g [5],[7]. Its high data rates, its low cost of deployment, its license-free use and its familiarity with the IEEE 802.3 standard [2] are enough reasons to choose it as wireless access technology in TrafficNet. The WDS is responsible for linking the UWD with the Backbone. It is only a link between these two parts and has not any other functionality related with mobility support. To avoid interferences

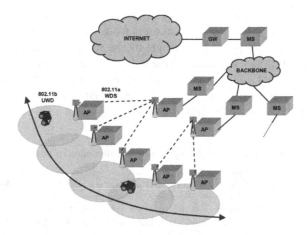

Fig. 1. TrafficNet architecture

between this subpart and the UWD, the wireless technology used in this subpart could be IEEE 802.11a [4] or WiMAX [8,9].

The backbone connects all Wireless Domains which cover the circulatory route in a pure L2 network. Due to the quantity of data traffic which has to tolerate and the large area which has to cover, the technology used in this part has to be a wired technology. IEEE 802.3 has been the chosen wired technology because of its familiarity with IEEE 802.11a/b/g technologies.

Two important requirements of this network are scalability and mobility support. A network like TrafficNet needs to be divided into several Broadcasts domains to achieve scalability support. Moreover, we have to design a communication protocol which will be responsible of both supporting mobility and reducing handover latencies. All these characteristics will be implemented by the MobiSwitch, a switching node placed between the Backbone and all Wireless Domains and Gateways (GW) of the network.

4 Scalability Support

TrafficNet will be a L2 metropolitan network with thousands of users using it at the same time. A pure L2 network architecture is attractive for its simplicity. However, current flat L2 solutions suffer from serious scalability problems when they have to support a large number of users. For example, some messages like broadcasts of mobility-related associations or broadcasts of ARP Requests can consume significant bandwidth. Moreover, L2 architectures based on Spanning-Tree topologies can present clear bottlenecks in the case of large networks.

In order to manage mobility of vehicular users, MobiSwitches have to send a mobility-related broadcast message for each vehicle which enters into their wireless domain. If we suppose 1 car every M seconds in a highway of L lanes per direction and N MobiSwitches in the system, every MobiSwitch needs to send a mobility-related message every $T_{BS} = M/2L$ seconds to the backbone, receive one every $T_{BR} = M/(2L * (N - 1))$ seconds from the backbone and distribute one every $T_T = M/(2L * (N - 1))$ seconds to the wireless domain.

If mobility-related message packet size is k bits, the bandwidth consumption will be $BW_{BS} = k/T_{BS}$, $BW_{BR} = k/T_{BR}$ and $BW_T = k/T_T$ respectively. And for average bandwidth of BW_{WD} Mbps in wireless domain, overhead of broadcasts will be $O_T = BW_T/BW_{WD}$.

Table 1. Overhead of mobility-related broadcast messages in the wireless domains

M	**L**	**N**	**k**	T_{BS}	T_{BR}	T_T	BW_{BS}	BW_{BR}	BW_T	**BW$_{WD}$**	**O$_T$**
1	2	100	1000	250 ms	2.5 ms	2.5 ms	4 kbps	400 kbps	400 kbps	2 Mbps	20%
1	3	100	1000	167 ms	1.68 ms	1.68 ms	6 kbps	600 kbps	600 kbps	2 Mbps	30%

We can see a very significant overhead due to mobility-related broadcast messages inside the wireless domains, which will affect badly TrafficNet performance (see Table 1).

[12] is a solution for the lack of scalability of large L2 networks but they do not have native support for mobility management, another critical requirement of TrafficNet. On the other hand, [11] is a solution to achieve scalability in large L2 network with mobility support but it is not optimized for vehicular environments in particular. So, we propose to divide TrafficNet into different broadcast domains: the wireless domains and the wired backbone.

Now, mobility-related broadcast messages will terminate in the backbone and so, $BW_T = 0$ and $O_T = 0$. BW_{BS} and BW_{BR} will not change but average wired backbone capacity BW_B is much greater than average wireless domain capacity BW_{WD}. BW_{BR} will be the worse of the two.

Table 2. Overhead of mobility-related broadcast messages in the backbone

M	**L**	**N**	**k**	T_{BS}	T_{BR}	BW_{BS}	BW_{BR}	**BW$_B$**	**O$_T$**	**O$_{BR}$**
1	2	100	1000	250 ms	2.5 ms	4 kbps	400 kbps	100 Mbps	0%	0.4%
1	3	100	1000	167 ms	1.68 ms	6 kbps	600 kbps	100 Mbps	0%	0.6%

Now, we can see a great drop in the overhead of broadcast messages (see Table 2). So, to divide TrafficNet into several broadcast domains is a very good improvement which will be implemented by the MobiSwitch. Moreover, in order to maintain the L2 connectivity, the MobiSwitch will have to act similar to a proxy ARP, which will also improve TrafficNet scalability.

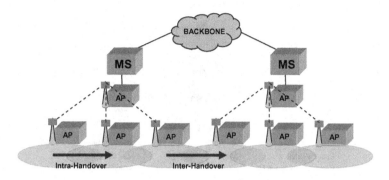

Fig. 2. Handovers in TrafficNet

5   Hierarchy-Limitations Support

TrafficNet will be a L2 metropolitan network with thousands of users using it at the same time. This behavior has an important impact in terms of bandwidth and resources consumption. In spite of having achieved scalability support with the division of TrafficNet into several broadcast domains, each MobiSwitch continues receiving information (mobility-related broadcast messages) about all vehicles in the system, irrespective of if they need to communicate with them or not.

With 10^6 vehicles in a metropolitan area on a given day and receiving one mobility-related broadcast message every $T_{BR} = 2.5ms$, the rate of update of the forwarding database of the MobiSwitch will be 400 updates per second. This value causes RAM and CPU requirements that are beyond core router capabilities supporting full BGP tables.

We propose to limit the distribution of mobility-related messages to MobiSwitches that need them, a quality achieved by the notion of From Neighbors (see Mobility Support). In other words, we want to exploit spatial locality inherent in vehicular environments and use it in order to predict the traffic.

6   Mobility Support

TrafficNet users will be mostly vehicles running along a circulatory route. They will perform a lot of "high-speed" handovers between different antennas which cover the route. In order to reduce these handover latencies, we introduce new location and mobility management protocols which exploit the high spatial locality of user movements in automotive networks. These protocols are played mainly by the MobiSwitch.

In TrafficNet there are two types of mobility, depending on the transition between the two corresponding access points. On the one hand, an intra-handover is performed when the two access points belong to the same MobiSwitch and, on the other hand, an inter-handover is performed when the two access points belong to different MobiSwitch (see Fig. 2).

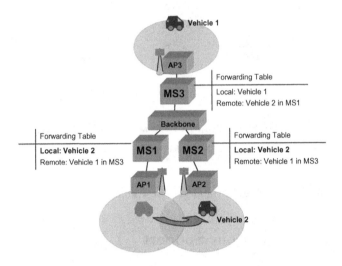

Fig. 3. Inter-handover problem

6.1   Intra-handovers

This type of transition does not cause any change in the state of the MobiSwitch that contains the two access points. The two access points and the vehicle involved are the only responsible nodes of this transition. So, the handover will be as fast as the access points and the vehicle wireless driver perform corresponding operations.

6.2   Inter-handovers

In this type of transition, the MobiSwitch has to implement a mechanism not only to allow handovers between access points of different MobiSwitch (different broadcast domain) but also to improve latencies due to these inter-handovers, since in this type of automotive network architecture, handover latencies are the most important problem in terms of delay in data communications.

When a vehicle performs an inter-handover, there will be two MobiSwitches in TrafficNet that will assume they have the same vehicle as local client, due to the non expiration of the corresponding timeout in the old MobiSwitch and to the immediately association of the vehicle to the new MobiSwitch (see Fig. 3). This temporary state has to be solved as soon as possible to reduce inter-handover latencies. If a vehicle connected to an access point of MobiSwitch1 performs an inter-handover to another access point that belongs to MobiSwitch2, MobiSwitch1 has to solve the problem of knowing, without waiting for the corresponding table timeout to expire and so, making the inter-handover latency smaller, that the vehicle no longer belongs to it.

The ideal way would be an explicit disassociation signal from the access point to its Distribution System (DS), in the same way access points send Gratuitous

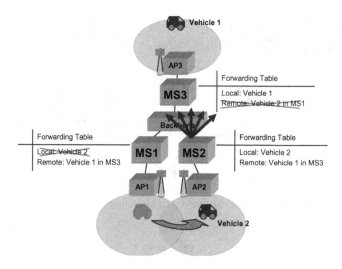

Fig. 4. Broadcast disassociation request

ARP to the DS for each new association. The disassociation would cause nodes in the DS (and so, MobiSwitches) to update their tables immediately, avoiding timeout expiration delays. However, since traditional transparent learning does not support explicit "negative" messages, access points do not currently include mechanisms to generate such messages.

To achieve this requirement, MobiSwitches will use new L2 messages between themselves. An alternative to the explicit disassociation message from the access point is an implicit disassociation message. This message can come from the MobiSwitch that knows that the vehicle has performed an inter-handover: the new MobiSwitch where the vehicle ends up with. The new MobiSwitch will be responsible to communicate to the old MobiSwitch that the vehicle belongs to it now (and, implicitly, that no longer belongs to the old MobiSwitch). But, how does the new MobiSwitch know which is the old MobiSwitch? It does not, unless it inspects all packets to detect the IAPP [6] message which contains this information, sent from the new access point to the old access point; and assuming that IAPP is in place. Since IAPP is not at all used and to inspect all packets is an inefficient solution, we discard this option. To answer this question, the solution is, for the new MobiSwitch, broadcast a new L2 message of disassociation request (DIS_REQ) about the vehicle to all MobiSwitches (see Fig. 4).

But this solution is inefficient, especially if it happens every time a vehicle changes of MobiSwitch (see Hierarchy-limitations Support). To avoid this inefficiency, we propose the use of From Neighbors Lists for each MobiSwitch. A From Neighbor List of one MobiSwitch will be a multicast group containing its From Neighbor MobiSwitches in the sense of the circulatory route (see Fig. 5).

Then, the special L2 messages of disassociation request will be sent in multicast to the multicast group only, since with high probability, the vehicle which has performed the inter-handover will come from a From Neighbor MobiSwitch.

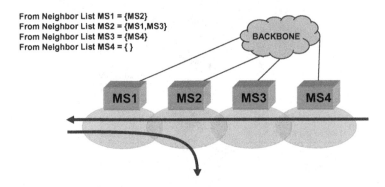

Fig. 5. From neighbor lists

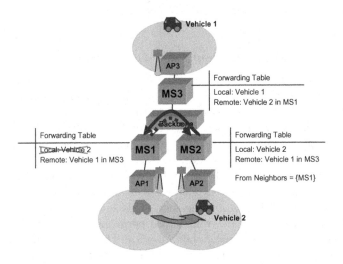

Fig. 6. Multicast disassociation request + unicast disassociation reply

To initialize and discover new neighbors, new L2 messages of disassociation reply (DIS_REP) will be sent due to the disassociation request signal. And, if the MobiSwitch which has sent the multicast disassociation request message does not receive the disassociation reply, it will send again the disassociation request message but now in broadcast mode to discover new From Neighbors (see Fig. 6).

So, every time that a vehicle changes of MobiSwitch, the new MobiSwitch has to send a message to its From Neighbors. Moreover, with a great probability, one of its From Neighbors will reply in unicast mode. In some cases (the vehicle is not associated to any of its From Neighbors), the MobiSwitch will have to send the message again but now in broadcast mode. Now, the overhead is not function of the total number of MobiSwitches of the backbone (see Scalability Support), but only of the number of From Neighbors, that in most cases, it won't be superior to two MobiSwitches.

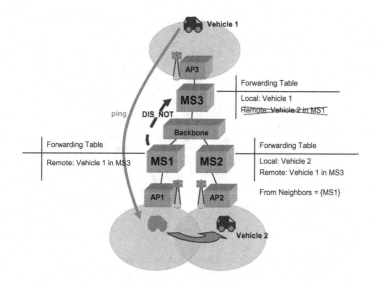

Fig. 7. Unicast disassociation notify (1)

As we previously said, when a vehicle performs an inter-handover, there will be two MobiSwitches in TrafficNet that will think they have the same vehicle as their local client. With the disassociation request and reply messages, the MobiSwitch will solve this temporary state as soon as possible. However, it is possible that another MobiSwitch, which has not been notified by the disassociation request signal, sends data for the vehicle to the old MobiSwitch (see Fig. 7).

To solve this situation, the old MobiSwitch will use another new L2 message, the disassociation notify message (DIS_NOT). When the old MobiSwitch detects wrong packets in terms of incorrect destination, it notifies the mistaken MobiSwitch with a disassociation notify signal. The mistaken MobiSwitch will receive this signal and will perform the operations to rediscover the new location of the corresponding vehicle (see Fig. 8).

In short, to achieve mobility support, MobiSwitches will send implicit disassociation signals as a solution to the lack of explicit signals from access points and moreover, to achieve hierarchy-limitations support, they will do this notification in multicast mode to the From Neighbors in order to avoid broadcast storms.

7   Testing

In order to test TrafficNet, we have emulated a network architecture similar to TrafficNet in a computer networking laboratory (see Fig. 9 and Table 3). This network architecture is not the same that TrafficNet but they are completely equivalents. The difference is that in our testbed there is only one access point per MobiSwitch, so, the Wireless Domain of each MobiSwitch only contains a

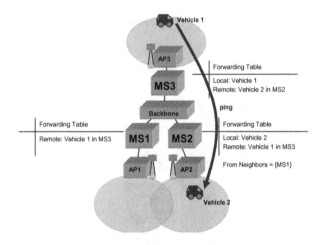

Fig. 8. Unicast disassociation notify (2)

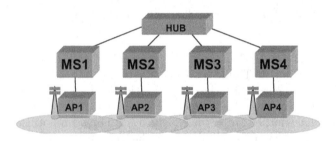

Fig. 9. Testbed architecture

User Wireless Domain. We suppressed the Wireless Distribution System since it is not necessary for testing the correct operation of TrafficNet (the Wireless Distribution System is only a wireless link which allows covering a larger area).

We have used four MobiSwitches because they are sufficient to test all types of configurations which can happen in real life (straight routes, crossroads, traffic circles, etc). Moreover, since in this testbed is not possible to use vehicles as traffic generators, we have used two laptops to generate simulated traffic by means of the use of Perl scripts. The basic idea is, depending on the type of the test, sending management traffic from laptops to different access points to cause a sensation of user mobility, or sending data traffic between the two laptops to check the correct operation of the system. However, it is important to bear in mind that handovers performed by the laptops are caused manually. The wireless device driver performs the handover when the script orders it and so, it does not waste time looking for new access points or verifying the signal intensity of its current access point.

Table 3. Testbed hardware

MS1	Pentium III-MMX 550 MHz - 128 MB RAM - Debian GNU/Linux 3.1 - Kernel 2.4.27 - Click Modular Router Linux kernel Driver
MS2	Pentium II 266 MHz - 64 MB RAM - Debian GNU/Linux 3.1 - Kernel 2.4.27 - Click Modular Router Linux kernel Driver
MS3	AMD Athlon 1 GHz - 256 MB RAM - Debian GNU/Linux 3.1 - Kernel 2.4.27 - Click Modular Router Linux kernel Driver
MS4	AMD Athlon XP 1800+ - 256 MB RAM - Debian GNU/Linux 3.1 - Kernel 2.4.27 - Click Modular Router Linux kernel Driver
Sniffer	AMD K6 300 MHz - 128 MB RAM - Debian GNU/Linux 3.1 - Kernel 2.4.27 - Click Modular Router Linux kernel Driver
AP1	Cisco Aironet 1200 Series Wireless Access Point 802.11g
AP2	Cisco Aironet 1200 Series Wireless Access Point 802.11g
AP3	D-Link AirPlus XtremeG DWL-2100AP 802.11g
AP4	U.S. Robotics 5450 Wireless Turbo Multi-Function Access Point 802.11g
HUB	3Com OfficeConnect 10/100 Mbps
Laptop1	Mobile AMD Athlon XP 2500+ - 768 MB RAM - Debian GNU/Linux 3.1 - Click Modular Router User-Level Driver - Broadcom WLAN 802.11g
Laptop2	Intel Pentium Mobile 1.4 GHz - 521 MB RAM - Windows XP Prof. - Intel WLAN 802.11b

Another important aspect in the testing is that some tests have been executed twice. We have implemented two versions of the MobiSwitch (using [13]), a version using From Neighbor Lists (multicast version) and another one without this optimization (simple version or broadcast version). Moreover, the values of the different timeouts (local vehicles, remote vehicles, From Neighbors) of forwarding tables of MobiSwitches used in these tests (around tens of seconds because Perl scripts operate around these delays) are values smaller than the values which have to be used in the real TrafficNet (around tens of minutes). Since in these tests distances are imperceptible and each MobiSwitch has only one access point, simulated vehicles perform inter-handovers more frequently than real vehicles and so, it is not necessary great timeouts to emulate the real TrafficNet.

7.1 Circulatory Routes

This first test checks the correct operation of TrafficNet in terms of mobility management. Vehicles do not generate data traffic and the only packets which pass through the backbone are mobility-related messages. We have divided this test into five subtests depending on different situations which is possible to find in real circulatory routes: straight circulatory route, zigzag (or mountain pass), long circulatory route, crossroad and traffic circle. Moreover, each subtest has been executed twice, first using the simple version of the MobiSwitch and second using the multicast version. In Table 4, we show the results of the subtests in terms of bandwidth consumption: number of transmitted packets and number of transmitted broadcast packets, due to users mobility.

Table 4. Circulatory route tests

		SIMPLE VERSION	MULTICAST VERSION
Straight Circulatory Route	#Packets	24	26
(8 vehicles - 2 MobiSwitches)	#Broadcast packets	16	10
Zigzag (or mountain pass)	#Packets	88	90
(8 vehicles - 2 MobiSwitches)	#Broadcast packets	48	10
Long Circulatory Route	#Packets	56	66
(8 vehicles - 4 MobiSwitches)	#Broadcast packets	32	16
Crossroad	#Packets	60	72
(12 vehicles - 4 MobiSwitches)	#Broadcast packets	36	20
Traffic Circle	#Packets	36	44
(12 vehicles - 4 MobiSwitches)	#Broadcast packets	24	24

These tests have checked the correct operation of TrafficNet in terms of mobility management and have served to compare the two implementations of the MobiSwitch to determine which of two is better in terms of bandwidth consumption.

The results show that whereas the quantity of packets in both versions is similar, the quantity of broadcast packets is higher in the simple version. So, at first sight, multicast version seems to be more efficient than simple version in terms of bandwidth consumption. For example, when a mobile vehicle crosses to a new MobiSwitch, the multicast group in the new MobiSwitch is created, and from here on all disassociation request messages generated by the new MobiSwitch will be sent in multicast mode.

On the other hand, multicast groups can be inefficient when a new vehicle arrives to one MobiSwitch which already have the multicast group initialized. The inefficiency is the delivery of the disassociation request message first in multicast mode and next, unnecessarily in broadcast mode, since not any MobiSwitch will reply. But this behavior only happens when a vehicle enters in the system the first time. There is another inefficiency of the multicast groups when a vehicle arrives to one MobiSwitch which already have the multicast group initialized but it does not contain the old MobiSwitch of the vehicle. The inefficiency is the delivery of the disassociation request message in multicast mode before sending the disassociation request message in broadcast mode. But also this behavior only happens one time for each From Neighbor of each MobiSwitch. And most of times, each MobiSwitch will have two From Neighbors at the most, due to the nature of circulatory routes.

To prove these assertions we will use two formulas to calculate the number of broadcast packets for each version and we will analyze them:

– Simple version:

$$\#Broadcast\_packets = N + \sum_{i=1}^{N} T_i \ . \tag{1}$$

where $N = \#$vehicles and $T_i = \#$transitions performed by $vehicle_i$

– Multicast version:

$$\#Broadcast\_packets = N + \sum_{j=1}^{K} V_j \ . \tag{2}$$

where $N = \#$vehicles, $K = \#$MobiSwitches and $V_j = \#$From Neighbors of $MobiSwitch_j$

(1) is correct. However, (2) is not in a complete way correct. There is a little behavior that the formula does not comprise. When a first vehicle $V1$ crosses from MobiSwitch $MS1$ to MobiSwitch $MS2$, it is possible that others vehicles which come from the same MobiSwitch $MS1$ arrive to MobiSwitch $MS2$ before MobiSwitch $MS2$ learns the new From Neighbor $MS1$ thanks to the inter-handover of the vehicle $V1$. So, these other vehicles will cause sending the DIS_REQ messages even in broadcast mode. This parameter depends on the delay of the first DIS_REP message. Therefore, it is not possible to calculate this value with precision:

– Multicast version:

$$\#Broadcast\_packets = N + \sum_{j=1}^{K} \left(V_j + \sum_{m=1}^{V_j} X_m \right) \ . \tag{3}$$

where $N = \#$vehicles, $K = \#$MobiSwitches, $V_j = \#$From Neighbors of $MobiSwitch_j$ and $X_m = $ random variable which represents the quantity of vehicles that arrive from each From Neighbor before the MobiSwitch receives the first DIS_REP message of this From Neighbor

However, the corresponding delay of the DIS_REP message will be often very low and so, in most of cases, X_m will be 0. Therefore, we can rewrite (3) in terms of expected value for $E(X_m) = 0$:

$$E\left(\#Broadcast\_packets\right) = E\left(N + \sum_{j=1}^{K} \left(V_j + \sum_{m=1}^{V_j} X_m \right) \right)$$

$$= N + \sum_{j=1}^{K} \left(V_j + \sum_{m=1}^{V_j} E\left(X_m\right) \right)$$

$$= N + \sum_{j=1}^{K} V_j \ . \tag{4}$$

In short, the correct two formulas which calculate the number of broadcast packets due to mobility-related messages are (1) and (4). The difference between them is that the number of broadcast packets in (1) depends on the quantity of transitions of each vehicle, a parameter which does not have limits over the time (more vehicles per second, more broadcast messages per second). On the other hand, the number of broadcast packets in (4) depends on the quantity of MobiSwitches and the quantity of From Neighbors of each MobiSwitch, both quantities static over the time (more vehicles per second, no more broadcast messages). In conclusion, the multicast version is much better than the simple version and it will reduce enormously the bandwidth consumption in the backbone.

7.2   Data Traffic

In this test we have used two MobiSwitches, $MobiSwitch1$ and $MobiSwitch2$ (see Fig. 10). This test checks the correct operation of MobiSwitches in terms of data transfer. There are two laptops acting as vehicles. $Laptop1$ is always associated to $access\ point$ 1 (for example, a vehicle which has had a road accident). Meanwhile, $laptop2$, which initially is associated to $access\ point$ 2, starts a ping to $laptop1$. Then, it crosses to $access\ point$ 1 and finally, goes back to $access\ point$ 2 and finishes the ping (for example, a vehicle which has seen the road accident and goes back to look for assistance; the ping can be interpreted as warning signals from $vehicle1$ to $vehicle2$ sent through TrafficNet).

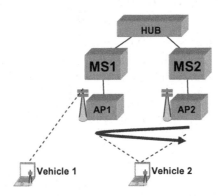

Fig. 10. Testbed

We have divided this test in several subtests depending on the initial state of the ARP tables of the two vehicles, the initial state of the forwarding table of the two MobiSwitches and if $vehicle2$ is already associated with $MobiSwitch2$ or not. Moreover, since multicast version is better than simple version, in these tests we will use only the multicast version.

Fig. 11 shows that in most of cases, the delay of the ping increases when the vehicle performs the inter-handover, but in other cases, the delay of the ping is almost null. However, there is high randomness in the different delays and in the different subtests. This strange behavior is due to the instability of the wireless transmission medium and to the randomness of the wireless device

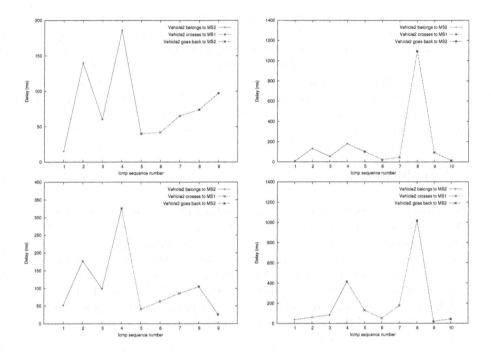

Fig. 11. Results of the data traffic

driver to perform handovers. In any case, most of delays are around milliseconds. However, it is important to bear in mind that handovers performed by the laptop are caused manually. The wireless device driver performs the handover when the script orders it and so, it does not waste time looking for new access points or verifying the signal intensity of its current access point. Therefore, inter-handover delays of these tests are smaller than real inter-handovers delays. So, if the wireless device driver of vehicular users is improved, the delays due to inter-handovers will be reduced. And in short, these tests have proved that TrafficNet supports mobility of vehicular users efficiently.

8   Future Work

This paper exposes the design of a L2 network architecture to provide connectivity to vehicular users in a metropolitan environment. There are many suggestions for future research to optimize some aspects of the architecture. Each MobiSwitch could have two groups of neighbors, the FROM group and the TO group, instead of only the FROM group. This second group could be used to suggest where a node is and to maintain an existing communication with a node that changes of network segment. Moreover, improvements in the wireless device driver of mobile users in terms of association and reassociation efficiency and the use of GMRP [1] as L2 protocol for implementing multicast flooding could be used. In the other hand, there are also many suggestions for future research to expand the functionalities of the architecture like to extend TrafficNet in the area of vehicular ad hoc networks, the development of new road applications or the development of new integrated terminals in vehicles to take advantage of benefits of TrafficNet. This last suggestion can turn into a great technological development for the automotive industry in the sense of being able to provide its cars with wireless connectivity to the Internet, an aspect very valued by vehicular users.

9   Conclusion

This research focuses on to design a new automotive L2 network architecture called TrafficNet. This network architecture, using IEEE 802.3 and 802.11 technologies, intends to support not only wireless communications to any type of vehicle driving along a circulatory route but also traffic management and road security services. The key node of TrafficNet is the MobiSwitch, a switching node with mobility management capability. The MobiSwitch has the functions of managing high mobility of vehicular users, to provide scalability support to the IEEE 802.11 and 802.3 technologies in metropolitan areas, and to optimize the use of network resources.

In this paper we show that with the concept of dividing TrafficNet in different broadcast domains we have managed to be able to use the L2 wired and wireless LAN technologies to cover a metropolitan area and with the concept of From Neighbors, we have managed to optimize mobility support for vehicular environments, to reduce inter-handover latencies and to optimize the use of network resources. Furthermore, we have implemented the MobiSwitch and tested the TrafficNet architecture in a computer networking laboratory. The results show that TrafficNet can be used to provide reliable wireless communications to vehicles driving along a circulatory route and, with the improvement of wireless device drivers of vehicular users, to provide efficient wireless communications. In short, this research has provided mobility and scalability support to the L2 wired and wireless LAN technologies optimizing it for automotive networks.

Acknowledgments. Work supported by the Ministery of Education of Spain under grant TEC2004-06437-C05-05 and by the project VI FP project EuroNGI-VNET.

References

1. 802.1d. IEEE Standard for Local and Metropolitan Area Networks. Media Access Control (MAC) Bridges. IEEE Standards (2004)
2. 802.3. Carrier Sense Multiple Access with Collision Detection (CSMA/CD) Access Method and Physical Layer Specifications. IEEE Standards (2002)

3. 802.11. Information Technology. Telecommunications and Information Exchange Between Systems. Local and Metropolitan Area Networks. Specific Requirements. Part 11: Wireless LAN Medium Access Control (MAC) and Physical Layer (PHY) Specifications. IEEE Standards (1999)
4. 802.11a. Supplement to IEEE Standard for Information technology. Telecommunications and Information Exchange Between Systems. Local and Metropolitan Area Networks. Specific Requirements. Part 11: Wireless LAN Medium Access Control (MAC) and Physical Layer (PHY) Specifications: High-speed Physical Layer in the 5 GHZ Band. IEEE Standards (1999)
5. 802.11b(Cor1). IEEE Standard for Information technology. Telecommunications and Information Exchange Between Systems. Local and Metropolitan Area Networks. Specific Requirements. Part 11: Wireless LAN Medium Access Control(MAC) and Physical Layer (PHY) Specifications. Amendment 2: Higher-speed Physical Layer (PHY) Extension in the 2.4 GHz Band. Corrigendum 1. IEEE Standards (2001)
6. 802.11f. IEEE Trial-Use Recommended Practice for Multi-Vendor Access Point Interoperability via an Inter-Access Point Protocol Across Distribution Systems Supporting IEEE 802.11 Operation. IEEE Standards (2003)
7. 802.11g. IEEE Standard for Information technology. Telecommunications and Information Exchange Between Systems. Local and Metropolitan Area Networks. Specific Requirements. Part 11: Wireless LAN Medium Access Control (MAC) and Physical Layer (PHY) Specifications. Amendment 4: Further Higher Data Rate Extension in the 2.4 GHz Band. IEEE Standard (2003)
8. 802.16. IEEE Standard for Local and Metropolitan Area Networks. Part 16: Air Interface for Fixed Broadband Wireless Access Systems. IEEE Standards (2004)
9. 802.16.2. IEEE Recommended Practice for Local and Metropolitan Area Networks. Coexistence of Fixed Broadband Wireless Access Systems. IEEE Standards (2004)
10. DSRC. http://grouper.ieee.org/groups/scc32/dsrc/
11. Hristea, C., Tobagi, F.: A network Infrastructure for IP Mobility Support in Metropolitan Areas. Computer Networks Journal, **38** (2002) 181-206
12. Perlman, R.J.: Rbridges: Transparent Routing. Sun Microsystems Lab. IEEE Infocom (2004)
13. Click Modular Router. http://www.read.cs.ucla.edu/click/
14. Hubaux, J.P., Capkun, S., Luo, J.: The Security and Privacy of Smart Vehicles. IEEE Securit and Privacy (2004)
15. Parno, B., Perrig, A.: Challenges in Securing Vehicular Networks. Workshop on Hot Topics in Networks, HotNets - IV (2005)
16. Raya, M., Hubaux, J.P.: The Security of Vehicular Ad Hoc Networks. SASN'05 (2005)
17. Gollan, L., Meinel, C.: Digital Signatures for Automobiles?!. Systemics, Cybernetics and Informatics (2002)
18. Raya, M., Jungels, D., Papadimitratos, P., Aad, I., Hubaux, J.P.: Certificate Revocation in Vehicular Networks. EPFL, Switzerland. LCA-Report-2006-006
19. Leinmuller, T., Buttyan, L., Hubaux, J.P., Kargl, F., Kroh, R., Papadimitratos, P., Raya, M., Schoch, E.: SEVECOM - Secure Vehicle Communication

A Protocol Stack for Cooperative Wireless Networks

Jorge García-Vidal, Manel Guerrero-Zapata, Julián Morillo-Pozo,
and David Fusté-Vilella

Technical University of Catalonia
Computer Architecture Dept.
Jordi Girona 1-3, E-08034 Barcelona, Spain
{jorge, guerrero, jmorillo, dfuste}@ac.upc.edu

Abstract. Nowadays, some of the more exciting research areas in networking are based on cooperation between network nodes. Examples of this are ad-hoc or sensor networks, cooperative physical layer techniques known as *cooperative diversity*, or other new cooperative mechanisms such as *Cooperative ARQ*. In many scenarios, this cooperation could be further exploited using new mechanisms that fall into the L2-L3 protocols, leading to a *cooperative stack*. These mechanisms allow an easy use of the resources of adjacent nodes to increase communication capabilities. This combines particularly well with the characteristics of wireless networks thanks to the broadcast advantage inherent in wireless transmission. This paper proposes a novel cooperative relaying scheme that exploits transmitter diversity and performs a fast path repair procedure at L2. All these operations are made transparently to the content of the forwarding tables of the nodes, thanks to the use of a new addressing scheme. This protocol could work together with other cooperative protocols such as Cooperative ARQ, leading to an integrated mechanism for frame relaying. Analytical and simulation results show that cooperative frame relaying clearly improves network resilience.

Keywords: Cooperative systems, Diversity methods, Land mobile radio diversity systems, Protocols.

1 Introduction

The very notion of communication protocol implies a joint and coordinated work between different nodes with the aim of transferring information. Traditionally, not all nodes of a network have the same role and responsibility in this task: end-hosts are usually only responsible of keeping their own communication flows, while other nodes, such as switches, routers, or access-points, are involved in making possible the coordinated operation of the network.

It is interesting to note that nowadays some of the more exciting research areas in networking are devoted to communication paradigms where this distinction disappears: In the area of application layer protocols, peer-to-peer (P2P) protocols have demonstrated their capacity to form distributed self-organized systems in which resources such as content, CPU cycles, storage or bandwidth are shared [1]. In ad-hoc or sensor networks, nodes can act either as end-points of a communication flow or as

J. García-Vidal and L. Cerdà-Alabern (Eds.): Wireless and Mobility, LNCS 4396, pp. 62–72, 2007.
© Springer-Verlag Berlin Heidelberg 2007

relays, and they must cooperate in order to maintain network connectivity. Other examples are the cooperative physical layer techniques known as *cooperative diversity* [8], or new cooperative mechanisms such as Cooperative ARQ ([4], [5], [9] and [10]).

We think that in many cases, a tighter cooperation among nodes of a wireless network would lead to major benefits. This cooperation would be established through mechanisms that usually fall into L2-L3 (i.e. data link and network layers) protocols, leading to a *cooperative stack* designed for allowing nodes to use the resources of adjacent nodes. We believe that this combines particularly well with the characteristics of wireless networks, since it exploits the broadcast advantage inherent in wireless transmission. Moreover, the cooperative use of antennas, RF chains, network interfaces, etc. of nearby nodes enables basic techniques for wireless transmission, such as spatial diversity, to be introduced.

In this paper, a novel cooperative relaying (C-Relaying) scheme is presented. It exploits transmitter diversity and performs a fast path repair procedure at L2. All these operations are made transparently to the content of the forwarding tables of the nodes, thanks to the use of a new addressing scheme. This protocol would work together with other cooperative protocols such as Cooperative ARQ (C-ARQ), leading to an integrated mechanism for frame relaying. By means of a simple analytical formulation and simulation analysis, it is shown that some important network performance metrics, such as path outage probability and packet loss ratio, are drastically improved.

We believe that exploiting cooperation at L2-L3 has some advantages over cooperative diversity schemes at PHY layer. No sophisticated hardware is required, and only changes in the firmware are needed. On the other hand, using cooperation at L2-L3 probably will increase latency and can lead to sub-optimal performance improvements. It is an open research issue to clearly identify under which conditions is preferable each type of cooperation.

A cooperative stack must tackle different aspects of the transport of frames through the network. As far as we know, ours is the first proposal where an integrated operation of addressing, relaying, ARQ and MAC is presented.

1.1 Related Work

Several researchers have raised the necessity of a cooperative stack. [6], for instance, discusses the cross-layer implications of a cooperative stack on the current architectures, although no specific mechanisms or protocols are described. [7] presents the idea of a cooperative transport. High capacity energy conduits are built using cascaded transmissions. Frame relaying is done at the physical layer, taking thus an opposite solution to the one presented in this paper. [13] studies the joint problem of transmission side diversity and routing. Cooperation is also exploited at the physical layer and the paper focuses on the problem of finding the minimum energy route. The Cooperative MAC of [3], can be seen as a particular case of our proposal for single-hop paths. Cooperative ARQ of [4], [5], [9] and [10] are also examples of cooperative mechanisms.

2 System Assumptions

This paper assumes a wireless network where nodes can use the resources of adjacent nodes, that we call *cooperators*, to increase their communication and processing capacities. The shared resources may be antennas, RF chains, network interfaces, memory or processors. One node might even completely take over the functions of another, in order to ensure that the movement or disappearance of nodes does not affect the operational status of the network.

Frame headers have four addresses fields: *Source address*, *Destination address*, *Transmission address* and *Reception address*. A *Frame ID* field, together with the source address field, uniquely identifies the frame. Frame header includes a field with several *flag* bits (*C-ARQ* bit, C-Relaying bit, *ACK* bit, etc). Other header fields, such as header error correction field, control field, protocol identifier, etc., are not relevant for describing the mechanism and will be not discussed in this paper.

The following conventions are used: Let N be a node of the wireless network. $R(N)$ is the set of nodes receiving the signal transmitted by S within certain parameters of quality (e.g. minimum signal-to-noise ratio (SNR) or maximum bit error rate (BER) values), whereas **Cloud**(N) is the set of N's cooperators, including node N itself.

Due to the broadcast nature of the wireless medium, when a node S transmits a frame addressed to another node D, the nodes of set $R(S) \cap$**Cloud**(D) will also receive the corresponding signal. We propose an addressing scheme which enables us to refer not only to the D nodes, but also to the set of nodes **Cloud**(D):

Address of node D : < @D, 0 >
Address of set Cloud(D): < @D, 1 >

where @D is a string of bits that uniquely identifies the wireless interface of node D.

The forwarding scheme proposed in this paper will be normally used together with a Cooperative ARQ (C-ARQ) protocol. C-ARQ works as follows: Assume that S sends a frame to D, using <@D, 1> as reception address. All nodes belonging to $R(S) \cap$**Cloud**(D) that can decode the frame must keep a temporal copy of it. If D receives a frame with incorrect bits, it can ask for a frame retransmission to the other nodes of **Cloud**(D). Given that we assume that nodes of **Cloud**(D) are in the proximity of D, if a node of **Cloud**(D) has a correct copy of the frame, it will be very unlikely that the corresponding frame retransmission will be erroneously received by D. Note that in case of NLOS (Near Line-of-Sight) and uniform scattering environment, the channels between S and nodes of **Cloud**(D) will be independent, provided that nodes of **Cloud**(D) have a separation of at least one half wavelength. For a large enough number of cooperating nodes, it will be very unlikely that all of these channels will be simultaneously in deep fading conditions. In other words, C-ARQ exploits *receiver diversity* [2] at L2. The C-ARQ flag bit will indicate the use of a C-ARQ protocol.

3 Cooperative Relaying

In this section we describe a Cooperative relaying (C-Relaying) mechanism that increases routing path resilience in wireless networks. The proposed mechanism exploits the following two facts:

- In case of NLOS and uniform scattering environment, it is unlikely that all channels between nodes of **Cloud**(S) and D will be simultaneously in deep fading conditions. In other words, it exploits *transmitter diversity* (see Fig. 1).
- Moreover, C-Relaying uses the fact that when a frame is forwarded through a routing path between two nodes, it is generally irrelevant which are the exact intermediate nodes that perform the relaying functions. The mechanism will choose different relay nodes depending on the channel conditions. It can thus be also seen as a *fast route restoration mechanism*, performed at layer L2, being transparent to the routing process at L3.

The proposed mechanism can be used together with C-ARQ, thus achieving increased network resilience.

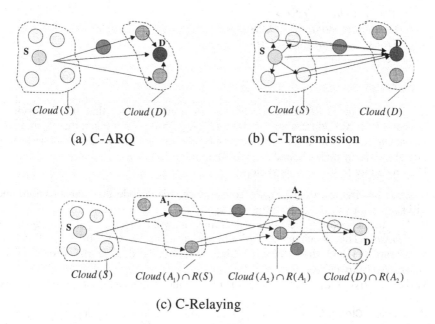

Fig. 1. (a) C-ARQ exploits receiver diversity, (b) C-Transmission exploits transmitter diversity, (c) Relaying is not done necessarily by nodes chosen by the routing protocol

Let us assume that S wishes to send a frame addressed to D$\notin$ **R**(S). We need to use a routing protocol (e.g. AODV [12]) to establish a routing path between the two nodes. Let us say that an ordered set of nodes $(A_0, A_1, A_2, ..., A_{n-1}, A_n)$ with A_0=S, A_n=D is a *path* between S and D where

$$A_i \in R(A_{i-1}), i=1...n.$$

At this point it is important to distinguish between nodes that *define* the path, i.e. the elements A_i that we call *anchor nodes*, and nodes that perform the actual packet forwarding function, that we call *relay nodes*. Normally, the anchor nodes will also be the relay nodes used in the communication, although it does not need always to be the case.

An element $L_i \in$ **Cloud**(A_i) is a candidate for performing relay functions when:

$$\begin{cases} L_i \in Cloud(A_i), \\ \quad L_i \in R(L_{i-1}), \\ A_{i+1} \in R(L_i) \quad . \end{cases} \tag{1}$$

Suppose that the routing protocol has determined a suitable path $(S, A_1, A_2, ... D)$ between nodes S and D on the basis of certain optimization criteria. It is assumed that all nodes of the i-th hop (i.e. nodes of **Cloud**(A_i)) know, at each moment, which node is the relay node L_i. When the i-th hop relay node forwards a frame generated by S and addressed to D, it will use the following header fields:

> *Source address : <S,0>*
> *Destination address: <D,0>*
> *Transmitter address: <A_i,0>*
> *Receiver address: <A_{i+1},1>*
> *C-ARQ flag = 1,*
> *C-Relaying flag = 1.*

Recall that, as the C-Relaying mechanism is used, the fact that the Transmitter address and Receiver address are <A_i,0> and <A_{i+1},1> does not mean that A_i and A_{i+1} are the actual nodes which forward the frame. We only require that nodes forwarding the frame (i.e. relay nodes L_i and L_{i+1}) fulfill conditions (1).

The procedure follows the next steps:

1. L_i sends the frame to A_{i+1}. A_{i+1}'s cooperators will decode this transmission, and will keep a copy of the transmitted frame.
2. If A_{i+1} unsuccessfully decodes the frame, it will trigger a *relay designation mechanism*. This mechanism will choose a node $L_{i+1} \in$ **Cloud**(A_{i+1}) fulfilling conditions (1) and that has been able to correctly decode the frame, as an *alternative relay node*.
3. This alternative relay node will perform the frame transmission process to the next hop.
4. If no node $\in$ **Cloud**(A_{i+1}) can decode successfully the frame after a given number of retransmissions, the frame will be discarded by node L_i. In this case the link can be declared as broken and a L3 rerouting process can be started.

If C-Relaying is not used, relay nodes must always be the anchor nodes (i.e. the relay designation mechanism will never be triggered). If C-ARQ is not used, relay nodes cannot ask for frame retransmissions to other nearby nodes. Note that, when C-Relaying is used, C-ARQ only has sense in the last hop, since we do not need that each anchor correctly decodes the frame as long as it goes forward along the established path.

Finally, it is interesting to discuss the situation where the current *anchor* node moves away or becomes out of operation. Potential relay nodes could be allowed to trigger by themselves the *relay designation mechanism*. However, this could lead to situations where several nodes consider themselves relay nodes of the i-th hop. A suitable *relay node duplicate detection* procedure must then be used, introducing more complexity in the mechanism.

4 Performance of Cooperative Relaying

The previously described mechanisms increase network resilience. Of course, depending on the scenario, the achievable benefits will be different. For instance, if nodes are quite far away from each other, cooperation cannot be exploited. On the other hand, when nodes are clustered, the benefits will be maximized.

This paper presents analytical and simulation results that show large performance benefits obtained through cooperation. Further work is needed to fully assess the performance of the proposed mechanism.

4.1 Analytical Results

Assume a communication path of H hops. In each hop, there are M-1 nodes that can cooperate with the anchor node. For simplicity, we assume that all the communication links that can be established between nodes of the i-th hop and nodes of the (i+1)-th hop follow the same statistics and are independent. Let P denote the outage probability for each of those links, i.e. the probability that the transmission conditions in the link are below a given level.

Let P_{hop} be the outage probability of a hop, and P_{path} be the outage probability for the path. A hop will be in outage when *all* the available communication links of the hop are in outage. The path will be in outage when *at least* one of the hops is in outage. Note that:

- For non-cooperative networks, there is a single available communication link for each hop (link from A_i to A_{i+1}).
- If we use the C-ARQ, C-Transmission or C-Relaying strategies alone, the number of available links is M for all hops.
- If we use the joint C-Transmission and C-ARQ strategies, the number of available links is M^2 for all hops.
- If we use the joint C-Transmission and C-Relaying strategies, the number of available links is M^2 for all hops, except the last one in which we only have the M provided by C-Transmission.

Let us define T as the average period of time during which a communication path is not in outage, measured in packet transmission time units. When the path is in outage, the routing protocol will trigger a route repair procedure that introduces an overhead of R, assumed to be constant and also measured in packet transmission times. Let us use, as the path resilience measure, the fraction of time during which the communication path is usable, defined as

$$r = \frac{T}{T + R} .$$

From the previous assumptions, we obtain the following expressions:

$$P_{hop} = P^\alpha ,$$

where:

- $\alpha = 1$ if no cooperation is used,
- $\alpha = M$ if either C-ARQ, C-Transmission or C-Relaying is used,
- $\alpha = M^2$ if both C-ARQ and C-Transmission are used.

$$P_{path} = 1 - \left(1 - P_{hop}\right)^H ,$$

where H is the number of hops, and

$$T = \frac{1 - P_{path}}{P_{path}} .$$

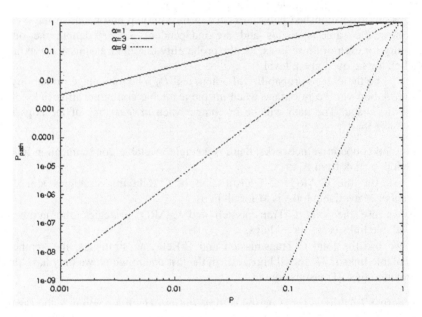

Fig. 2. P_{path} versus P for non-cooperative relaying, C-Relaying without C-ARQ, and combined C-Transmission and C-ARQ. M=3 and H=3.

In Fig. 2, 3 and 4 we show P_{path} and r for different values of P and R, with M=3, H=3. In the figures can be seen that for moderate to high values of P, the cooperative scheme leads to large improvements in terms of network resilience.

This model is useful as its highlights the factors that impact on the network performance. It predicts huge differences in the performance of cooperative and the non-cooperative relaying. However, in real life other effects, such as routing protocol inefficiencies, etc., will impact system performance.

In the next section we present results from a simulation model, where more realistic conditions are assumed.

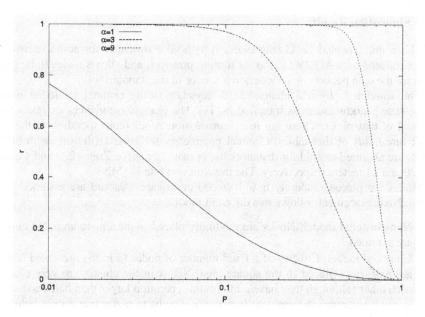

Fig. 3. r versus P for non-cooperative relaying, C-Relaying without C-ARQ, and combined C-Transmission and C-ARQ. M=3, H=3 and R=10.

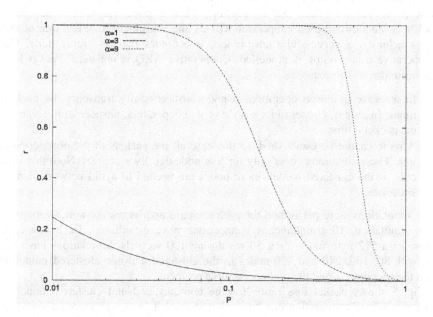

Fig. 4. r versus P for non-cooperative relaying, C-Relaying without C-ARQ, and combined C-Transmission and C-ARQ. M=3, H=3 and R=100.

4.2 Simulation Results

We have implemented (in C language and python) a simulator for ad-hoc networks. The simulator uses AODV [12] as its routing protocol, and allows nodes to be set to forward the data packets in a cooperative way or in the standard way.

The simulated physical channel is a Rayleigh fading channel modelled with a finite-state Markov chain, as specified in [11]. The channel parameters are taken from Table I of that paper. There are four transmission zones (corresponding to the four SNR thresholds of that table). Channel parameters for zone 1 (the one with higher SNR) are assumed to hold for distances lower than 12 meters. Zones 2, 3 and 4 end at 15, 20 and 24 meters respectively. The transmission rate is 1Mb/s.

Nodes are placed randomly in a 100x100 m^2 square area and are assumed to be static. Node placement follows two different models:

- Non-clustered model: Nodes are randomly placed in the square area. No clusters are assumed.
- Clustered model: Clusters of a fixed number of nodes (3 in the presented results) are uniformly placed in the square area. Nodes in the cluster are very close to each other (although they have a minimum separation larger than half wavelength in order to ensure independent transmission paths to nodes that do not belong to the cluster).

When we use cooperation, cooperator nodes must be closer than 12 m. From our transmission channel model, this ensures an almost error free transmission channel between cooperator nodes and its anchor. When a node transmits erroneously a packet, a randomly chosen cooperator will try the transmission. When one of these nodes achieves a successful transmission, it becomes the new relay node. Only Cooperative transmission is modelled. Cooperative ARQ is not used. Packet losses can occur due to two reasons:

- In the case of non-cooperation, a node unsuccessfully transmits the packet 8 times. In case of cooperation, a node or its cooperators, unsuccessfully transmits the packet 8 times.
- A route cannot be established. In this case all the packets of the connection are lost. These situations occur only for low node density scenarios. Note that in the case of the clustered model, more nodes are needed to avoid network partition situations.

Five simulations were performed for each scenario and its results were averaged. In each simulation, 10 simultaneous connections were established. Each connection transmits a 512-byte frame each 50 ms during 100 seconds. Simulations have been run with 80, 160, 240 and 320 nodes in the clustered and non-clustered model and with the cooperative and the non-cooperative protocol.

Fig. 5 shows packet loss ratios for the non-clustered and clustered models. In scenarios where cooperation can be exploited, packet loss experiences a significant reduction. In the non-clustered scenario this happens when the expected number of cooperator nodes is large enough. In the clustered scenarios the reduction appears when the number of nodes guarantees a connected network. For instance, in the case of 320 nodes and non-clustered scenario, packet loss ratio is of 20%. When

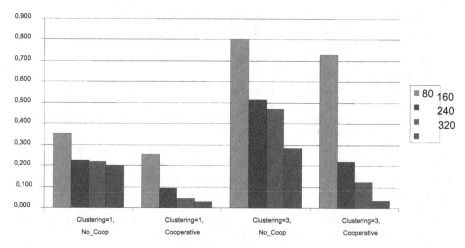

Fig. 5. Packet loss rate

cooperation can be exploited, the packet loss ratio drops to 3%. For the same number of nodes and clustered scenario (i.e. around 106 clusters) packet loss ratios are 28% and 3.4% respectively.

5   Concluding Remarks

In this paper we have presented an integrated proposal of addressing scheme, MAC, ARQ and frame relaying which allow node cooperation in wireless networks. The results presented in this paper show that, for scenarios where this cooperation can be exploited, large gains in terms of reduced packet loss ratio or increased network resilience can be achieved.

In our opinion, the presented results give interesting hints for designing a cooperative stack. However, there are still many open issues, like which are the scenarios for which cooperation is better exploited at physical layer or at L2-L3 layers; signaling overheads, security aspects, etc.; and what mechanism must be devised to incentive cooperation between nodes.

Acknowledgments. This work has been supported by the Ministry of Education of Spain under grant TEC2004-06437-C05-05, and by the VI FP project EuroNGI.

References

1. S. Androutsellis-Theotokis, D. Spinellis, "A Survey of Peer-to-Peer Content Distribution Technologies", ACM Computing Surveys, Vol 36, No. 4, December 2004.
2. A. Goldsmith, "Wireless Communications", Cambridge University Press, 2005.
3. P. Liu, Z. Tao, and S. S. Panwar, "A Cooperative MAC Protocol for Wireless Local Area Networks," IEEE ICC'05, 2005.

4. A. Miu, H. Balakrishnan, C. E. Koksal, "Improving Loss Resilience with Multi-Radio Diversity in Wireless Networks", ACM Mobicom 2005, Cologne.
5. J. Morillo, J. García-Vidal, A. Pérez-Neira "Collaborative ARQ in Energy-constrained Wireless Networks", Third ACM/SIGMOBILE Workshop on Foundation of Mobile Computing DIAL-M-POMC 2005.
6. V. Srivastava, M. Motani, "Cross-layer design: a survey and the road ahead", IEEE Communications Magazine, December 2005.
7. R. Ramanathan, "Challenges: A Radically New Architecture for Next Generation Mobile Ad Hoc Networks", ACM Mobicom 2005, Cologne.
8. A. Nosratinia, T.E. Hunter, A. Hedayat, "Cooperative Communication in Wireless Networks", IEEE Communications Magazine, October 2004.
9. P. Monti, M. Tacca, A. Fumagalli, "Optimized Transmission Power Levels in a Cooperative ARQ Protocol for Microwave Recharged Wireless Sensors", IEEE ICC'05, 2005.
10. B. Zhao, M. C. Valenti, "Practical Relay Networks: A Generalization of Hybrid-ARQ", IEEE JSAC, Vol. 23, No. 1, January 2005.
11. Qinqing Zhang and Saleem A. Kassam: "Finite-State Markov Model for Rayleigh Fading Channels". IEEE Transactions on Communications, VOL. 47, NO. 11, pp. 1688-1692, Nov 1999.
12. Charles E. Perkins, Elizabeth M. Belding Royer, Samir R. Das: Ad hoc On-Demand Distance Vector (AODV) Routing. RFC 3561, November 2003.
13. Amir E. Khandani, Jinane Abounadi, Eytan Modiano, Lizhong Zheng, "Cooperative Routing in Wireless Networks", Allerton Conference on Communications, Control and Computing, October, 2003.

Cross Layer Routing and Medium Access Control with Channel Dependant Forwarding in Wireless Ad-Hoc Networks

Anders Nilsson[1], Per Johansson[2], and Ulf Körner[1]

[1] Lund University, Dept. of Communication Systems, Box 118, SE-221 00 Lund, Sweden
`andersn@telecom.lth.se, ulfk@telecom.lth.se`
[2] University of California, San Diego, Calit2, 9500 Gilman Drive, La Jolla, CA, 92093, USA
`pjohansson@ucsd.edu`

Abstract. Wireless ad hoc networks have the last 10 years gained a lot of attention within the research community. A wireless ad hoc network is a special type of wireless network where nodes are typically mobile and doesn't rely on any fixed infrastructure to operate correctly. Much work has been done on developing robust and stable routing algorithms that consider the dynamic nature of an ad hoc network: nodes are very mobile and enter and leave the network in random ways. Much work has also been done on developing medium access control (MAC) algorithms that consider many wireless characteristics such as interference and the hidden terminal problems. Little work has so far been done on developing joint routing and MAC layer solutions that consider the variations of the wireless channel. We present a solution where the routing protocol can cooperate with the MAC layer to provide power control and channel dependent forwarding. By establishing non-disjoint multiple paths between each source and destination, nodes may be able to avoid links that are currently in a deep signal fade by choosing a more beneficial next hop path.

1 Introduction

Mobile ad hoc networks are networks where all nodes are typically wireless and do not rely on any fixed infrastructure to operate correctly. Nodes that wish to communicate with each other but are not within direct communication range need to rely on intermediate neighbors to forward their data toward the final destination. Before this can happen a routing protocol will have to establish routing paths between each source and destination. These protocols will have to take into account the node mobility; a path that was available just a few minutes ago might not be usable anymore because one or more wireless nodes towards the destination have moved away.

Medium access control (MAC) protocols determine who should be allowed access to the physical medium. In a wireless environment, if two nodes transmit at the same time they will cause interference which may result in loss of data. A common solution to this problem is to only allow a single node to transmit at the same time, thus enabling successful transmissions and preventing collisions from occurring. The most popular wireless MAC layer protocol today is IEEE 802.11 DCF [1][2] that is being used in almost in every laptop computer as a wireless LAN technology. IEEE 802.11 can be

J. García-Vidal and L. Cerdà-Alabern (Eds.): Wireless and Mobility, LNCS 4396, pp. 73–86, 2007.

used in both infrastructure mode to gain access to the Internet, or in ad hoc mode for easy communication between nodes without the need for an access point.

Recently there has been work that considers the current interference situation when setting up access to the wireless medium [3].If we know the current interference situation at our intended destination, we can make more intelligent decisions on whether we should transmit or not. If we also know the gain or path loss between ourselves and the destination it will be possible to do power control; we could set the power level to a value such that a certain SINR threshold is achieved. What would be even better is if we could coordinate the different transmitters and their power levels. If they transmit at the same time and at the appropriate power level, throughput could be improved and interference can be controlled.

Another popular research topic is that of multi path routing. If we setup multiple path betweens a source and a destination is is easy to switch to a new path if the old path breaks. This will also enable the possibility for load balancing between different routes, and to distribute the load in the network. A special type of multi path routing is non-disjoint multi path routing. In this type of routing, every source and intermediate node on the path towards the destination has one or more next hop candidate nodes. This is in contrast to node-disjoint routes where a source has multiple paths to a destination, but no paths share any nodes. In the same way, link-disjoint routes don't share any links. By having a non-disjoint routing scheme we can let each forwarding node make a forwarding decision based on the best current channel conditions. If the signal strength on a link to one next hop neighbor is in a current bad state due to fading, it can choose another next hop, that is currently in a better fading situation.

2   On Demand Multpath Link State Routing

In this paper, we present a cross layer solution where the MAC protocol can perform power and interference control by querying a number of possible candidate terminals. Each candidate is a possible next hop forwarder toward the destination, as determined by the upper layer routing protocol.

For this scheme to work successfully we need a routing protocol that can setup multiple non-disjoint paths to destinations. The routing protocol should also be able to provide the MAC layer with information about possible candidates.

We are using a hybrid on demand scheme that consists of two parts: the route *setup* part and the route *calculation* part. The route calculation part consists of calculating the cost toward different destinations using a link state database. The link state database can be created either by listening on other nearby data transmissions and overhearing or forwarding routing messages. It could also be created in a more proactive way as is in OLSR [4] or Fiseye State Routing [5].

While multiple routes can be calculated using the link state database, this calculation can not ensure that loops will not exist when packets are transmitted and forwarded by intermediate nodes. When a packet arrives at an intermediate node, where multiple next hop candidates exist, the forwarding node can not be sure that this packet has not already passed through one of the candidate nodes. One way of solving this problem is to use source routing. However, since source routing is performed at the source node based on information included in the link state database (or in the routing cache), which is not updated frequently enough to include the channel state information, source routing can never be channel dependent. Another solution to the loop problem would be to include a record route option, where each hop is recorded. Each intermediate node can then make sure the packet is not forwarded to the same node twice.

In our solution, we use an on demand route setup phase that create loop free routing table entries. When a node is about the send a packet to some destination, it first searches its routing table. If an entry can not be found, the node searches the link state database to see whether it can calculate one or more paths to the destination. If it can't do this either, it issues a *Route Request*, RREQ, message. This enables the protocol to fall back and behave as a normal on demand routing protocol such as AODV [6], but where each rebroadcasting node also adds the previous link to the RREQ packet. Each forwarding node also adds this link information, and any link information it finds in the RREQ packet. This information will update the link state database for each of the forwarding nodes.

If the node do find a path in the link state database, it unicasts a *Route Enforce*, RENF message to each of its neighbors that it determines can be used as a next hop forwarding node towards the final destination. Each of these messages includes the link state information of each forward hop as perceived by the sending node. Each node that receives this RENF message creates a forward and backward routing table entry, between the source and the destination. The node then forwards the message along the path toward the destination as specified in the RENF. Similar to the source node, each forwarding node consult its own link state database creates and then sends a new RENF message to each of its own neighbors that it determines can be used used for reaching the destination. Note that each RENF message associated between a source and destination setup can only be forwarded once. Any subsequent RENF messages from the same source destination setup phase are dropped. This prevents loops and enables each intermediate node to have unique but multiple routing table entries toward a destination.

Each entry in the routing table maps the source of the route to the destination, and possibly a multiple number of next hops. This differs from a normal routing table, which only routes according to the destination and through a specified next hop. The source address of the route is needed in order to simplify the loop freedom criteria, as the originating source node has reserved multiple routes towards the destination. While it may be possible to create routing table entries that are loop free without using the source address, which can later be reused by other nodes, there will be less multiple paths. This is because when the route is being setup, the path doesn't allow a packet to visit a previous node again. This means that any intermediate node that wishes to reuse the route also will not be able to visit these nodes, thereby limiting the number of multiple paths. This is also in contrast to normal shortest single path routing schemes where *shortest* is the most important objective. Here, we wish to create redundant routes that can be used in case the link of the shortest next hop goes into a bad fading phase.

Since this is an on demand routing protocol, routing table entries will time out if they are not being used. Because multiple redundant routes are used, this protocol is not so sensitive to "link breaks" as normal single path protocols. Also, since the MAC protocol performs power control, link breaks will only occur when the link destination is no longer reachable. This protocol has no route repair or local repair feature as for example AODV does. Even though routes are redundant, they need to be refreshed every now and then. This is done by issuing a new RENF, controlled by a refresh timer. The timeout value of this timer should depend on the mobility of the node, and the network in general, but how to determine this value is out of scope of this paper.

3   Multipath Power and Interference Control

So far we have only described how a routing protocol can setup multiple paths to a destination that enables each intermediate node to make an independent relaying choice. However, in order for this scheme to allow us to make channel dependent forwarding decisions, we also need a MAC protocol that can evaluate the state of the channel towards the different next hop candidates. To make this possible we need to exchange information across layers. The MAC protocol needs information about different candidate next hops. The routing protocol also uses information, provided by the MAC protocol during receptions and transmissions, about the status and capacity of the different links. This information is included in the link state database.

3.1   Diversity and Relaying Node Selection

In our scheme, the MAC layer performs both Medium Access Control procedures and take the relaying decision. By evaluating different candidate nodes, as described below, in a query-reply evaluation procedure, the protocol is able to determine the best possible next hop. Not only do this allow us to determine the candidate with the best channel conditions, but it also allows us to perform power control, and implicitly interference control.

Please consider Figure 1. Here we see a simulated example of the signal variations in a Rayleigh fading channel when the terminal is moving at 2.5 m/s. The small circlets indicate packet reception instants and we can see how large the signal variations are for this simple scenario. When we are in a deep fade it will not be possible to receive even at the lowest rate, while at good instants it will be possible to receive at the maximum rate. If one candidate is currently in a deep fade, one can argue that some other candidate might be in a more advantageous situation situation due to the channels being independent. If the candidates are placed about a half a wavelength apart, it is generally enough to create independent radio channels (less than 0.1 meter for 2.4GHz).

Consider this fading situation in a single path scheme. If the channel towards our next hop is in a bad fading state, it may not be possible to transmit to that node at all, until the channel comes into a more favorable phase. If we instead use a muti path scheme as we are proposing, we might be able to choose a better next hop, and perhaps even transmit at a higher rate, and lower power.

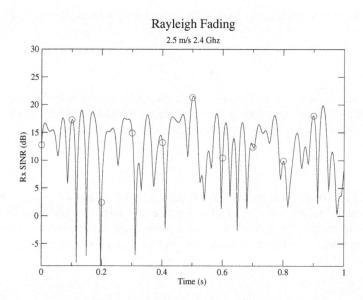

Fig. 1. Packet reception for a Rayleigh fading channel at 2.5 m/s mobility at 2.4 GHz

3.2 Extended Multi Path Power Control Mac Protocol

In standard 802.11 DCF, a terminal may use a simple RTS-CTS cycle to inform its neighbors about its intended transmission. RTS stands for Request To Send and CTS stands for Clear To Send. This makes all neighbors defer their transmissions for the duration of the scheduled transmission. In our protocol, MPPOW, we extend this cycle by including two new messages, DTS and ATS. These abbreviations stand for Determine To Send (DTS) and Acknowledge To Send (ATS).

In MPPOW, whenever a node wants to send a packet, it multicasts a RTS message by indicating which two or more destinations that it wishes to transmit to. It also includes information about the power level used to transmit the RTS, and how many more users that are used to transmit in parallel, *Nusers*.

When a neighbor indicated in the RTS receives this message, it calculates the current path gain to the transmitter. This is done by comparing the transmit power level as indicated in the RTS to the power level at which the RTS was received. The ratio between these levels is the gain, G:

$$G = \frac{P_{rx}}{P_{RTS}} \qquad (1)$$

The node then uses this gain to calculate the data power level, *Pdata*, which the actual data packet will use. When calculating this power level, the node takes into account the needed SINR target ratio, μ^*, which depends upon the current data rate. It also takes into account the current noise level, and the estimated interference level as described below. By using these values, the node is able to calculate the minimum power level, *Pmin* needed to achieve the SINR target ratio. This calculation is performed in the following way:

$$P_{min} = \frac{\mu^* P_{noise}}{G} \qquad (2)$$

While *Pmin* is the minimum transmit power needed by the transmitter for the receiver to successfully receive the packet at this time instant, the data power level, *Pdata*, that the node will propose will have include an additional interference budget ξ:

$$P_{data} = \frac{\mu^* \xi P_{noise}}{G} \qquad (3)$$

This is done both to compensate for other interferences and noise that may start during the transmission, but also to allow for an extra budget that enables other nodes to transmit in parallel. By having this budget we increase the level of interference the receiver can tolerate during the transmission. In fact, it can tolerate an additional interference level of *Pai*:

$$P_{AI} = \frac{G}{\mu^*}(P_{data} - P_{min}) \qquad (4)$$

So, if we allow N transmissions to run in parallel in addition to our own, the maximum tolerable interference, *Pmti* we can accept is:

$$P_{MTI} = \frac{P_{AI}}{N} \qquad (5)$$

This value, *Pmti* is a constraint put on each possible parallel transmitter. Whenever they are about to schedule a new transmission they have to make sure that the amount of received interference at the already scheduled receiver does not exceed *Pmti*. It should be noted that this type of power control scheme is very close to the one used in [2].

Initially, each of these power calculations are performed with regard to the SINR target ratio, μ^*, of the highest physical layer rate. If, during these calculations it is found that either *Pdata* or *Pmin* is higher than the maximum transmit power, the target rate will be lowered to the next highest rate, and μ^* is updated accordingly. This means that the power control procedure tries to maximize the link rate under a given maximum power constraint, and only updates the power levels accordingly. It is possible to design other schemes that for example considers a certain power level that a node wishes to use, and instead modify the data rate accordingly. This would also make sense, because a higher rate typically translates into higher power, because the μ^* is higher for the higher rates. It is also possible to define and design other non linear cost functions that takes more parameters and aspects into account. This could for example be maximum forward progress, or remaining battery lifetime.

Each destination that receives an RTS replies by sending a CTS in the order they were listed in the RTS. For example if node 1 transmits an RTS $1 \rightarrow 2,3$ to destination nodes 2 and 3, node 2 will first send a CTS, and then node 3 will send a CTS. Just as with the RTS, the CTS include the power level used for transmitting the CTS. In addition to this, the CTS include the power level *Pdata* that was calculated as described above.

$$RTS(i \rightarrow j, h) = \{i, j, h, Prts, Pmap, Nusers, PayloadSize, DataRate\} \quad (6)$$

$$CTS(j \rightarrow i) = \{j, i, rr, Nusers, Pmap, Pdata, Pmti, Pcts, duration, rate\} \quad (7)$$

$$DTS(i \rightarrow j) = \{i, j, Pdata, Pdts, duration, dataOffset, rate, Nusers\} \quad (8)$$

$$ATS(j \rightarrow i) = \{j, i, Nusers, Pmti, Pats, duration, dataOffset, rate\} \quad (9)$$

When the initiating node has received all the CTS messages it expects, or they have timed out, it chooses an appropriate destination, sets its corresponding power level *Pdata*, pick an appropriate transmission *rate* and calculates the *duration*. In addition to this, it also calculates the *dataOffset*, the time in μs until the transmission is scheduled to start. The node transmits a DTS that includes these values; *Plevel, rate, duration, dataOffset* as well as the power level used to transmit the DTS. This informs neighboring nodes about the scheduling of the transmission, and allows them to determine the start and end time as well as how much interference the transmission will cause them. When the receiving node receives the DTS, it replies by sending an ATS. This ATS includes in addition to the information contained in the DTS, the value *Pmti* that states the Maximum Tolerable Inference that it can accept before it will be unable to successfully receive the packet. Other neighboring nodes that wish to transmit in parallel may do so, as long as they don't exceed this value at the scheduled receiver. The ATS is needed because there might be possible interferers close to the receiver that did not receive the DTS, and therefore needs to receive the ATS to learn about the scheduled transmission.

3.3   Next Hop Selection Procedure

A very important step of this whole cross layer solution is the selection of the next hop forwarding node. This decision is based both upon the information gained by the MAC protocol during the RTS-CTS-DTS-ATS signaling phase, and information provided by the routing protocol. This means that the selection of the next hop is based on information gained from two different time scales, a short MAC time scale and a longer average routing time scale.

After the MAC signaling phase, we now have enough information to choose the next hop depending on the quality of the links. But, even if we choose the perceived *best link* and forward the packet to that next hop, it does not necessarily mean that it is the *best path* to the destination. The link to the next hop candidate might be very good, but if conditions after that hop seems to be unfavorable according to the link state of the routing protocol, it would still be a bad choice.

We determine the best next hop relaying node in the following way:

1. Determine what candidates to include in the MAC signaling phase by evaluating the link state database. This database has been updated by the routing protocol. The candidates with the least cost will be used in the evaluation.
2. Perform the MAC signaling evaluation.
3. Determine the short term cost, C_{STi} to each next hop i based upon the MAC evaluation.

4. Determine the average long term cost, C_{LTi} to each next hop i based upon the link state database.
5. Determine the routing cost, C_{RCi} to the final destination through each next hop i based upon information in the link state database.
6. Determine the current path cost, C to the final destination through each next hop by subtracting the long term cost from the short term cost and adding this difference to the routing cost: $C = ((C_{STi} - C_{LTi}) + C_{RCi})$.
7. Choose the next hop relaying node with the least current cost, C.

Another important question here is how we determine the actual cost of each link, ie. the metric. In most routing protocols for ad hoc networks used today, a simple hop count metric is used. This is a fairly simple and robust metric that considers the fact that more hops means that more resources and capacity have to be used for transferring a packet to its destination. This is especially true in a wireless ad hoc network, where one transmission not only affect other transmissions on the same link, but all other possible transmissions opearating on the same channel in the area around the node, and around the receiver.

Other metrics and more sophisticated cost functions are also possible. In the simulations performed for this paper we used a metric that defined the cost of a link as the inverse bit datarate. This makes sense if we consider the following case: consider two links where one link has a bitrate of 1Mbps and the other has 2Mbps. Since the data transmission duration on the 1Mbps link is twice as long as the duration for the 2Mbps link, it makes sense that the cost of that link is also twice as high.

Figure 2 shows the theoretical maximum throughput that the extended version of the protocol is able to achive for different 802.11 physical layers, packet sizes and number of users. Here we can clearly see that the packet size used for each transmitted packet is a very important parameter. When the packet size is small, the signaling overhead induced is simply more than the protocol can handle, and standard 802.11 will always be more efficient. However, the reason that the difference between MPPOW and 802.11 is larger for 802.11b, is the long preamble size. 802.11b uses a preamble that takes $144\mu s$ to transmit, while 802.11a uses a $16\mu s$ preamble. Since this time is added to every frame transmitted, i.e. RTS, CTS, DTS etc, this translates into a lot of overhead, reducing the performance of the protocol.

When the packet size is larger, MPPOW becomes more efficant than 802.11, both from a system wide view as well from an individual users perspective, when the number users tranmitting is either two or three or more. If only one node is transmitting the overhead is simply too much, and we can't reach any improvement in throughput. It should be pointed out that these figures only show the maximum throughput on a single link, and doesn't consider the multi-path and power control features provided by the protocol. The conclusion that can be drawn from these figures, is that if the packet size isn't too small, throughput especially from a system perspective can be increased, if users are transmitting in parallel. This means that channel contention will also be lower and the throughput increase for flows over several hops will be higher.

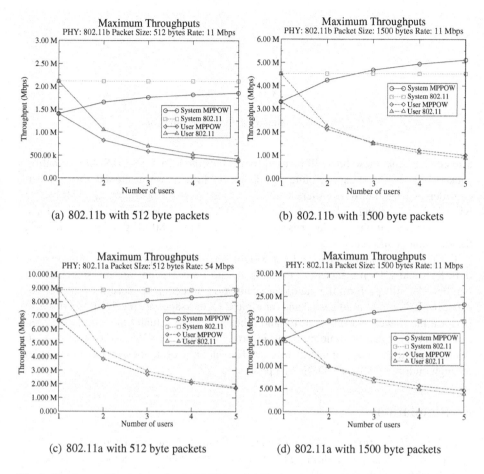

(a) 802.11b with 512 byte packets

(b) 802.11b with 1500 byte packets

(c) 802.11a with 512 byte packets

(d) 802.11a with 1500 byte packets

Fig. 2. Maximum Throughput for MPPOW and 802.11 DCF for different 802.11 PHYs and packet sizes. The number of users trying accessing the channel either in parallel or in alteration is also shown.

3.4   Lite Multi Path Power Control Mac Protocol

As we saw in the previous section, the MAC protocol described in section 3.2 relies on a quite heavy signaling phase that takes place before each packet is transmitted. If two nodes wish to transmit in parallel, the RTS-CTS-DTS-ATS phase will be performed twice. This means a lot of overhead. Still, we may gain from this if two packets are transmitted in parallel, so that one transmitter does not have to wait for the other to finish. But, the overhead is also heavily dependent upon the type of physical layer used. In 802.11b for example, which is used for simulations in this study, the preamble and physical layer headers is always transmitted at 1Mbps, even though the data payload can be transmitted at a higher data rate such as 11Mbps. This means that the 192 overhead bits in 802.11b, can be regarded as 2112 overhead bits with the 11Mbps datarate. If we

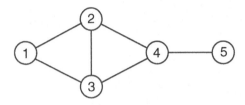

Fig. 3. Network setup used during the simulations

also consider that these bits will be used for each of the RTS-CTS-DTS-ATS signaling packets, the overhead can be quite significant. In fact, as we discussed above, if we consider two parallel transmitters with 1500 bytes payload operating at 11Mpbs, we will not gain anything and only slightly for 5.5Mbps, but more for 2Mbps and 1Mbps. If an other type of physical layer is used, such 802.11a or 802.11g in "g-only mode", the situation is different.

For this reason we also have a light weight version of our protocol. In this version, only RTS and CTS messages are exchanged, and transmissions are not scheduled in parallel. We still perform the candidate evaluation procedure as described above, because the RTS is still multicasted and multiple CTS messages are received. We still also perform the power and rate control, and other nodes are actually allowed to transmit in parallel. This can be done by using information from the CTS, as long as they do not interfere with an ongoing transmission. They are however, not scheduled in parallel through multiple RTS-CTS-DTS-ATS phases.

4   Simulations

The protocols described in this paper were implemented and evaluated in the Qualnet simulator [7]. Qualnet is a discrete event network simulator that includes a rich set of very detailed models.

Figure 3 describes the network setup used for the simulations in this study. The traffic used in the simulations are UDP Constant Bit Rate (CBR) 275kbps data flows between node 1 and node 5. This is a fairly simple network setup, but it still provide intermediate node with multiple next hop candiates at several nodes, i.e. node 1,2 and 3. Each of the available links fades according to the Ricean distribution, see figure 1. This means that although the indpendent distances between each of the nodes never changes, the signal strength still varies a lot. This can be compared to a situation where the whole network is moving with a certain speed through the environment, although the network topology never changes. This technique allows us to completely specify the network topology as we wish to, but we still have fading links as if the nodes were moving through a variable environment.

Our ODMLS routing protocol combined with the MAC used the lite MAC version of MPPOW. RTS and CTS messages were transmitted at 15dBm at 1Mbps. The physical layer used in all the simulations were 802.11b, and the routing protocols used for comparison were AODV [6] and OLSR [4]. AODV and OLSR used the 802.11 MAC protocol.

Figure 4 shows the instantaneous delay during 8 seconds for both ODMLS/MPPOW and AODV/802.11. In figure 4(a) Ricean fading with a K-factor of 1 is used and in figure 4(b) a K-factor of 6. In 4(b) where fading is less severe we only see a significant difference in delay between AODV and ODMLS during two half a second long periods, at 8.5s and 9.5s. During these periods, the link AODV uses goes into a bad fading phase. For the duration of such a phase, AODV will experience several unsuccessful packet transmission attempts over the link, which increases the packet end-to-end delay. During periods like these, ODMLS/MPPOW is able to avoid the bad links through the next hop diversity selection. When fading becomes severe, i.e. a lower K factor, the bad fading phases comes more rapidly and longer. Longer in this case for AODV, in fact longer than the interarrival time of packets, causes a build up of the queue length resulting in longer queuing delays. Although AODV might be triggered to believe the link is broken, and to start a route repair procedure, it still takes a long to repair the route. Even if the route repair is successful, the new link will soon become bad again. Here we clearly see the benefits of diversity forwarding, where bad links can be avoided on a per packet basis.

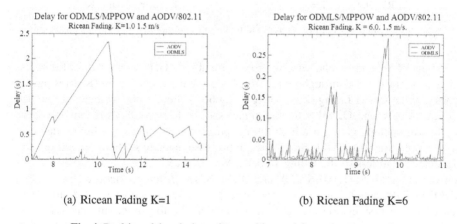

(a) Ricean Fading K=1   (b) Ricean Fading K=6

Fig. 4. Realtime delay during a 8 second interval for various protocols

In figure 5 we see the average end-to-end delay instead of the instantaneous for different protocols, but this time also for OLSR and different K-factor velocity speeds. The main observation here is that during the faster fading case of K=0 (Rayleigh Fading, figure 5(a)), delay increases for OLSR at higher mobility. This stands in direct relation to the rate of the topology updates sent by OLSR to update its link state. As the mobility increases, the OLSR link state database will become more and more inaccurate. For AODV it is actually the direct opposite; as the mobility increases AODV will more and more often believe the link to be broken, causing it to repair the route. The reason that the performance AODV increases with higher velocity, even though it is not mobility in terms of topology movement, is that when the route is first setup, the first RREQ that is received at the destination will determine the route. This route may not be the most optimal route. As the fading velocity increases, AODV will more often believe the route to be broken, and therefore repair the route. The chances that a good path is eventually chosen therefore increases. ODMLS/MPPOW maintains a low delay as long it manages to find new valid and good next hop relays, which it does.

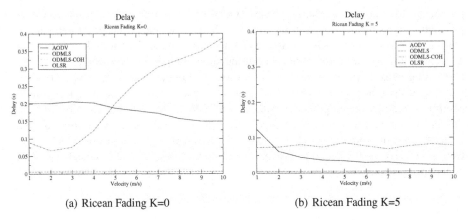

(a) Ricean Fading K=0   (b) Ricean Fading K=5

Fig. 5. End-to-end delay during different fading factors and mobilities for various protocols

In figure 6 we can see the same improving trend for AODV as we did for the delay. The reason for the low throughput for AODV during the faster fading (K=0) is packet drops. For the slower fading situation (K=5, fig 6(b)), there is no significant difference between AODV and ODMLS for the higher speeds. Here, AODVs repair procedure is effective enough, giving it a high throughput, but at the price of a higher delay as we saw in figure 5(b). ODMLS/MPPOW in this case maintains a high throughput and low delay regardless of the fading velocity. We also see two different curves for two versions of ODMLS; ODMLS-COH and ODMLS. The difference between these is that ODMLS-COH includes an extra feature where a failure to receive an ACK after data transmission is first regarded as a transmission failure due to fading. This means that the transmitter will wait for a duration as long as the coherence time of the channel, before retransmitting. In the simulations this value is preset to a known channel coherence time and gives a slight throughput improvement, mainly for K=0.

However, this comes at the price of a slight increase in delay, which can be seen in the lower part of figure 5(a) at close examination. While the gain of doing this isn't very high, the gain in our simulations is roughly a 7% increase in throughput for K=0, but less than 1% for K=5.

The channel coherence time is a parameter that could be provided by the physical layer. It could for example be determined by looking at the time difference between the events where the signal crosses a certain reference level. Other methods that depend on the type of physical layer used is also possible.

Figure 7 confirms that packet drops cause the lower throughput for AODV and OLSR. If we compare Figure 7 and figure 6 we can see the close relation between delivery ratio and throughput; when the packet delivery increases, so does the through-put, as expected. ODMLS manages to deliver a high number of packets, but without the

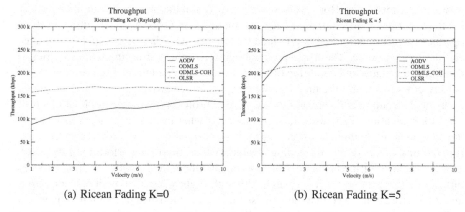

Fig. 6. Throughput in kbps during different fading mobilities and Ricean K factors for various protocols

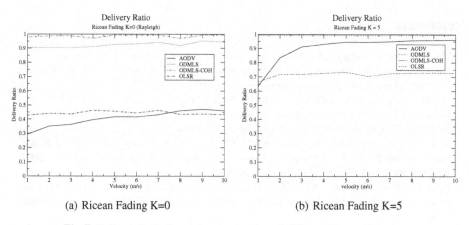

Fig. 7. Delivery Ratio for various protocols and different Ricean K factors

coherence time feature (retransmission hold-off), the packet drop ratio is around 10% for K=0. For K=5 almost all packets are delivered.

5   Discussion and Conclusion

We have presented a cross layer solution that defines and specifies a MAC and a routing protocol that interact in order to create efficient diversity forwarding. The routing protocol (ODMLS) is semi reactive and operates by setting up routes on demand, but maintains a link state database that is continuously updated by using a promiscuous mode operation, as the one specified in 802.11, and listening to other data and control traffic. The routing protocol setup multiple non-disjoint paths between a source and destination and presents the MAC layer with a set of candidate next hop forwarding nodes. The MAC protocol evaluates the candidates presented by the routing protocol, and performs power, rate and interference control in addition to implementing the diversity forwarding capabilities. Both protocols are involved in the process of routing a packet, but they operate on different timescales and on different horizons. The routing protocol operates on information that is provided by the link state database, which is averaged and filtered over time. The MAC protocol operates on a shorter timescale and tries to determine the status and condition of a link with an ms resolution. The routing process is truly cross layer, and the final routing decision is actually made the MAC protocol, by using the routing table created by the routing protocol in combination with its own fast link evaluation. This faster link evaluation is what enables it to adapt to bad fading situations. Even though power control is performed which improves performance, it is the link diversity and the fading awareness that improves performance the most. This has been confirmed by a control experiment, where the power control feature was turned off. The gain was still very high, although slightly less than with power control, and it therefore confirmed that the highest gain is accomplished through link diversity.

The presented solution displays a significant performance gain, which has been verified through a set of simulations in a 5 node network topology.

References

1. IEEE Computer Society LAN MAN Standards Committee. *Wireless LAN Medium Access Protocol (MAC) and Physical Layer (PHY) Specification, IEEE Std 802.11-1997.* The Institute of Electrical and Electronics Engineers, New York, 1997.
2. A. Muqattash and M. Krunz2006. A single-channel solution for transmission power control in wireless ad hoc networks. In *Proceedings of the 5th ACM international symposium on Mobile ad hoc networking and computing, Tokyo, Japan*, May 2004.
3. M. Cesana, D. Maniezzo, P. Bergamo, and M. Gerla. nterference aware (ia) mac: an enhancement to ieee802.11b dcf. In *Proceedings of the IEEE Vehicular Technology Conference 2003, VTC fall 2003, Orlando, Fl, USA*, October 2003.
4. P. Jacquet, P. Muhlethaler, T Clausen, A. Laouiti, A. Qayyum, and L. Viennot. Optimized link state routing protocol for ad hoc networks. In *IEEE International Multi Topic Conference*, 2001.
5. Guangyu Pei, Mario Gerla, and Tsu-Wei Chen. Fisheye state routing: A routing scheme for ad hoc wireless networks. In *Proceedings of IEEE International Conference on Communications, ICC*, pages 70–74, 2000.
6. C. Perkins. Ad-hoc on-demand distance vector routing. In *Second IEEE Workshop on Mobile Computing Systems and Applications*, 1999.
7. Scalable Networks. Qualnet network simulator, version 3.9. 2005.

An Energy-Efficient Low-Latency Multi-sink MAC Protocol for Alarm-Driven Wireless Sensor Networks

António Grilo[1,2], Mário Macedo[1,3], and Mário Nunes[1,2]

[1] INESC, Rua Alves Redol, No 9,
1000-029 Lisboa, Portugal
[2] IST/UTL, Av. Rovisco Pais,
1096 Lisboa, Portugal
[3] FCT/UNL,
2825 Monte da Caparica, Portugal
{mario.nunes, antonio.grilo}@inesc.pt,
mmm@fct.unl.pt

Abstract. This paper presents a novel MAC protocol for Wireless Sensor Networks (WSN)s designated Tone-Propagated MAC (TP-MAC). This protocol is specially suited for early warning and tracking applications, where sensor nodes generate sporadic asynchronous traffic (mainly consisting of uplink alert messages and downlink control messages) with stringent latency requirements. This protocol aims to maximize energy-efficiency while minimizing latency in source-to-sink and sink-to-source communication. This difficult objective is achieved integrating scheduled channel polling (i.e. synchronized low power listening) with rapid fast path establishment based on the propagation of short wake-up tones. An analytical model was used to compare TP-MAC with SCP-MAC. The results show that TP-MAC is able to achieve better target latencies even when its duty-cycle is lower during periods of inactivity. The results also show that the advantage of using TP-MAC increases with the hop-distance between source and sink.

Keywords: Wireless Sensor Networks, Early Warning and Tracking, MAC, Energy-Efficiency, Scheduled Channel Polling.

1 Introduction

Wireless Sensor Networks (WSNs) have motivated intense research, in academia, industry and on the military sector due to the potential to support distributed micro-sensing in environments for which conventional networks are impractical or when the required sensor density demands a robust, secure and cost-effective solution. WSNs rely on large numbers of cheap devices, able to collaborate in distributed in-network data fusion and processing tasks, with final results that are equivalent to those obtained with centralized processing. An example of the latter is Homeland Security Early Warning and Tracking of Chemical, Biological Radiological, Nuclear and Explosive (CBRNE) agents, Toxic Industrial Materials (TIM), and other terrorist threats. In fact, this is generally regarded as one of the future WSN main applications.

J. García-Vidal, L. Cerdà-Alabern (Eds.): Wireless and Mobility, LNCS 4396, pp. 87–101, 2007.
© Springer-Verlag Berlin Heidelberg 2007

Homeland Security Early Warning and Tracking is one of the WSN application scenarios addressed in the FP6 IST project Ubiquitous Sensing and Security in the European Homeland (UbiSeq&Sens). The overall objective of UbiSeq&Sens is to provide a comprehensive architecture for medium and large scale WSNs, with the full level of security required to make them trusted and secure for all applications.

Homeland Security Early Warning and Tracking poses interesting requirements on the WSN networking aspects, namely the requirements for low duty cycles (in order to assure maximum autonomy and minimum maintenance) and low latency in source-to-sink alert notifications (in order to assure a timely response to CBRNE/TIM threats). Current WSN MAC protocols usually trade-off one for the other, not supporting them simultaneously. The Tone-Propagated MAC (TP-MAC) protocol [1], presented in this paper, tackles this problem, supporting ultra-low duty cycles in periods of no activity, providing at the same time fast path establishment based on quick wake-up tone propagation in the beginning of activation periods. This paper extends the initial specification presenting a more comprehensive description, this time addressing synchronization and multi-sink support issues. This paper also proposes an analytical model for performance evaluation and discusses some obtained results.

The rest of this paper is organized as follows. Section 2 presents the WSN MAC protocols that were most relevant for this work. Section 3 presents TP-MAC. Section 4 presents an analytical model that will be used for the performance evaluation and comparison with SCP-MAC, made in section 5. Finally section 6 concludes the paper.

2 Related Work

Many techniques and MAC protocols have been developed for WSNs, in order to lessen the sources of inefficiency in wireless access, such as idle listening, collisions, message overhearing and control packets overhead [2]. We will focus on scheduled contention-based protocols, and low-power listening, as they are more related to our work.

Contention-based protocols are more flexible than Time-division multiple-access (TDMA) protocols, because they can provide more flexibility in multi-hop communications, and are more prone to topologic changes. The IEEE 802.11 standard [3] was designed for wireless LANs and also for ad hoc networks. In its Distributed Coordinated Function (DCF), it uses a contention protocol - Carrier Sense Multiple Access with Collision Avoidance (CSMA/CA), inherited from the MACAW protocol [4] – that has inspired some WSNs specific protocols, because it has satisfactory performance in avoiding collisions. Namely, the protocol messages sequence - RTS (Request to Send), CTS (Clear to Send), Data, and ACK (Acknowledge) – are used by other contention protocols.

S-MAC [5] is a scheduled contention-based protocol. Nodes are active (listening and transmitting) for some time, and asleep for the remaining time of a fixed period. In the active time, it uses the basic ideas of the IEEE 802.11/MACAW contention protocol for data exchange. A technique, named *virtual clustering*, permits that nodes adopt and propagate time schedules that synchronize the active time of the nodes in the sensor network. SYNC packets are exchanged to keep the nodes' schedules synchronized and compensate for clock drifts. However, *virtual clustering* leads to existence of multiple schedules [6], because they are generated locally by the initiative of the nodes. This is somehow a source of inefficiency, because nodes in the frontier of more than one schedule have more active times. In [6] is also presented an algorithm to achieve a unique global schedule, but convergence is very slow (in the order of several minutes). Other techniques are used by S-MAC in order to avoid overhearing, and excessive control packets overhead (such as message passing).

S-MAC duty cycle, and therefore its energy efficiency, can be tuned by acting on the active time duration. However, its fixed cycle of operation is not flexible to adapt to different load conditions. Some protocols addressed this problem, namely T-MAC [7].

The basic idea of T-MAC, which mainly differentiates it from S-MAC, is that active time duration is not fixed, but finishes when no activation events (i.e., communication activity) in the media occur for a chosen timeout. However, as its authors note, T-MAC suffers from the *early sleeping* problem: briefly, in a chain of four nodes, if the first node wants to communicate till the fourth, through the second and the third, the third node can still hear the first communication (between the first and the second), and remain active, but the fourth node goes too early to sleep state. This is a major drawback, because in WSNs the communication is mainly oriented to the sinks, in chain communication patterns. The authors propose two solutions for this problem, but the first solution (a Future Request to Send packet, issued by the third node) seems only to be effective to maintain the fourth node awoken, and not for subsequent nodes. Consequently, T-MAC seems to have a latency problem.

In order to reduce the latency, the research team of S-MAC also proposes a *fast path algorithm* [6], with additional and staggered active times along the path, between a node and the sink. However, the fast path must be reserved hop by hop, in the first packet communication. *Adaptive listen* [8] is another technique described in the context of S-MAC. Nodes that hear neighbors' protocol exchange messages, wake up for a short time, after the full data transmission ends, to check if they have transmissions for them, instead of going to sleep till the next active time. Analysis and simulations show the effectiveness of this solution.

The Data-gathering MAC (D-MAC) protocol presented in [9] includes an adaptive duty-cycle like T-MAC. However, its main purpose is to minimize the node-to-sink latency in convergecast[1] networks, where all sensing data converges to only one sink node. D-MAC uses staggered synchronization so that a data packet heard by a node at one level of the tree in one slot is transmitted to the next level in the following slot. The node is then allowed to sleep until the reception slot for its level occurs again.

Another approach, different from the scheduled schemes, is low-power listening (LPL) [10], used by B-MAC [11], and by WiseMAC [12]. It is a very simple mechanism designed to minimize the energy spent in idle listening: receiving nodes periodically poll the media for activity, and if there is no activity, they return to sleep state for the rest of the period; the sender node can wake up the receivers by sending a preamble. Poll durations can be very small, just the time to detect the preamble. However, preamble must last for an entire poll period, as nodes are not supposed to be synchronized. Nevertheless, this simple scheme can be effective in applications with low data traffic.

---

[1] Sometimes designated "reverse multicast".

More recently, a new scheduled contention protocol was proposed. SCP-MAC (Scheduled Channel Polling MAC, [13]) combines the advantages of LPL and scheduled protocols. Nodes that have data to transmit contend in a first contention window for tone transmission; nodes that win the contention transmit a tone. Possible collisions in tone transmission are allowed, because what is important is the presence of the tone. The potential receiving nodes poll the media for short time (around 2-3 ms), just enough to detect the tone. If there is no tone, the receiving nodes return to the sleep state. If there is a tone, they remain woken up for a further data transmission. Actual data transmission can be done with a second contention window, only with the winners of the first contention window, and with RTS-CTS exchanges.

Tone polls, and the tones themselves, are synchronized by the scheduled times, in the S-MAC way, and therefore can be very short. The long preambles of LPL are not needed. In this way, SCP-MAC proves to be much more efficient than LPL. Moreover, as contention is done in two consecutive windows, they can be smaller. Further use of adaptive listening in conjunction with SCP-MAC, is a hypothesis that the authors foresee. However, SCP-MAC presents a significant dependency between duty-cycle and transmission delay, since longer polling periods imply that the hop-by-hop transmission from sender to receiver also takes longer. This can be problematic in medium and large scale WSNs, specially in scenarios that require the combination of ultra-low duty cycles with low latency transmission (e.g. long-term deployment of alarm-driven applications), which is the main problem addressed by TP-MAC.

3   Tone-Propagated MAC (TP-MAC)

In order to achieve low duty cycle, the proposed TP-MAC protocol inherits some features from other MAC protocols, namely synchronized wake-up periods (S-MAC, SCP-MAC), and synchronized wake-up-tone announcement of data availability associated with scheduled channel polling (SCP-MAC). However, in TP-MAC the wake-up-tones are propagated across the WSN so that the nodes in the path from source to destination are woken-up as quickly as possible, before the arrival of the heralded data packets. In this way, TP-MAC is able to achieve low delivery latency even if the WSN node duty-cycle is extremely low, preventing or at least ameliorating the early-sleeping problem.

TP-MAC is based on the convergecast communication paradigm, assuming that the WSN is organized in a logical tree topology, associated with one sink, which corresponds to the root node. This imposes some cross-layer constraints on the network (i.e. routing) layer, which is not a real limitation, since most typical WSN scenarios require convergecast of sensor data towards sink nodes. Moreover, unlike D-MAC, TP-MAC supports the existence of multiple sinks in the network (and thus the coexistence of multiple overlaid logical trees – see below), but for sake of simplicity its basic mechanisms shall be first described assuming that there is a single sink node.

In a tree structure rooted at the sink node, it is possible to define different levels defined by the minimum hop distance relative to the sink node. In this way, the sink node constitutes level 0 and the level number increases as hop distance to the sink node increases. The establishment of network levels is at the core of the wake-up-tone propagation mechanism.

TP-MAC establishes super-frame periods for channel access, each starting by a synchronization wake-up-tone and two wake-up-tone propagation windows (upstream and downstream[2]), followed by a data transmission window (see Fig. 1). The size of the tone propagation window can be different for upstream and downstream, depending on the latency requirements. The channel access method in the transmission window can be based on any MAC protocol, e.g. CSMA/CA, S-MAC, T-MAC, SCP-MAC, etc.

The synchronization tone marks the beginning of the super-frame structure. This tone is periodically activated by the sink node and slowly propagated downstream to announce the transmission of a broadcast synchronizing/re-synchronizing SYNC packet in the data transmission window. The procedures supported by this synchronization tone are many, as shall be seen later.

The wake-up-tone propagation windows allow the announcement of data and establishment of fast paths from source to destination.

While no data traffic is generated, each node only has to poll the channel once in each wake-up-tone propagation window (only in the slot that corresponds to its level), and sometimes also in the synchronization slot. The nodes are allowed to sleep during the rest of the super-frame.

When a node has data to transmit, it first sends a wake-up upstream tone (e.g., for sensing data destined to the sink node), or a waking downstream tone (e.g., for control messages issued by the sink node to sensor nodes). The wake-up-tone propagation window structure guarantees that nearby nodes in the next upper/lower level listen to the generated wake-up-tone. They then propagate the tone upstream/downstream, as it can be seen in the tone propagation windows of Fig. 1. If a node detects a wake-up-tone in the last slot of a propagation window, then it shall only propagate it in the next super-frame. The tone propagation mechanism, which resembles the data propagation mechanism of D-MAC, assures that nodes within some hop distance are woken-up in just one operation cycle, forming a fast-path before actual data arrives. The maximum distance that a wake-up tone can reach in a single super-frame is equal to the number of tones in each tone propagation window, which is a configuration parameter.

The nodes that form a fast path stay active in the data transmission window, for a pre-defined time interval, which is dimensioned to keep those nodes active until the announced data arrives. The timeout mechanism is similar to that defined in T-MAC.

TP-MAC nodes only poll the media for a number slightly above two times per cycle (two polls, respectively for upstream and downstream propagated tones in each super-frame, and more seldom for the synchronization/re-synchronization tone), propagating the wake-up tones fast and deeply through the network (and thus opening fast data transmission paths). In this way it is possible to achieve low latencies simultaneously with low duty cycles.

One side effect of the TP-MAC protocol is that downlink propagation of wake up tones may result in waking up all nodes of the network. This behavior is an advantage when downstream data has to be broadcasted, and a handicap for other downstream

---

[2] In this paper, upstream and downstream definitions are relative to a WSN convergecast tree, considering the sink node at the top.

traffic patterns. Nevertheless, if the applications do not demand stringent latency requirements for downstream traffic, the downstream tone propagation window can be eliminated and the synchronization slot can be also used for data announcements. The frequency of the synchronization tone can be configured as to match the required latency. This solution decreases the duty cycle even further.

Another side effect is that for the upstream tone propagation the nodes in adjacent branches of the tree at levels above the source may be also woken-up, since they also detect and propagate the wake-up-tones. This behavior can cause some energy inefficiency. However, it is compensated by the ultra-low duty cycle required to achieve the intended delivery latencies.

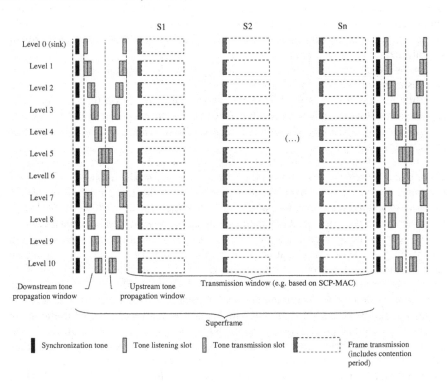

Fig. 1. TP-MAC super-frame structure and hierarchical wake-up-tone propagation

3.1 Synchronization / Re-synchronization

Like D-MAC, TP-MAC requires a global schedule spanning all levels of the logical tree. Being the root of the logical tree and natural destination of sensing data, the sink node is in a privileged position to initialize the WSN imposing the global schedule. Like in other scheduled MAC protocols, special SYNC packets are periodically issued in TP-MAC to re-synchronize the WSN and eliminate the effects of clock skew. In TP-MAC, these SYNC packets are firstly issued by the sink and propagated downstream in sequential super-frames. Each SYNC packet carries the sink node identifier and the current hop distance to the sink (which increases each time the

SYNC packet is propagated), allowing each receiving node to know its level in the tree. In order to announce the transmission of a SYNC packet in a super-frame, each issuing node precedes that super-frame by the transmission of a synchronization tone. Since the SYNC period is known by all nodes, the latter only have to listen to the synchronization tone in those specific super-frames where its transmission is expected. In case for some reason the synchronization tone is not heard, the node continues to poll the synchronization slot at the beginning of each subsequent super-frame until a synchronization tone is detected.

While this technique can be effective after the WSN is initiated, some difficulties arise just after deployment, when WSN nodes have no idea either about the global schedule or even about each other's schedules. A similar problem arises when new nodes are added to the network and must listen to a SYNC packet, before being admitted in the scheduled tree. One way to solve the problem is to force unsynchronized nodes to continuously listen to the channel until a SYNC packet is received. This procedure is energy consuming and risks draining the batteries, even before the network starts effective operation (especially when there is a large hiatus between WSN deployment and the initialization by the sink). The solution adopted in TP-MAC is to use LPL-based synchronization (see Fig. 2). SYNC packets are preceded by a long preamble, long enough to span the polling period of unsynchronized nodes (this period is a configuration parameter). Once the nodes detect any activity, they remain woken-up during the remaining of the preamble, in order to receive an ensuing SYNC packet. If the activity detected corresponded indeed to the preamble of a SYNC packet, those nodes get all the information needed to synchronize with the WSN. Otherwise, those nodes return to periodic polling the channel.

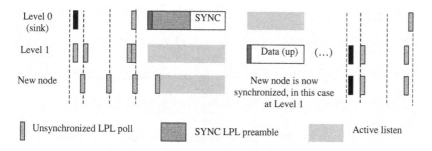

Fig. 2. TP-MAC LPL-based synchronization. The example considers a new node that is distant one hop from the sink node. Notice the long preamble of SYNC packets as compared to other packets.

3.2 Multiple Sink Nodes

Until now the description of TP-MAC only considered the existence of one sink node, located at the root of the tree. TP-MAC also supports the existence of multiple sink nodes, which is essential to satisfy the robustness and resiliency requirements of the UbiSeq&Sens Homeland Security Scenario. However, a single schedule is assumed, which means that the WSN must be fully initialized by an initial sink node, before additional sink nodes can join while adopting the initial schedule. The procedure to become a new sink is the same already described to initialize the WSN, i.e. the new sink activates the synchronization tone in the beginning of a superframe and in the subsequent transmission window it transmits a SYNC packet with its own identifier and hop distance to the sink equal to 0. This SYNC packet is propagated throughout the network in the usual way. Each receiving node creates an additional record for the new sink and adopts his new position in the tree in addition to the positions it already occupies relative to other existing sink nodes. This means that as the number of sinks increases, the number of times a node has to poll the channel during the tone propagation windows also tends to increase (there may be exceptions when a node is in such a position that it polls the same slot for two or more trees with different sinks). In the limit, a node may have to poll all slots in the wake-up tone propagation windows. The number of sinks should thus be limited in order not to affect energy-efficiency too much.

Since wake-up tones do not bear any information about the destination address, which may eventually be a multicast address, when a node belongs to two or more trees, each detected wake-up tone must be propagated in every other tree it belongs to, until the end of the current tone propagation window. While this technique presents the disadvantage of unnecessarily waking-up nodes in trees towards which the packet will not be sent, it keeps latency low since it avoids interrupting the propagation of

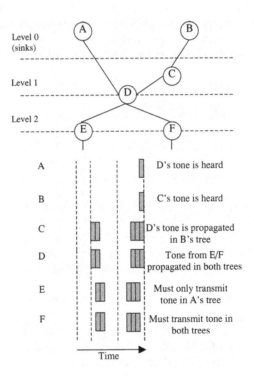

Fig. 3. Support of multiple sinks in TP-MAC

tones in any of the trees the node belongs to. This also solves a problem that arises when a node must poll the tone propagation window in two succeeding slots (one for each different tree to which the node belongs). Since the detection of a tone in the first of those slots would require it to be propagated in the ensuing slot, while the latter should also be polled, there would be a conflict if the detected tone was not propagated in every other tree. Fig. 3 illustrates this mechanism in a WSN comprising two sink nodes. In the example, node E generates a data packet directed to sink node A, while node F generates a data packet directed to sink node B. Since nodes E and F are in possession of the data packets, they know the respective destinations. Node E only transmits the uplink tone relative to level 2 (tree of sink node A), while node F must transmit two uplink tones because the tone relative to level 3 (tree of sink node B) falls in the slot that should be polled in level 2 (tree of sink node A). A similar situation happens at node D, which must transmit the received tone in both trees.

4 Analytical Model

In this section, we propose an analytical model for the performance evaluation of TP-MAC, based on a previous analytical model developed for SCP-MAC [13]. This model will also allow comparison of TP-MAC and SCP-MAC duty cycles for the same intended delivery latency.

Suppose that a data packet has to be routed to the sink node, and that the packet originator node is at distance of N_hops from the sink. This number is also the level of the node in the TP-MAC convergecast tree. We also admit that SCP-MAC delivers the packet through the minimum hop count path, and therefore this number is the same for a SCP-MAC network.

Considering that the packet is generated just after one SCP-MAC wake-up period, the worst-case delivery latency for SCP-MAC is approximately given by:

$$Td\_SCP \cong N\_hops \times Tp\_SCP \ , \qquad (1)$$

where Tp_SCP is the cycle period of the SCP-MAC protocol. Expression (1) only applies if we assume, as it is the case for the sake of simplicity of the analysis, that there is just one single node that wants to communicate with the sink, and therefore there are no collisions with other transmissions. Moreover, in expression (1) we neglect the times of the SCP-MAC tone transmission, the time required for the second contention window and the packet transmission time at the last hop, because they are typically small. But, on the other hand, as we are about to equate expressions for delivery latency of the two protocols, in order to make a comparison of their duty cycles, all these terms cancel because they are equal in both protocols.

Delivery latency expression for TP-MAC is a little bit more complex.

The first term of the total latency is a TP-MAC cycle period, Tp_TP, which accounts for the worst case, when a packet is generated just after the tone propagation windows elapse. In terms of tone propagation and packet transmission, this first cycle is always lost.

Hereafter, we recommend the reader to follow the subsequent reasoning with the help of the Figure 1.

If the node level, *N_hops,* is lower or equal than the number of tones, *N_tones,* say for instance level 3, we can see that the tone is completely propagated to the sink in the propagation window of a second cycle. Subsequent data transmission can be done in a number of *N_hops* of consecutive data transmission slots of that cycle. The time required for these transmissions is equal to $(N\_hops-1) \times Tts\_TP$ (where *Tts_TP* is data transmission slot duration), plus the packet transmission time, and that of the SCP-MAC protocol overhead, the time durations of the tone propagation windows, and of the synchronization tone. We consider, in the following analysis, a time of $N\_hops \times Tts\_Tp$, which is enough to account for those terms.

If *N_hops* is greater than *N_tones,* say for instance 8, another extra TP-MAC cycle, is needed. In the second cycle, propagation of the upstream tone and actual packet transmission are done only till level 6, because nodes in the levels above it, are still asleep (upstream tone could not reach them in the second cycle). In the third cycle, tone propagation is done till the sink, awaking a number of *N_tones* levels. Actual transmissions of the packet, in the third cycle, are done within a time equal to $N\_tones \times Tts\_TP$ in that cycle.

It is interesting to note that the delivery latency in the upstream direction remains the same for nodes from level 7 till level 12. Propagation and transmission patterns only change in the second cycle, and remain the same in the third cycle.

When we increase the level from 12 (a multiple of *N_tones*) to level 13, another cycle is needed, and the number of cycles needed to transmit the packet is four.

With this reasoning we are able to derive the following expression:

$$Td\_TP \cong \left(\text{ceiling}\left(\frac{N\_hops}{N\_Tones} \right) \right) \times Tp\_TP +$$
$$\min(N\_hops, N\_tones) \times Tts\_TP$$

Now it is worth to simplify this expression. If we approximate *Tts_TP* by the TP-MAC period, *Tp_TP,* divided by the number of slots of the data transmission window, *Nt_slots,* the above expression becomes:

$$Td\_TP \cong \left[\frac{\text{ceiling}\left(\frac{N\_hops}{N\_tones} \right) + \min(N\_hops, N\_tones)}{Nt\_slots} \right] \times Tp\_TP . \qquad (2)$$

Expressions (1) and (2) are of great utility, because they allow us to estimate the value of the TP-MAC period, needed to achieve the same expected latency as with the SCP-MAC protocol.

For SCP-MAC, we have one poll per cycle, and its poll frequency is given by the expression:

$$F\_poll\_SCP = \frac{1}{Tp\_SCP} . \qquad (3)$$

Rigorous poll frequency estimation for TP-MAC, with data transmission in the upstream direction, is not an easy task, because as we have seen before, nearby nodes of those located in the minimum hop path, also form woken-up branches.

In order to compare the duty cycles of SCP-MAC and TP-MAC, we assume that the network remains silent for the most part of the time, and only sporadically has data to be delivered. We believe that this assumption is true for a large number of applications.

For TP-MAC, we have two polls per cycle, and more seldom one poll for the synchronization tone. If we define Nc_st_TP, as the number of TP-MAC cycles between two consecutive polls for the synchronization tone, the poll frequency for TP_MAC, for the quiet state of the network, is given by the expression:

$$F\_poll\_TP = \frac{\left(2 + \dfrac{1}{Nc\_st\_TP}\right)}{Tp\_TP} . \tag{4}$$

The relation between the duty cycles of the two protocols is given by the following expression:

$$\frac{DC\_TP}{DC\_SCP} = \frac{F\_poll\_TP}{F\_poll\_SCP} .$$

Using expressions (1) through (4), and equating the delivery latencies, the last expression becomes:

$$\frac{DC\_TP}{DC\_SCP} \cong \left(2 + \frac{1}{Nc\_st\_TP}\right) \times$$

$$\left[\text{ceiling}\left(\frac{N\_hops}{N\_tones}\right) + \frac{\min(N\_hops, N\_tones)}{Nt\_slots}\right] \times . \tag{5}$$

$$\frac{1}{N\_hops}$$

Expression (5) can give the relation of the duty cycles of the two algorithms, in the quiet state of the network, needed to achieve the same target latency of a transmission, in the upstream direction, to the sink.

The relation of the two duty cycles decreases, as the number of hops increases. Therefore, TP-MAC becomes more energy efficient as the network size grows.

It is interesting to derive a limit for expression (5), as N_hops increases to high numbers. The ceiling term of expression (5) obeys the following inequalities:

$$\frac{N\_hops}{N\_tones} - 1 < \text{ceiling}\left(\frac{N\_hops}{N\_tones}\right) < \frac{N\_hops}{N\_tones} + 1 .$$

Therefore the ceiling term, divided by N_hops, approaches $1/N\_tones$, as N_hops approaches infinity.

In expression (5), $\min(N\_hops, N\_tones) = N\_tones$ when $N\_hops > N\_tones$. Consequently, its division by N_hops approaches 0, as N_hops increases.

Therefore, the following expression can be written:

$$\lim_{N\_hops \to \infty} \frac{DC\_TP}{DC\_SCP} = \left(2 + \frac{1}{Nc\_st\_TP} \right) \times \frac{1}{N\_tones} . \tag{6}$$

TP-MAP efficiency increases, as more tones are added, because more deeply and faster the wake-up tones are propagated to the sink, and data is transmitted. As the number of polls of TP-MAC remains the same for each cycle, lower latencies are achieved for the same duty cycle, or, conversely, lower duty cycles are obtained, for the same target latency. A large wake-up-tone propagation window becomes more attractive as the wake-up time increases, in order to minimize this overhead (typical wake-up times are in the order of 2 ms [14], which is approximately the expected duration of one wake-up-tone). However, it is not possible to increase indefinitely the number of tones, in order to achieve lower latencies, keeping the duty cycle unchanged, as this requires more data transmission slots, and greater tone propagation windows. On the order hand, if we increase the number of tones, in order to reduce the duty cycle keeping the latency unchanged, cycle periods become wider, demanding a decrease of the number of cycles between consecutive synchronization tone polls (i.e. Nc_st_TP), which has the opposite effect of raising the duty cycle.

5   Results

In this section some numerical results are displayed in two figures, in order to compare expected performance of the two MAC protocols.

Fig. 4 shows the poll period of the two protocols as a function of the target latencies, for a hop distance of 25 hops. The TP-MAC parameters are: number of tones: 6; number of transmission slots: 10; synchronization tone period: 5 cycles. The poll period of TP-MAC is slightly more than twice that of SCP-MAC, which means that, under the considered assumptions, it requires approximately one half of the SCP-MAC duty cycle, for the same target latency.

Fig. 5 shows the ratio between the duty cycles of TP-MAC and SCP-MAC as a percentage, for different numbers of hops, and different sizes of the wake-up tone propagation window. All other TP-MAC parameters are the same as those of Fig. 4. It is worth to note that TP-MAC duty cycle decreases with increasing number of hops, but that its energy efficiency gain, with respect to SCP-MAC, stabilizes for high numbers of hops. Higher number of tones can give higher energy efficiency gain. For instance, for 10 tones, we can obtain a duty cycle as low as 22% of the SCP-MAC duty cycle, for large network sizes.

These numbers seem to be very promising. We believe that TP-MAC can achieve very low duty cycles for the same target latency when compared with pure SCP-MAC, or equivalently very low latencies for the same duty cycles.

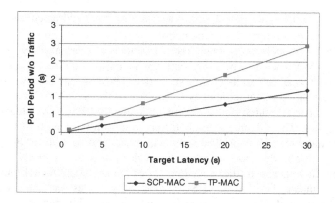

Fig. 4. Poll periods of TP-MAC and SCP-MAC as a function of the target latency

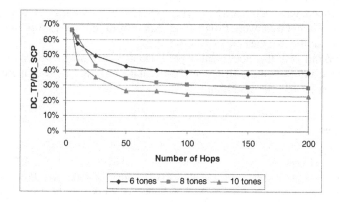

Fig. 5. Ratio between the duty cycles of TP-MAC and SCP-MAC as a function of the number of hops, and size of the wake-up tone propagation window

6   Conclusions

This paper has presented Tone-Propagated MAC (TP-MAC), a novel MAC protocol for WSNs, specially suited for early warning applications, where the traffic generated by sensor nodes (mainly alert messages) is sporadic, but has stringent latency requirements.

TP-MAC is based on a multi-sink multicast/convergecast tree WSN topology, supporting fast data path establishment, propagating short wake-up tones upstream and/or downstream between adjacent tree levels. This fast-path establishment mechanism does not incur on latency penalty for the transmission of the first packet of a stream, and it allows TP-MAC to achieve lower duty-cycles in periods of inactivity. The reliance on a tree topology is not a big limitation from the point of view of the authors, since it is typical in most WSN applications. The existence of a global schedule is essential to the operation of TP-MAC. The method used to establish and maintain this global schedule has also been addressed, as well as the mechanism for support of multiple sink nodes.

An analytical model to evaluate the performance (normal duty-cycle versus latency) of TP-MAC has also been presented, which allows a direct comparison with SCP-MAC. Performance results clearly show that TP-MAC can achieve much lower duty cycles, for the same target latency (e.g., 49% of the SCP-MAC duty-cycle for a 25-hop path between source and sink), or equivalently, very low latencies for the same duty cycles. This advantage tends to increase with the length of the path, and stabilizes for more than 50 hops. The analytical model was derived for the quiet state, as we believe that is the most common network state in many WSN applications. However, simulations and further development of the analytical model must be done, in order to compare TP-MAC and SCP-MAC duty cycles and latencies in other realistic scenarios, with increased contention and inter-flow interference.

Acknowledgments. The work described in this paper is based on results of IST FP6 project UbiSec&Sens. UbiSec&Sens receives research funding from the European Community's Sixth Framework Programme. Apart from this, the European Commission has no responsibility for the content of this paper.

The information in this document is provided as is and no guarantee or warranty is given that the information is fit for any particular purpose. The user thereof uses the information at its sole risk and liability.

References

1. Grilo, A., Macedo, M., Nunes, M.: Tone-Propagated MAC (TP-MAC): A Low Duty-cycle Low Latency MAC Protocol for Wireless Sensor Networks. In: Proceedings of the Performance Control in Wireless Sensor Networks Workshop (hold in conjunction with the IFIP Networking Conference 2006). Coimbra, Portugal (2006).
2. Heidemann, J., Ye, W.: Energy Conservation in Sensor Networks at the Link and Network Layers. In: Bulusu, N., Jha, S. (eds.): Wireless Sensor Networks: A Systems Perspective. Artech House Inc. (2005) 75-86
3. IEEE: Wireless LAN Medium Access Control (MAC) and Physical Layer (PHY) Specifications. IEEE Std. 802.11 (1999).
4. Bharghavan, V., Demers, A., Shenker, S., Zhang, L.: MACAW: A media access protocol for wireless LAN's. In: Proceedings of the ACM SIGCOMM. London, UK (1994) 212-225
5. Ye, W., Heidemann, J., Estrin, D.: An Energy-Efficient MAC protocol for Wireless Sensor Networks. In: Proceedings of the IEEE Infocom. New York (2002) 1567-1576
6. Li, Y., Ye, W., Heidemann, J.: Energy and Latency Control in Low Duty Cycle MAC Protocols. In: Proceedings of the IEEE Wireless Communications and Networking Conference (WCNC 2005). New Orleans, LA, USA (2005)
7. van Dam, T., Langendoem, K.: An adaptive energy-efficient MAC protocol for wireless sensor networks. In: 1st ACM Conference on Embedded Networked Systems (SenSys 2003). Los Angeles, USA (2003) 171-180
8. Ye, W., Heidemann, J., Estrin, D.: Medium Access Control With Coordinated Adaptive Sleeping for Wireless Sensor Networks. The IEEE/ACM Transactions on Networking, Vol. 12, No. 3. (2004) 493-506

9. Lu, G., Krishnamachari, B., Raghavendra, C.: An Adaptive Energy-Efficient and Low-Latency MAC for Data Gathering in Wireless Sensor Networks. In: Proceedings of the 18th International Parallel and Distributed Processing Symposium (IPDPS 2004). Santa Fe, NM, USA (2004)

10. Hill, J., Culler, D.: Mica: A wireless platform for deeply embedded networks. IEEE Micro, Vol. 22, No. 6. (2002) 12-25

11. Polastre, J., Hill, J., Culler, D.: Versatile Low Power Media Access for Wireless Sensor Networks. In: Proceedings of the 2nd ACM SenSys Conference. Baltimore, MD, USA (2004) 95-107

12. El-Hoiydi, A., Decotignie, J.-D.: WiseMAC: An Ultra Low Power MAC Protocol for the Downlink of Infrastructure Wireless Sensor Networks. In: Proceedings of the 9th IEEE International Symposium on Computers and Communications (ISCC'04). Alexandria, Egypt (2004) 244-251

13. Ye, W., Silva, F., Heidemann, J.: Ultra-Low Duty Cycle MAC with Scheduled Channel Polling. In: Proceedings of the 4th ACM Conference on Embedded Networked Sensor Systems (SenSys 2006). Boulder, Colorado, USA (2006)

14. Körber, H., Wattar, H., Scholl, G., Heller, W.: Embedding a Microchip PIC18F452 based commercial platform into TinyOS. Workshop on Real-World Wireless Sensor Networks (REALWSN'05). Stockholm, Sweden (2005)

Adaptive QoS Reservation Scheme for Ad-Hoc Networks

Rafael Paoliello-Guimarães and Llorenç Cerdà-Alabern

Polytechnic University of Catalonia
Computer Architecture Department
Jordi Girona 1-3, E-08034 Barcelona, Spain
{rafael.guimaraes, llorenc}@ac.upc.edu

Abstract. Achieving QoS (Quality of Service) in Mobile Ad-hoc NETworks (MANET) has been a research topic in the last years. In this paper we describe an adaptive QoS reservation mechanism for Multirate Ad-hoc Networks. The mechanism is targeted for sources requiring a bandwidth allocation. The scheme consist of the nodes initially computing the available bandwidth for new reservations, using the state information advertises among the neighbors. Then, the nodes adjust the available bandwidth by measuring the effective transmission rate achieved while transmitting packets. Simulation results show that the available bandwidth computed by the proposed scheme adapts fast and accurately to changing network conditions.

Keywords: Ad-hoc wireless networks, adaptive QoS, bandwidth reservation.

1 Introduction

Over the last years, ad-hoc networks have captured the attention of researchers and also of the general public. The flexibility it provides due to the fact that no infrastructure is needed to deploy a wireless network is one of the most attractive features this technology. However, along with the flexibility, lots of problems arise due to the possible mobility of the network nodes, the variability of the radio channel characteristics, the scarcity of resources etc.

Providing Quality of Service (QoS) in these scenarios is a non trivial problem. However, since real time applications are likely to be typically demanded in ad-hoc networks, QoS provisioning for such networks has become an active research area.

Some of the proposals done so far (like SWAN [8]) are based on the DiffServ idea, i.e., on the classification of traffic into classes that are served with different priorities by the network. Others like the Flexible Quality of Service Model (FQMM) [9] combine a reservation mechanism for high-priority traffic and service differentiation for low-priority data. Other proposals may be found in the literature facing the problem in a different way. Examples are INSIGNIA

J. García-Vidal and L. Cerdà-Alabern (Eds.): Wireless and Mobility, LNCS 4396, pp. 102–112, 2007.

[5] (which uses in-band signaling) and CEDAR [7] (which defines a "backbone" in order to reduce signaling overhead).

None of these proposals is based on a reservation-based approach. However, we believe that such an approach has a number of advantageous properties: Due to the interference among the nodes, the available capacity decreases rapidly as new connections are established in a wireless ad-hoc network. This may cause a sudden QoS degradation of a significant number of connections when congestion occurs. A CAC based on the reserved bandwidth allows looking for paths that can accommodate new connections, or block them if not enough resources are available. Thus, offering a "proactive" control approach, that prevents congestion.

Few proposals can be found in the literature using a resource reservation-based approach. This is motivated by the difficulties on measuring the available bandwidth of a node in a wireless ad-hoc network. One example is the Ad hoc QoS On-demand Routing (AQOR) [10]. AQOR introduces a resource reservation-based routing and signaling algorithm that tries to provide end-to-end QoS support, in terms of bandwidth and end-to-end delay. The proposal, however, provides a superficial analysis of the bandwidth consumed by a connection and the computation of the available bandwidth for the establishment of new connections in a given node.

In [2,3,4] we have investigated a bandwidth reservation-based scheme to provide QoS in wireless ad-hoc networks. The mechanism works purely on the network layer, and the information about the available bandwidth at a given node is computed using static state information about reserved bandwidth advertised among the neighbors.

In this paper we extend our previous work by proposing an adaptive bandwidth reservation-based scheme. This is motivated by the imprecision of the state information, caused mainly, by the movement of the nodes. The method consists of measuring the effective transmission rate while the node is transmitting packets. These measures are used to adjust the available bandwidth, initially computed using state information.

The paper is organized as follows: we first explain a revised version of the algorithm that we proposed in [3] in section 2. Then in section 3 we present how we can use information provided by the MAC layer about the network state in order to make the mechanism more adaptive and, finally, in section 4 we present some simulation results that shows its feasibility. For the simulations, we applied our reservation mechanism to the *Ad hoc On-Demand Distance Vector Routing* (AODV) [6], although it could be easily applied to other ad-hoc routing protocols.

2   Bandwidth Reservation for QoS Provisioning

The basis of our original mechanism is the computation of the available bandwidth (AB) by each node in the network (see [2,3,4]). This is done in a distributed way, avoiding as much as possible unnecessary interchange of signaling messages.

In this first proposal, all the information is static, i.e. based on the bandwidth reservations made by ongoing connections.

The mechanism is developed with the assumption that we are dealing with multirate wireless ad-hoc networks, i.e., ad-hoc networks where nodes may use different transmission rates when transmitting to different neighbors. The chosen transmission rate usually depends on the distance between nodes and the wireless channel conditions.

2.1   The Basis of Bandwidth Reservation

Our mechanism assumes the existence of two traffic classes: one for traffic that demands QoS requirements and another for best effort traffic. Although we use this assumption throughout the paper, with minor modifications the mechanism could be adapted to work with other traffic classes as well. Besides this, we also assume that the MAC used is able to isolate the traffic classes in such a way that QoS traffic has priority over best effort (we could, for instance, use 802.11e).

The goal of our *bandwidth reservation mechanism* is to provide rate allocation (e.g. peak or sustainable rate) and, at the same time, remain as simple as possible. The solution provides QoS for realtime flows introducing as little overhead as possible in the network. In order to do that, it piggybacks information on signaling messages that most ad-hoc routing protocols already provide (HELLO messages, for example).

If we want to compute the amount of bandwidth that is available for a given node to use for new reservations, we should first investigate the amount of bandwidth that is already being consumed by active flows. By knowing this value, we may just subtract it from the total bandwidth dedicated to QoS traffic in order to obtain the currently available bandwidth.

In order to know how much bandwidth is available for a node to use, we must take into account all transmissions that directly affect its opportunities to transmit. In the case of a CSMA-based wireless MAC protocol, the bandwidth of a node is consumed whenever:

case 1)   It transmits data to a neighbor;
case 2)   One of its neighbors is transmitting data (if the node senses that the medium is being used, it remains in silence);

Representing this in an analytical way, we may state that the load impact of all transmissions on a node i is given by [1]:

$$LD_i = \left(\underbrace{x_i}_{Case\ 1} + \underbrace{\sum_{j \in \mathcal{N}_i} x_j}_{Case\ 2} \right) = \sum_{j \in \mathcal{N}_i^+} x_j \qquad (1)$$

---

[1] Although we use a *sum* operator in the load demand computation, in fact this is a bit pessimistic, since some of these transmissions may overlap in time.

where:

$$x_j = \sum_{k \in \mathcal{N}_j} \frac{r_{jk}}{v_{jk}} \tag{2}$$

and

- LD_i is normalized load demand of all transmissions on node i ($0 \leq LD_i \leq 1$);
- x_i is the normalized total traffic generated or relayed by node i;
- r_{jk} is the amount of traffic reserved for transmission from node j to k (in bps);
- v_{jk} is the transmission rate used between nodes j and k (in bps);
- $\mathcal{N}_i$ is the set of neighbors of node i;
- $\mathcal{N}_i^+$ is the set of neighbors of node i and node i itself;

Once we have computed the load demand on each node of the ad-hoc network, we could define the amount of bandwidth dedicated to QoS traffic as Q and state that the following *QoS constraint* should be respected in order to provide QoS guarantees for realtime flows:

$$LD_i \leq Q, \forall i \tag{3}$$

In other words, by guaranteeing this condition in every node of the network, we can guarantee that the channel occupancy due to the transmission of QoS traffic observed by any MN is never greater than Q.

Of course, due to collisions and other minor MAC issues, the QoS traffic transmitted by the MNs may consume more bandwidth than the computed QoS Load Demand. We shall assume that the parameter Q is dimensioned to cope with this in a way that delays remain acceptable for QoS connections.

2.2 The Maximum Available Bandwidth in Each Mobile Node

Since we have stated that, in order to guarantee the QoS requirements of accepted connections, we should have $LD_i \leq Q$ for every node, we can define the maximum available bandwidth for the establishment of new connections through a node as the difference between the amount of bandwidth dedicated to QoS flows (Q) and the amount of traffic generated by on-going connections (LD):

$$MAB_i = Q - LD_i \tag{4}$$

And, consequently, we could rewrite the QoS constraint as:

$$MAB_i \geq 0, \forall i \tag{5}$$

2.3 The Call Admission Control

After defining the distributed mechanism to compute the *maximum available bandwidth* at each node of the network, we shall use this value to decide if a new connection fits in a given node. Then, if we integrate this admission control into a routing protocol (no matter if the protocol is proactive or reactive), we will not only be able to accept or refuse connections based on available bandwidth, but also to find the less congested path for this new connection, distributing the traffic more equally throughout the ad-hoc network.

The Call Admission Control (CAC) should guarantee that, just after accepting a new connection the *MAB* remains non-negative for all nodes in the network (as it was beforehand). However, since we know that the transmission of a node only impacts on the load demand computation of its one-hop neighborhood, we can restrict the CAC to guaranteeing that the *MAB* is non-negative for the nodes in the candidate path and all their one-hop neighbors. Defining the available bandwidth (*AB*) of a node as:

$$AB_i = \min\{MAB_j\}, j \in \mathcal{N}_i^+ \tag{6}$$

We may restrict ourselves to guaranteeing that the *AB* of every node in the path is non-negative.

Since we know that the load demand of a node is impacted by every transmission in the neighborhood, we may state that for establishing a new reservation of r bps the following CAC should be checked in every node of the path:

$$AB_i \geq \sum_{y\in((\mathcal{N}_i^+\cup\mathcal{N}_j^+)\cap path)} \frac{r}{v_y} \tag{7}$$

where

- i represents the current node in the path;
- j represents the next node in the path (to which i will transmit);
- v_y is the transmission rate from node y toward its next hop in the path.

3 Using MAC Information to Adapt

The mechanism presented before is completely based on the computation of the so called Available Bandwidth of a node. This value, however, may not reflect the network conditions at a given moment. In wireless networks, conditions vary and state information becomes "imprecise". Thus, a QoS mechanism should somehow take into account this dynamic behavior of the network and adapt to its conditions. We, thus, propose to use information about the current wireless channel condition in order to provide a more adaptive *AB* computation.

The basis of our proposal is to use information that can be provided by the MAC layer in order to compute the instantaneous "effective" transmission rate. This measurement can then be used to compute the node's *AB*, which was based on a fixed value (Q) in our previous proposal.

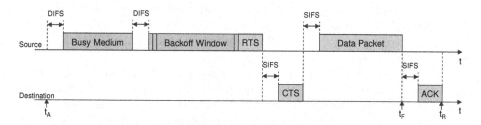

Fig. 1. Data transmission on 802.11

In the case of an 802.11 network, for example, the transmission of a data packet is always acknowledged in order to guarantee the reception of the packet by the destination (see figure 1). This characteristic can then be used to measure the amount of time that it takes to transmit a given data packet.

If we are able to obtain the timestamp (t_A) that marks the instant of time when the MAC layer of a given node i gets a new packet to be transmitted to node j and the timestamp (t_R) of the instant when the corresponding ACK packet is received by node i, we may compute their difference and obtain the total time that it took to transmit the data packet. If we then divide the size of the transmitted packet (L) by the time it took to transmit it $(t_R - t_A)$, we can obtain the instantaneous "effective" transmission rate.

$$v_{ij}^{eff} = \frac{L}{t_R - t_A} \qquad (8)$$

Note that this value already takes into account every possible event that may delay the transmission of a packet (e.g., transmission of neighbors, the hidden node problem), since if any problem happens, a retransmission will occur and, consequently, the instantaneous "effective" transmission rate will decrease.

After computing this value, in order to avoid fluctuations in the measurements and thus provide a more robust estimation, we compute an Exponentially Weighted Moving Average (EWMA) of the "effective" transmission rate. At the same time, we normalize the value by dividing it by the "nominal" transmission rate between the nodes.

$$V^{eff}(k) = \alpha \times V^{eff}(k-1) + [1 - \alpha] \times \beta \times \frac{v_{ij}^{eff}}{v_{ij}} \qquad (9)$$

Where $V^{eff}(k)$ is the estimated V^{eff} at iteration k. The parameter α controls the reaction of the measurement. Smaller values of α can lead us to fast reactions to changes in the network conditions but, in the other hand, it may cause that short instabilities in transmissions impact hugely on on-going reservations. The election of this parameter, thus, should be a trade-off between fast response and robustness.

Clearly, V_k^{eff} in (9) converges to $\beta \times \frac{v_{ij}^{eff}}{v_{ij}}$. The parameter β (which may vary from 0 to 1) states that the measured "effective" transmission rate can not be completely reserved for QoS traffic. In fact, although we are able to measure the "effective" transmission rate in the MAC layer, we can not use it completely without increasing delays. We should instead use just a portion (β) of this value for QoS reservations.

Once the "effective" transmission rate is computed based on measurements performed in the MAC layer, this value can be used to compute an "adaptive available bandwidth" for node i. Since we know that, in the current moment, the node is able to transmit at a given rate, the difference between this value and the amount of traffic that it is really transmitting can be seen as the amount of bandwidth that is still available for new connections:

$$AB_i^{adaptive} = V_i^{eff} - x_i \tag{10}$$

By doing this, we may have an $AB^{adaptive}$ computation that is more responsive to the network conditions, since any event that may interfere with transmissions directly impacts in the measured V_i^{eff}.

Nevertheless, in order to measure the V^{eff}, a node must be already transmitting some data. That means that if a node is neither generating nor relaying data packets, it won't be able to compute the $AB^{adaptive}$. This may be a problem, since many times the CAC is executed before a node starts to transmit anything.

In order to solve this issue, we propose to keep the computation of the AB by the original "static" way (we shall refer to it as AB^{static}) and, in parallel, compute it by the "measurement" way. We, then, use the AB^{static} whenever the node does not have a measured value to base the CAC on. By doing this, the original way is used only before the node starts any transmission and when the node remains in silence for a long period of time. In this latter case, the measured values are no longer trustful, since network conditions may have changed a lot.

Using this strategy, even if a node does not have a measurement to base its CAC on, it receives information from its neighbors that reflects their measurements. In this way, although the node is not transmitting yet (or has spent a long period of time without transmitting), it may have at least an idea of what is going on in the neighborhood. By doing that, the CAC can surely perform better than if the node just took a blind decision.

4   Simulation

In order to evaluate our proposal, we performed simulations under scenarios that shows that by using MAC layer measurements the mechanism outperforms our previous proposal. These simulations give us an idea of the advantages of monitoring transmissions on the MAC layer in order to obtain information about the current state of the network.

All simulations were performed using ns-2 [1]. Routing is performed by a modified version of the Ad-hoc On-demand Distance Vector (AODV) protocol [6] that includes the needed extensions to implement our mechanism. The parameters that were used for all simulations are presented on table 1.

Table 1. Parameters used on simulations with ns-2

Parameter	Value
Area	Square of 1000m x 1000m
MAC Protocol	802.11 with multirate and RTS/CTS
Tx Rate 1	11Mbps (100m range)
Tx Rate 2	2Mbps (300m range)
QoS Flows	CBR, 600Kbps (500 bytes UDP packets)
α parameter	0.99
β parameter	0.8
Q parameter	0.175

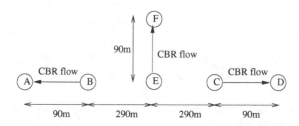

Fig. 2. Simulation topology for the 1st scenario

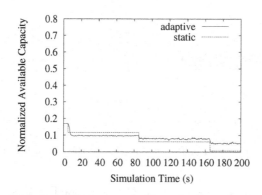

Fig. 3. Available Bandwidth on node E on the first simulation scenario

In the first simulation scenario, six nodes are placed as depicted by figure 2. After 5 seconds of simulation, node E starts a CBR connection towards node F. After other 80 seconds, node B starts transmitting to node A and after other 80 seconds, node C starts its transmission to D.

The total simulation time is 200 seconds. Note that RTS/CTS signaling packets are sent at 2 Mbps, thus, node E can hear the transmissions from nodes B and C, but nodes B and C do not interfere each other.

Figure 3 shows both the available bandwidth computed using equation (6) (without using measurements in the MAC layer) and the available bandwidth

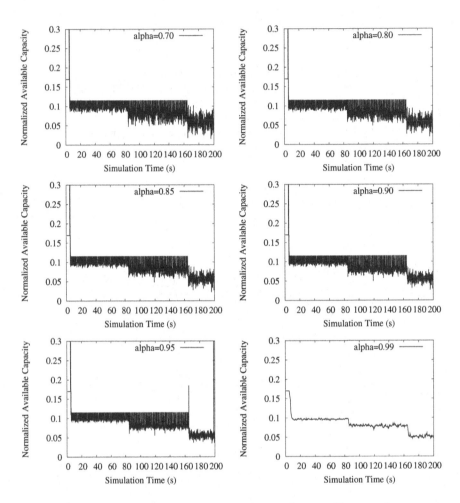

Fig. 4. Instability in measurements due to the use of low α values

based on measurements (using equation (10)) on node E . We shall refer to these available bandwidths as AB^{static} and $AB^{adaptive}$, respectively . Notice that this node is in the neighborhood of the other two transmitters (B and C). Therefore, AB^{static} is 0.12, 0.66 and 0.011 when 1, 2 and 3 connections are established respectively.

In this graph it is possible to see that the two mechanisms for obtaining the available bandwidth are similar in the first 160 seconds (when only two nodes are transmitting). After that, when the third connection starts, the difference between them increases. That happens mainly due to two reasons: First because nodes B and C can transmit simultaneously, while node E computes AB^{static} adding all bandwidth consumed in the neighborhood. Secondly, by the fact that the busy period of wireless medium (and thus the adaptive available bandwidth) does not vary linearly with the number of connections.

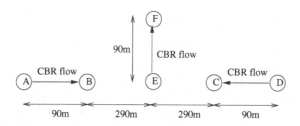

Fig. 5. Simulation topology for the 3nd scenario

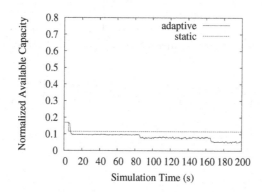

Fig. 6. Available Bandwidth on node E on the third simulation scenario

Still using this scenario, we conducted several simulations with different α value (see equation 9), trying to figure out the impact of this parameter in the stability of the algorithm (see graphs of figure 4). The higher the chosen α the more stable the available capacity value obtained. However, increasing this value very much may have a negative impact on the response time of the system. Variations on the available capacity of the node would only be noticed after a while. The parameter α should be as small as possible without compromising the robustness of the system.

In figure 4 it is possible to see the measurements of the available capacity when using different α values. One can notice by quickly analyzing these graphs that values below 0.99 provide a very unstable "effective" transmission rate measurement. All simulations that use low α values (up to 0.95) present lots of fluctuations.

Finally, in the last simulation scenario (figure 5), we invert the direction of the flows from B→A to A→B and C→D to D→C. By doing that, these flows are not taken into account in the computation of the available bandwidth of node E. Nevertheless, when these transmissions are taking place, E is not allowed to transmit to F (due to the reception of a CTS), what should impact on its *AB* computation. This can be seen in figure 6, where the available bandwidth on node E is quite different when using measurements and when not using them.

5   Conclusion

In this paper we propose an adaptive QoS bandwidth reservation scheme for wireless ad-hoc networks.

First, the nodes estimate the available bandwidth by taking into account the reserved bandwidth in the neighborhood. Then, while the nodes transmit packets, they estimate by measurements the "effective" transmission rate. This value is used to continously adapt the available bandwidth to the network conditions. A CAC based on the available bandwidth allows looking for paths that can accommodate new connections, or block them if not enough resources are available. Thus, offering a "proactive" control approach, that prevents congestion.

Simulation results show that the available bandwidth computed by the proposed scheme adapts fast and accurately to changing network conditions.

Acknowledgments. This work was supported by CAPES - Brazil, the Ministry of Education of Spain under grant CICYT TEC2004-06437-C05-05 and the European NoE EuroNGI.

References

1. The Network Simulator ns-2.
2. L. Cerda, M. Voorhaen, R. Guimaraes, J. Barcelo, J. García, and C. Blondia. A Reservation Scheme Satisfying Bandwidth QoS Constraints for Ad-Hoc Networks. *Lecture Notes in Computer Science (LNCS)*, 3427:176–, Feb 2005.
3. L. Cerda, M. Voorhaen, R. Guimaraes, J. Barcelo, J. García, J. Morillo, and C. Blondia. A Reservation Scheme Satisfying Bandwidth QoS Constraints for Multirate Ad-Hoc Networks. In *IST Mobile and Wireless Communications Summit*, Jun 2005.
4. R. Guimaraes and L. Cerda. Bandwidth Reservation on Wireless Networks. In *Proceedings of the 12th European Wireless Conference*, Apr 2006.
5. S. Lee, G. Ahn, and A. T. Campbell. Improving UDP and TCP performance in mobile ad hoc networks with INSIGNIA. *IEEE Communications Magazine*, 39(6):156–165, Jun 2001.
6. C. Perkins and S. D. E. Belding-Royer. RFC 3561: Ad hoc On-Demand Distance Vector Routing, Jul 2003.
7. R. Sivakumar, P. Sinha, and V. Bharghavan. CEDAR: A COre-Extraction Distributed Ad Hoc Routing Algorithm. *IEEE Journal on Selected Areas in Communications*, 17(8):1454–1465, Aug 1999.
8. A. Veres, G. Ahn, A. Campbell, and L. Sun. SWAN: Service Differentiation in Stateless Wireless Ad Hoc Networks. In *Proceedings of the Conference on Computer Communications (IEEE Infocom)*, Jun 2002.
9. H. Xiao, W. G. Seah, A. Lo, and K. C. Chua. A flexible quality of service model for mobile ad hoc netowrks. In *Proceedings of the IEEE Vehicular Technology Conference*, May 2000.
10. Q. Xue and A. Ganz. Ad hoc QoS on-demand routing (AQOR) in mobile ad hoc networks. *Journal of Parallel and Distributed Computing*, (63):154–165, 2003.

DiffServ in Ad Hoc Networks

Tor Kjetil Moseng and Øivind Kure

Centre for Quantifiable Quality of Service in Communication Systems (Q2S)*
Norwegian University of Science and Technology (NTNU)
O.S. Bragstads plass 2E, N-7491 Trondheim, Norway
{torkjeti,okure}@q2s.ntnu.no

Abstract. In this paper we study the expected difference between the
QoS classes in an ad hoc network. The results have a direct bearing on
the suitability of extending a fixed DiffServ architecture into an ad hoc
network. Through simulation, we analyze the number of classes that can
be used in the ad hoc network with separation between the observed
QoS in the different classes. The results clearly depend on the type of
traffic run in the network. With well behaved CBR traffic, the ad hoc
network supports no more than four classes, but with more aggressive
traffic like TCP no more than two classes are supported. In addition,
there is a fairness problem; the performance for a particular flow is not
well distributed among the nodes.

1 Introduction

In an ad hoc network the nodes communicate over a shared wireless channel.
There is no infrastructure and the nodes must operate as a router to forward
traffic to destinations that are multiple hops away. Ad hoc networks therefore
have different characteristics compared to fixed networks. A common channel
with hidden and exposed nodes combined with node movement are aspects that
necessitate different solutions and mechanisms. The dynamic nature of the links
and their capacity makes providing Quality of Service (QoS) more challenging
than in comparable sized fixed networks.

One of the most promising QoS architectures for fixed networks is the DiffServ
architecture [3]. DiffServ is a QoS architecture that divides each flow into a
defined class, and treats all packets on a per-hop basis based on which class the
packets' flow belongs to. DiffServ solves the scalability problems in the IntServ
QoS architecture [4]. IntServ is a flow-aware architecture that does not scale if the
number of source-receiver pairs become too high. The DiffServ architecture uses a
6-bit Differentiated Service Code Point (DSCP), which is in the Type of Service
(ToS) field in the IP-header, to define a packet's treatment in the network.
This treatment gives the per-hop behaviour (PHB) in each intermediate node

---

* "Centre for Quantifiable Quality of Services in Communication Systems, Centre of
Excellence" appointed by the Research Council of Norway, funded by the Research
Council, NTNU and UNINETT. http://www.q2s.ntnu.no

J. García-Vidal and L. Cerdà-Alabern (Eds.): Wireless and Mobility, LNCS 4396, pp. 113–125, 2007.

that belongs to the network domain. The domain's policies will therefore give the definite treatment. Packets receiving similar forwarding behaviour belong to the same PHB class - or DiffServ class. The differentiation among the classes is typically given by the buffer capacity, buffer drop probability and packet scheduling technique. DiffServ defines one Expedited Forwarding (EF) class, twelve Assured Forwarding (AF) classes (i.e. four classes, each with three drop probabilities) and one Best Effort (BE) class.

In this paper we explore the number of QoS classes that can be supported in an ad hoc network. Standard DiffServ based IP networks use 5 different QoS classes. Clearly an IntServ based architecture is feasible, but our work aims at exploring the number of classes ad hoc networks can sustain assuming a DiffServ based architecture. By sustaining we mean the number of classes where the end to end performance for flows in the various classes differs markedly. This will be the starting point in defining a suitable QoS architecture or less drastically, suitably mapping schemes between the standardized DiffServ classes and the corresponding classes in ad hoc networks.

There are several proposals for QoS architecture for ad hoc networks. The number of aggregation classes range from two classes [15] up to four classes based on 3GPP's class definitions [1], [21]. However none of the different proposals make a stringent argument for the number of aggregation classes selected. It is therefore beneficial to analyze the maximum number of classes in a network where there is still some separation between the observed behaviour of flows mapped to the different classes. The separation in behaviour is clearly a function of the per node behaviour for each class. We use the standardized per hop behaviour in DiffServ with one Expedited Forwarding class, a set of Assured Forwarding classes and a Best Effort class. The Assured Forwarding classes differ in terms of drop probability and in the fraction of the forwarding resources allocated to the class. Through simulations we find the separation in terms of the performance characteristics loss and delay for different number of aggregation classes. The degree of unpredictability in how the ad hoc network will influence the various traffic classes is likely to be a function of the type of traffic run in the aggregation classes. Well behaved CBR traffic is relatively easy to deal with compared to more aggressive traffic like TCP. We will therefore perform a sensitivity analysis for different types of traffic in the "lowest" aggregation class, which we call the BE class for simplicity.

QoS architectures for the ad hoc network in today's literature include proposals like INSIGNIA [14], ASAP [20], FQMM [19] and SWAN [2]. INSIGNIA is an end-to-end resource reservation based protocol that reserves one of two bandwidth levels. ASAP extends INSIGNIA with hard and soft reservation modes to utilize the resources better. FQMM combines IntServ and DiffServ where only the highest prioritized classes may use IntServ because of its per-flow guarantee and lack of scalability. SWAN is a class based approach that use probing for admission control of the real-time packets and rate control for the best-effort packets. All these architectures are only intended for the ad hoc network and need mapping of some kind in gateways for Internet connectivity. There is some research that cover the interconnection point between a fixed and an ad hoc network [7], [8], [9], [18], [6], and [16]. However, these approaches require mapping between two different architectures in the gateways. [7], [8], [9], [18] and [6] extend SWAN to cope with the interconnection point, while [16] considers inter-domain agreements and proposes a framework to help the ad hoc and fixed network to cooperate. Clearly, using the same architecture in both the fixed and ad hoc networks would be beneficial.

The rest of the paper is structured as follows: Section 2 describes the simulation setup. Section 3 and Sect. 4 give the results from the simulations. Section 5 presents a different view on the network considering fairness. And finally, conclusions in Sect. 6.

2   Simulation Setup

The main goal with the simulations was to make a sensitivity analysis on the number of classes in the network. The number of sources were kept constant in our network, so in order to increase the number of classes in the network, we chose to split up the lowest aggregated class (here: the BE class) in more classes. Also, we wanted to see how the performance depended on the type of traffic in the network. We started therefore with only well behaved traffic like CBR traffic. We then introduced TCP as aggressive traffic in the lowest aggregated class, i.e. the BE class. The TCP sources was only restricted by their sending window that was set to 64 kB. The now more aggressive BE traffic increased the offered load to the network, compared to the scenario with only well behaved CBR sources. Also, the load was different for different number of classes since the number of BE nodes was varied. However, even though this can explain some of the results, the conlusions found in this paper are still valid.

Regarding the buffer scheduling and buffer management mechanisms, we wanted to keep it simple. To fully exploit mechanisms like WRR and RED, which are used in the standard DiffServ architecture, one need to do a sensitivity analysis on how to best configure them. This was evident when we did a few simulations with RED as our buffer management. With the same RED parameters for all priority classes, there was a non-existent separation among the CBR traffic classes. Based on this, we used Strict Priority and Drop Tail as our buffer scheduling and buffer management mechansims, respectively. However, studies with different buffer scheduling and buffer management mechanisms will be a part of our future work.

The simulations were done using the J-sim network simulator, version 1.3 and patch 3, with the wireless extension package [12]. A 1500 x 300 meters area was used with a total of 40 nodes. 18 of these nodes were selected as a source and divided into a set of classes, varying from two to six. A random receiver was by each source elected from the remaining 22 nodes. The sources were divided into the following class distribution (EF:AF1:AF2:AF3:AF4:BE): (3:0:0:0:0:15) for two classes, (3:6:0:0:0:9) for three classes, (3:3:3:0:0:9) for four classes, (3:3:3:3:0:6) for five classes and (3:3:3:3:3:3) for six classes.

Each source sending CBR traffic, transmits with a fixed rate from 5 to 30 kbps according to the scenario, 10 replications - each with a different seed, running for 200 seconds. Each source started sending packets after a negative exponential distributed waiting time to avoid the same starting time. The average packet size was 358 bytes[1]. The interdeparture time varies according to a negative exponential distribution with mean equal to the data rate. Every node drew a new starting point for each repetition and moved within the simulation area according to the Random Waypoint model with a 2 m/s mobility. The IEEE 802.11 MAC-layer was used with 2 Mbps capacity and 250 meters transmission range. Each class' buffer size was computed from the buffer delay restriction placed on each of the classes: 3 kB (EF), 18 kB (AF1), 31 kB (AF2), 44 kB (AF3), 57 kB (AF4) and 70 kB (BE) were used. The reactive routing protocol AODV [17] was used as routing protocol in the simulations. The AODV buffer was set to 64 kB. By setting the RTS-threshold to zero, every packet was sent with an RTS/CTS handshake first. The AODV HELLO mechanism was disabled, which means that link breaks were discovered by retransmissions.

3   Results

To compare the results we chose loss and delay to illustrate the differentiation between the QoS in the classes. The loss is an average over all packets for each source in the aggregate, while the delay is an average for all received packets for each source in the aggregate. This gives a packet's view of the network and tells the probability of loosing a packet and gives the expected delay for a packet. A different view, from a node's point of view, reflects the fairness in the network and is explained and discussed in Sect. 5.

As we expected, the packet loss in the EF class is independent of the number of classes in the network. This is shown in Fig. 1. What is also shown is that the BE class's packet loss is independent of the number of classes in the network, and quite similar to the EF class's packet loss. One could have expected that the BE loss would increase for more classes in the network, but this effect seems to be minimal. Lower priority and larger buffer size gives EF and BE, respectively, nearly the same packet loss. Packet loss because of buffer overflow on the IP-level is not common when only around 10% of the dropped packets are due to buffer overflows. The high packet loss is caused by the high traffic intensity in the network and no existing route between source and receiver. The CBR sources will send at the same data rate independent of the network conditions and whether a valid route exists. All the noise on the shared channel leads to retransmissions and disrupts the packets, while no existing route leads to packet drops in the AODV buffer. This will consequently lead to a high loss rate. However, the loss rates will not change the paper's conclusions.

In terms of differentiation, the delay is different from the loss. Starting with two classes, the nodes receive the same treatment for low load, but when the load

---

[1] The packet size was drawn from a distribution; 128 byte packet with a 0.2 probability, 256 byte packet with a 0.5 probability and 512 byte packet with a 0.3 probability.

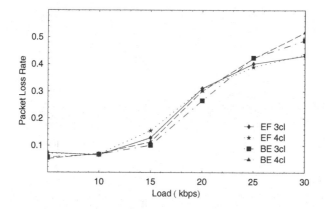

Fig. 1. EF and BE loss with CBR BE traffic

increases the difference between the EF and BE packets become more evident. From bit rates higher than 10 kbps, the EF packets are differentiated from the BE packets (Fig. 2 (a)). When we introduce another class in the network, the same pattern appear, as shown in Fig. 2 (b). The only difference is that the behaviour is equal up to 15 kbps. For higher bit rates, the classes are differentiated. The EF packets get the lowest delay, followed by the AF1 packets and BE packets in that order. This is as expected because of the priority and the smaller buffer sizes for higher prioritized classes.

Increasing to four classes (Fig. 2 (c)) show the exact same pattern, where AF1 and AF2 are between the EF and BE classes - AF1 with lower delay than AF2. But when five classes are introduced, the differentiation gets a bit blurred, as Fig. 2 (d) shows. Again, the classes show different values from 10 kbps and above. However, the classes are not completely separated over the entire load range. The EF and AF1 classes cannot be separated from each other, and also, the AF2 and AF3 classes intercept at 20 kbps. Incrementing further with one class in the network blurs the pattern even more. So, to fully separate the classes from each other above the delay knee (i.e. the point where the classes start to differentiate), the number of classes must be kept below five. The long delays must be commented. The long delays observed in Fig. 2 are insufficient for most flows. The reason for the long delays is the simulation setup that causes high traffic intensity in the network. However, the delay values are, as the loss rates in Fig. 1, a function of the simulation setup and will not change the conclusions in this paper. With the setup, the EF and AF traffic are not close to an acceptable operational point. Still we compared the delay to illustrate the degree of separation even heavy disturbance. Due to the heavy loss, the detailed perturbation of the curves is of less interest since the paths' packets are lost and will affect the average delay. Another issue is that there is a large variation on what delay the packets experience. The large buffer sizes combined with the traffic intensity produced some worst case delays for some packets, which is reflected in the high average delays in Fig. 2.

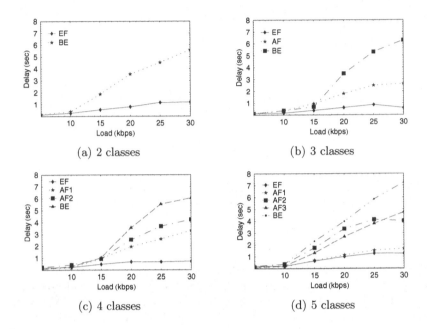

Fig. 2. Differentiation in terms of delay with CBR BE traffic

4   Aggressive Best-Effort Traffic

For the first results, described in Sect. 3, all traffic was well behaving. Each packet was sent according to a constant bit rate scheme. However, more aggressive traffic like the Transport Control Protocol (TCP) [11] are likely to affect the degree of separation between the classes. The simulation was therefore repeated with TCP traffic in the lowest aggregated class (i.e. the BE class). We used the TCP Reno version [13] as it is a well deployed version. Our TCP sources had no bandwidth limits - they were only restricted by the sending window, which was set to 64 kB (no restrictions on the receiving window).

Fig. 3 (a) and (b) show the packet loss for three and four classes in the network, respectively, as a function of the load. The load on the x-axis is in this section for the nodes running CBR, while the BE nodes run TCP and are, as mentioned, only restricted by the sending window. As seen from Fig. 3 the CBR nodes have a very high packet loss that is quite stable independent of the bit rate. As mentioned in Sect. 3, the reason for the high loss is because of the high traffic intensity in the network and no existing route. The traffic intensity on the channel is even higher here than in Sect. 3 when TCP was not present. The number of packets sent by a BE node can be over 10 times the number sent by an EF node for low bit rates. Opposed to the EF nodes, which send packets at fixed rate independent of the channel conditions and whether there exists any valid route to the receiver, the BE nodes throttle their sending rate down to zero if no acknowledgements are received or no valid route exists. However, if

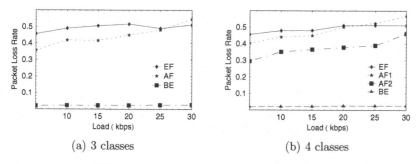

(a) 3 classes   (b) 4 classes

Fig. 3. Packet loss rate with TCP BE traffic

there exist a good path, TCP increases its sending window exponentially and
the transmission rate is then also increased substantially. Since TCP only sends
many packets when the path is good, the loss probability is much lower than
what is experienced in the classes with CBR traffic. As we could expect, both
AF1 and AF2 experience lower loss than the EF class because of the larger
buffer sizes, with AF2 lower than AF1. This is true until the curves intercept at
25 kbps.

The packet loss for the EF class in the two classes scenario is higher than the
loss in the three and four classes scenario. This is due to, as discussed previously,
the reduction in the number of BE nodes from the two to three classes scenario
(i.e. from 15 to 9 nodes). The same behaviour is seen for five and six classes
where the loss is even lower - the number of BE nodes is for those cases further
reduced. One could argue that the number of TCP sources should have remained
constant for all the simulations. By decreasing the number of TCP sources as
more classes are included, the EF class should be better off with more classes.
However, as is shown in Fig. 4, the separation is lost for more than two classes.
This means that our conclusions still hold. A constant number of TCP sources,
say nine TCP sources[2] for all number of classes, would only have given better
differentiation with two classes compared to more classes in the network.

Considering the delay, two classes in the network (Fig. 4 (a)) show that the
EF and BE nodes are differentiated for all bit rates. But the separation is already lost when three classes are in the network (Fig. 4 (b)). That is, there is
separation between the classes, but the classes are not differentiated based on
their relative importance since BE experiences lower delay than AF1. The same
pattern also appears for four classes (Fig. 4 (c)). The introduction of aggressive
traffic like TCP degrade the in-between classes (here: AF1 and AF2) relative
to the aggressive traffic itself. As long as there is no MAC layer priority the
access to the channel will be a function of the traffic load from the neighbours.
The upcoming IEEE 802.11e [10] standard aims to provide priority at the MAC
level. This standard could be a possible enhancement in our model to strengthen

---

[2] 9 TCP sources are used for three and four classes in the network. Using 9 TCP
sources instead of 15 would therefore only have increased the separation with two
classes in the network, which are already separated.

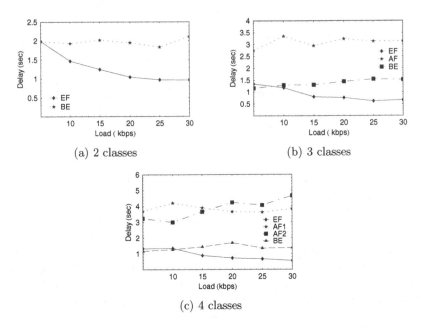

(a) 2 classes

(b) 3 classes

(c) 4 classes

Fig. 4. Differentiation in terms of delay with TCP BE traffic

the differentiation between the classes. The local IP scheduling differentiation only affects the packet handling on the node and not the channel access. For four classes the effect of packet scheduling is marginally compared to the overall delay. The delay is filtered through a high packet loss. The packet loss mostly affects the absolute level of delay, and not the relative performance. So, it is seen that the differentiation between the classes when nodes are transmitting aggressive traffic is lost already at three classes in the network. This is in contrast to the case where every node was well behaved in Sect. 3.

5   Fairness

The results that were presented in Sect. 3 and Sect. 4 were found from a packet's view of the network. From the packet's view the loss and delay values are averaged over all packets that are lost and received, respectively, by each node in an aggregated class for all repetitions. In this view, the packet has a certain probability for being lost and a certain delay it could expect, given the packet's class.

A different view of the network is from the node's point of view. The node's view considers the fairness aspect of the network. How is the loss and delay distributed among the nodes, and which loss and delay values can a new entering node expect? The aspect of fairness is a familiar problem in wireless conditions and is hard to deal with [5]. In our simulations, the results given in this section are averaged over all nodes' individual loss and delay in an aggregated class for

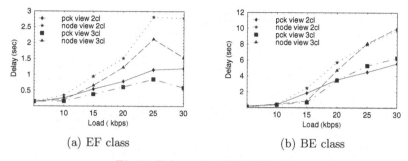

(a) EF class   (b) BE class

Fig. 5. Delay with CBR BE traffic

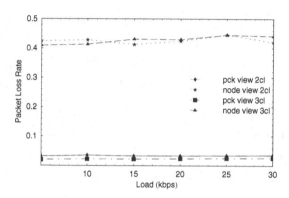

Fig. 6. BE loss with TCP BE traffic

all repetitions. As an example let us use one node with bad conditions where TCP restrict the number of packets to 500 with only 100 received i.e. a 0.8 loss probability, and a node with good conditions that send 20000 packets of which 19900 packets are received, i.e. a 0.005 loss probability. Equal weight among these two nodes results in an average 0.4 loss probability, while from a packet's view there would be an average 0.01 loss probability. A new entering node will therefore expect a 0.4 loss probability in the network; even the network has a 0.01 loss probability as seen by the packet view.

With only well behaved CBR traffic the packet loss is only slightly different from the packet's view. Because the nodes are all transmitting nearly the same number of packets, and major packet drops like no valid route exist under both views, the loss do not differ much. The delay, on the other hand, shows more difference between the views. Nodes with only a few packets reaching the destination have generally higher average delays, and these will in the node's view get a higher weight and increase the class' average delay compared to the packet's view. So, if a node's view gives higher delay than the packet's view, it means that some nodes receive relative poor performance and will therefore increase the average delay since the nodes' weight is increased. This is seen in Fig. 5 (a) where the node's view doubles the average EF delay seen under the packet's

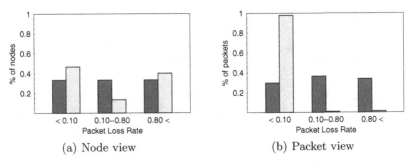

(a) Node view   (b) Packet view

Fig. 7. Loss distribution (TCP BE traffic)

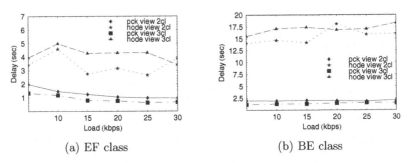

(a) EF class   (b) BE class

Fig. 8. Delay distribution (TCP BE traffic)

view. Also, the average BE delay is substantially increased for higher bit rates -
around 50% higher (Fig. 5 (b)). This shows fairness problems in the network.

Although the network gave fairness problems with only well behaved sources,
introducing TCP only increase the unfairness in the network. Fig. 6 presents the
packet loss for the BE nodes to show the great difference between the two views.
The packet loss is several orders higher in the node's view than in the packet's
view, both for two and three classes in the network. Because a node with a bad
route will get equal weight as a node with a very good route, as described above,
the packet loss rate is shifted upwards. In the simulations a TCP node with a
very good route may send 50 times more than a TCP node with a bad route
in our simulations. As already stated: even though the packet loss rate in the
network is low, the probability for packet losses for an individual node is much
higher due to the shared wireless channel. Another illustration on the fairness
problems is the loss distribution difference between the packet's and the node's
view. As an example, Fig. 7 (the EF class is represented by the dark grey bars,
while the light bars represent the BE class) shows the loss distribution for one
replication of the two classes scenario where the EF class sends 5 kbps CBR and
the BE class sends TCP traffic. According to Fig. 7 (a) there are several nodes
that experience a loss probability above 0.8, however according the packet's view
in Fig. 7 (b) almost all packets experience a loss probability below 0.1 in the

network (this is especially true for TCP nodes). This shows that some nodes receive good performance at the expense of the rest of the nodes.

The same effect as the node's view has on the packet loss is also present for the delay. The delay for EF nodes is more than doubled for the two classes scenario, and around four times higher when running three classes in the network (see Fig. 8). This implies that some nodes experience a very high delay that is spread over the total received packets in the aggregate for all replications under the packet's view, but is only spread over the number of nodes under the node's view, which increases the average delay. The delay is even worse for the TCP nodes (i.e. the BE class). This is because, as already mentioned, the big difference in the number of packets that are sent and received on a good versus a bad route. In addition, the high number of packets received on a good route experiences generally a low delay, while the bad route experiences generally a high delay. So when each node gets the same weight, the average delay increases around 10 times dependent on the number of classes in the network (see Fig. 8 (b)).

We see that we need more explicit mechanisms to ensure fairness in the network. Nodes that control the channel transmit flows that have relative few hops to the receiver, and we therefore need more global mechanisms rather than only local mechanisms in order to distribute the performance more evenly. A different buffer scheduler, e.g. WRR, could give a fairer share to the different queues in one node, but there are nodes that do not forward any traffic. If these nodes only transmit aggressive TCP traffic, they seem to control the shared channel as their own dedicated channel. Therefore, not only a fair buffer scheduler is needed, but also a mechanism that takes more global effects into count as regards network fairness.

6   Conclusions

The different context of wireless ad hoc networks compared to fixed networks necessitates different techniques in providing QoS in the network. Several QoS architectures have been proposed for the ad hoc network independent of the fixed network. We investigate in this paper the suitability of using a class based QoS architecture in the ad hoc network. More precise, we investigate the number of classes an ad hoc network can support while maintaining separation between the classes.

Based on simulations a maximum of four classes are supported when the traffic is well behaved, i.e. CBR type traffic. Once more aggressive traffic sources like TCP are running in classes with large buffers, the ad hoc network is barely able to support two different classes. Also, the highest prioritized classes, which send CBR traffic, experience a high loss because of the interference from the aggressive TCP traffic run in the lowest prioritized class. We must therefore shape the aggressive traffic in some way. By restricting the aggressive traffic, more QoS classes could be separated and other types of traffic could have a higher probability of accessing the shared channel.

The number of classes supported was also investigated from a fairness point of view. In the simulations, the performance was distributed unevenly among the nodes in the network. Some nodes received good performance at the expense of others. There were nodes that could not get access to the channel because others were controlling the channel - especially with aggressive TCP flows. In order to ensure fairness for all flows independent of number of hops, we cannot rely only on local mechanisms - we also need some global mechanism.

In future work we will investigate suitable mechanisms for shaping the aggressive traffic in the network. Different mechanisms for the buffer management and scheduling will be a first step; some initial simulations showed that RED ensured a differentiation of TCP traffic from the higher prioritized CBR traffic quite well. However, a sensitivity analysis of the parameters will be required. Our analysis is aimed at ad hoc networks with no MAC layer QoS mechanisms. The new IEEE 802.11e MAC layer with up to four priority classes will clearly provide a better support for a class based QoS architecture.

The simulations indicated that it is possible to use the default DiffServ architecture in ad hoc networks given some strong assumptions on the traffic behaviour; aggressive traffic need to be shaped in order to ensure timely access for higher prioritized traffic. Secondly, there need to be additional mechanisms to ensure fairness between the nodes in the network.

References

1. 3rd Generation Partnership Project (3GPP). Quality of Service (QoS) concept and architecture (release 6). Technical Specification Group Services and System Aspects, TS23.107 v6.1.0, March 2004.
2. G.-S. Ahn, A.T. Campbell, A. Veres, and L.-H. Sun. SWAN: Service Differentiation in Stateless Wireless Ad Hoc Networks. volume 2, pages 457–466. 21st Annual Joint Conference of the IEEE Computer and Communications Societies (INFOCOM), June 2002.
3. S. Blake, D. Black, M. Carlson, E. Davies, Z. Wang, and W. Weiss. RFC 2475: An Architecture for Differentiated Services. Informal, The Internet Society, December 1998.
4. R. Braden, D. Clark, and S. Shenker. RFC 1633: Integrated Services in the Internet Architecture: an Overview. The Internet Society, June 1994.
5. C. Chaudet, D. Dhoutant, and I.G. Lassous. Performance issues with IEEE 802.11 in ad hoc networking. *IEEE Communications Magazine*, 43(7):110–116, July 2005.
6. S. Crisstomo, S. Sargento, M. Natkaniec, and N. Vicari. A QoS Architecture Integrating Mobile Ad-Hoc and Infrastructure Networks. pages 897–903. The 3rd ACS/IEEE International Conference on Computer Systems and Applications, 2005.
7. M.C. Domingo and D. Remondo. A Cooperation Model between Ad Hoc Networks and Fixed Networks for Service Differentiation. pages 692–693. IEEE International Conference on Local Computer Networks, November 2004.
8. M.C. Domingo and D. Remondo. Analysis of VBR VoIP traffic for ad hoc connectivity with a fixed IP network. volume 4, pages 2834–2837. 60th IEEE Vehicular Technology Conference, VTC2004-Fall, September 2004.

9. M.C. Domingo and D. Remondo. A cooperation model and routing protocol for QoS support in ad hoc networks connected to fixed IP networks. pages 390–395. Telecommunications, 2005. Advanced Industrial Conference on Telecommunications/Service Assurance with Partial and Intermittent Resources Conference/E-Learning on Telecommunications Workshop. AICT/SAPIR/ELETE 2005, July 2005.

10. IEEE 802.11 WG. IEEE Std 802.11e/D10.0, Draft Amendment to Standard for Information Technology Telecommunications and Information Exchange Between Systems LAN/MAN Specific Requirements Part 11: Wireless Medium Access Control (MAC) and Physical Layer (PHY) Specifications: Medium Access Control (MAC) Quality of Service (QoS) Enhancements, September 2004.

11. Information Sciences Institute, University of California for Defense Advanced Research Projects Agency (DARPA). RFC 793: Transmission Control Protocol. Protocol Specification, September 1981.

12. J-sim network simulator. http://www.j-sim.org, accessed June 2006.

13. V. Jacobson. Modified TCP Congestion Avoidance Algorithm. Technical Report. Email to the end2end-interest Mailing List. URL: ftp://ftp.ee.lbl.gov/email/vanj.90apr30.txt, April 1990.

14. S.-B. Lee, G.-S. Ahn, X. Zhang, and A.T. Campbell. INSIGNIA: An IP-Based Quality of Service Framework for Mobile Ad Hoc Networks. *Journal of Parallel and Distributed Computing, Special Issue on Wireless and Mobile Computing and Communications*, 60(4):374–406, April 2000.

15. X. Li and L. Cuthbert. Multipath QoS Routing of supporting DiffServ in Mobile Ad hoc Networks. pages 308–313. SNPD/SAWN'05, May 2005.

16. Y.L. Morgan and T. Kunz. PYLON: An Architectural Framework for Ad-Hoc QoS Interconnectivity with Access Domains. 36th Annual Hawaii International Conference on System Sciences (HICSS'03) - Track 9, January 2003.

17. C. Perkins, E. Belding-Royer, and S. Das. RFC 3561: Ad Hoc On-Demand Distance Vector (AODV) Routing. Experimental Protocol, The Internet Society, July 2003.

18. Chen ShanShan and A.J. Kassler. Extending SWAN to Provide QoS for MANETs Connected to the Internet. pages 503–507. 2nd International Symposium on Wireless Communication Systems, September 2005.

19. H. Xiao, W.K.G. Seah, A. Lo, and K.C. Chua. A Flexible Quality of Service Model for Mobile Ad-Hoc Networks. volume 1, pages 445–449. IEEE 51st Vehicular Technology Conference Proceedings (VTC), May 2000.

20. J. Xue, P. Stuedi, and G. Alonso. ASAP: An Adaptive QoS Protocol for Mobile Ad Hoc Networks. volume 3, pages 2616–2620. IEEE International Symposium on Personal, Indoor and Mobile Radio Communications (PIMRC2003), September 2003.

21. Bosheng Zhou, A. Marshall, and Tsung-Han Lee. A cross-layer architecture for DiffServ in mobile ad-hoc networks. volume 2, pages 833–838. International Conference on Wireless Networks, Communications and Mobile Computing, June 2005.

Analytical Evaluation of the Overhead Generated by a Routing Scheme with Subnets for MANETs

Johann López, Steluţa Gheorghiu, and José M. Barceló

Technical University of Catalonia (UPC), Department of Computer Architecture, C/Jordi Girona 1-3, 08034 Barcelona, Spain
{johannl, steluta, joseb}@ac.upc.edu

Abstract. Most of the current topological based routing algorithms used in MANETs treat all the nodes in the network like independent peers, making them not scalable with respect to the number of nodes in the network. Since hierarchical routing techniques have been known to afford scalability in large networks (e.g. Internet), and taking advantage of the existence of scenarios in which the nodes of a MANET can be aggregated in a natural manner, we propose a two level hierarchical routing scheme for MANETs. In this paper we present the main components and an analytical performance evaluation of our proposal, with the number of control packets per second as the metric of our interest. The evaluation shows a significant overhead reduction from $\Theta(N^2)$ to $\Theta(N)$. However, a trade-off between the # of nodes in the network and the complexity of the system has to be achieved.

1 Introduction

Research efforts have been focused on the Mobile Ad-hoc Networking (MANET) [1] area as consequence of the important role performed by mobile communications. A MANET is mainly a multi-hop wireless network without infrastructure, in which the nodes must behave simultaneously as hosts and as routers.

Since MANETs are multi-hop networks, the routing has become one of the main research issues in this area. A number of routing proposals have been developed which can be generally classified in either Topology-based routing, or Position-based routing approaches. None of the current topology-based routing protocols (e.g. AODV [2], OLSR [3]) are scalable with respect to the number of nodes increment, because the control packets exchanging relies on flooding and they assume a flat structure (e.g. flat addressing space), the number of control packets increases as the number of nodes grows up.

A logical solution to improve the scalability of the routing in networks is "to keep, at any node, complete routing information about nodes which are close to it (in terms of hop distance or some other nearness parameter), and lesser information about nodes located further away" [8]. This is the main idea behind the hierarchical routing schemes, like the one used in Internet, in which nodes are aggregated into sets (subnets) to be handled as a single routing entity. It means that every node will maintain one entry per destination for the closer nodes (other members of its subnet), and one entry per subnet for the remote nodes. An example of this kind of efforts is the work

J. García-Vidal and L. Cerdà-Alabern (Eds.): Wireless and Mobility, LNCS 4396, pp. 126–143, 2007.

presented in [5], which shows improvements in the scalability when address aggregation is used in a static Ad-hoc network with AODV protocol.

On the other hand there are some scenarios in MANETs with heterogeneous environments where some nodes have extra capabilities (e.g. processing, transmission range, power supply) or responsibilities (e.g. speed of movement, position in the network, etc), and can be grouped following logical or geographical constraints. Some examples could be found in Emergency Networks [4], and Wireless Mesh Networks WMN [23, 24]. Taking advantage of these environments we proposed a two level hierarchical routing scheme for MANETs in [10]. Figure 1 shows an example of the scenario to which our proposal is directed.

The adoption of nodes aggregation in MANETs under such environments encloses the solution of the following challenges: Grouping nodes (clustering), address allocation and registration, neighborhood and neighboring subnets discovery, the routing into the subnet and inter-subnets, mobility between subnets (node movement reallocation) and finally how to manage the established connections.

We would like to emphasize that the majority of the aforementioned challenges (except the inter-subnet routing) are not exclusive of our proposal. They are open issues in wireless ad-hoc communications, and therefore many solutions can be found in the literature. We have chosen the solutions which better adapt to the mentioned environments, or take some basic ideas behind them to build our own solutions.

In this paper we focus on the intra-subnet and the inter-subnet routing block. We propose a routing scheme with subnets that takes into account the particularities of MANETs. In addition we present an extended analytical evaluation of the overhead generated by routing mechanism. The mobility management between subnets is out of the scope of the performance evaluation. However we will introduce in this paper the basic idea about this challenge.

The rest of the paper is organized as follows: section 2 shows the related work and previous attempts of scalable routing proposals for MANETs. A generic description of the network environment and the model used in the evaluation are given in section 3. Then, we present the basic idea and a description of the proposed mechanism in section 4. Analytical evaluation of the overhead generated by our proposal is presented in section 5. Finally, we have the conclusions and future work.

2 Related Work

Most of the existing ad hoc routing proposals make use of globally distributed topology information. They flood routing information to the entire network, and despite of the optimizations to reduce the impact of this flooding these kinds of proposals do not scale well with respect to the number of nodes in the network. Since hierarchical techniques have long been known to afford scalability in networks (e.g. Internet), several proposals have been made around this idea.

One of the simplest proposals is the address aggregation for AODV [5]. In this work the authors refines the AODV protocol for scenarios in which nodes are constrained in an area (e.g. a vehicle) forming a group, and one of the nodes is designated to become responsible for the routing of the remaining group nodes. This node must support the maintenance of a subnet sequence number. They leave as an open issue

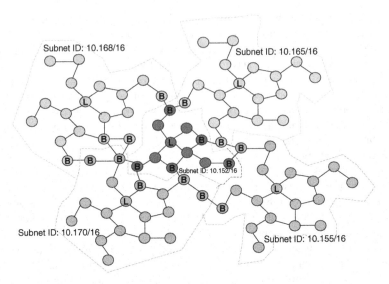

Fig. 1. Example of a MANET with nodes grouped in subnets. The "L" denotes the leader nodes.

the formation and leadership election of the subnets, and they do not consider the movement of the nodes between the subnets.

There are proposals in which nodes are treated differently depending on their distance from the destination. For example the Zone Routing Protocol ZRP [13] and the Fisheye State Routing FSR [18]. The global query flooding suggests that these approaches may scale badly with a large number of nodes.

On the other hand we have the Geographic based routing mechanisms, like for example GLS [14], which are the known mechanisms that scale well in large MANETs. Geographic routing requires that endpoints of communications find each other's current location. This location information can be absolute if the nodes use a global positioning system (e.g. GPS, GALILEO), or relative if it is distance estimation (on the basis of signal strength, delay, etc), such as Dream [15] and LAR [16]. However these proposals are best suited for small networks because are flooding based proposals. The geographical approaches can be severely limited as location information is not always available and can mislead among other networks.

In order to acquire scalability some hierarchical solutions for ad-hoc networks have been proposed. Some examples of these proposals are LANMAR [17], Landmark [19] and L+ [20]. In these proposals specific nodes are elected as cluster heads, and these cluster heads in turn select a higher-level cluster head, up to some desired level. Additionally, recent work has been conducted to apply peer-to-peer routing principles to MANETs. In [21], the authors propose an initial design of a routing scheme based on dynamic addressing principles, similar to the used in peer-to-peer, and taking into account the particularities of MANETs. The main problem of this former proposal is the address space exhaustion. In fact the compatibility with IP networks is also one main of the weaknesses of the multilevel clustering approaches.

None of the aforementioned proposals are directed to scenarios involving group mobility [25]. Additionally, none of them takes advantage of the heterogeneity (extra capabilities) of the node: It means that some nodes could perform some extra-functionalities in order to collaborate with the routing tasks.

3 Network Model

We are proposing a two level hierarchical routing scheme for MANETs, which is compatible with IP networks. In our scheme nodes are grouped following physical or environmental constraints. These groups have explicit Leader nodes (cluster heads), and the address allocation is relative to them. Our scheme only uses the IP address to indicate the node's location in the network.

3.1 Model Assumptions

The nodes are randomly located throughout the network area following a two-dimensional uniform distribution. The node movement over the network also follows a uniform distribution.

The nodes organize themselves into clusters, forming an area of dynamic size around a leader node. However, for the scope of this study we assume the formed areas of fixed size. Each cluster will correspond to an IP subnet; therefore, the nodes constrained in the same area will share the same IP address prefix. When a node moves from one subnet to another, it has to acquire a new IP address corresponding to the new IP subnet.

A leader node is a node with some extra capabilities (e.g. transmission rate, power supply, speed of movement, etc); an example of a leader node could be a node that resides in a truck or another kind of vehicle. In addition, the nodes in coverage with nodes pertaining to other subnets (Border nodes) have to perform some extra functionalities in order to collaborate with the inter-subnet routing (manage the inter-subnet topology).

Each node has a single interface card with a fixed transmission radius. If the distance between a pair of nodes is less than the transmission radius, then a bidirectional link connects them and they are considered to be neighbors. Otherwise, the nodes are not connected (Gupta/ Kumar model) [26].

In order to isolate the performance of our proposal with respect to the number of nodes in the network N, it is assumed that the average node density (network area is proportional to N) and the node speed are constant. The average number of nodes subsumed in a subnet is also considered constant.

3.2 Model Notation

The parameters used to model the network are:

- N: Number of nodes in the network.
- k: Number of subnets in the network.
- R_{Tx}: Average transmission radius of a node.
- v: Average node speed.
- T_b: Average life time of a link. $T_b = 1/\mu$.
- μ : Average link state change rate. It is proportional to the node speed.

- N_k: Average number of nodes subsumed by a subnet. $N_k = N/k$.
- d_k: average size (diameter) of the subnet in terms of hop count.
- A_k: Average area covered by a subnet.
- x: Average number of border nodes per subnet.
- η: Average subnet crossover rate.
- h_p: Frequency of the hello messages.
- o_p: Protocol optimization factor (broadcast).
- λ_i: Average number of route creation for routes to nodes located into the same subnet.
- t_p: Average rate of topology messages (proactive protocol).

4   Routing Scheme Description

Nodes keep complete routing information about other nodes that are close to them, and less information about nodes located further away from them.

In our proposal the IP address is not used like an identifier, and it is only used to indicate the node's location into the topology of the network The IP address of a node is dynamic and changes when the node switches to other subnet, reflecting the new node's location in the network. Each node has a globally unique identifier (user friendly) that does not change during its lifetime. We can give the responsibility of the node identity to higher layers (e.g. Host Identity Protocol).

Each node has a Local Routing Table containing information about how to reach (next hop) those nodes belonging to its subnet, and a Global Routing Table with information (border node IP address) of how to reach each subnet in the network. The intra-subnet routing is responsible of maintaining the local routing table, while the inter subnet routing protocol is responsible of maintaining the Global Routing Table.

In order to optimize the control packets exchange, the Intra and Inter-subnet routing functional block shares information obtained by mechanisms pertaining to other functional blocks. Therefore, in this section we also present the basic ideas behind the subnet formation and mobility between subnets blocks.

4.1   Subnet Formation

The subnet formation is composed of a grouping and address allocation mechanism. Since a subnet is formed around a leader node, the number of subnets will depend on the number of leader nodes in the network. In our study, a leader node is designated and configured statically for each subnet in order to group the nodes. In any case, a distributed cluster-head election mechanism can also be introduced. The leader nodes broadcast hello messages (beacons) periodically, announcing their subnet IP prefix and other information (e.g. the distance to the leader node, which is equal to zero initially), such that nodes under its coverage acquire the necessary information to configure their IP address with the same IP prefix of the announced subnet. The address configuration implies address construction and duplicate address detection (DAD). A node performing DAD sends a message to the announced leader asking if

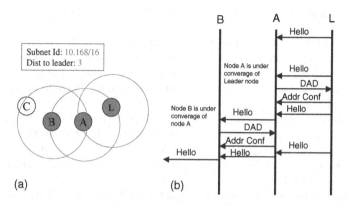

Fig. 2. Subnet Formation Block. **(a)** The coverage of subnet 10.168/16 is incremented because node A has became member of the subnet, and now node B is under coverage of the subnet and it will attach to it. **(b)** Message exchange during the subnet formation for the example presented in figure (a).

the requested IP address is available or not. Upon the reception of this message the leader node verifies the requested address in its registration table. If the address is available the leader assigns (registers) the target address to the requesting node, then it replies a confirmation message. Otherwise, a reject message is sent back to the requesting node. Once the nodes are configured they will forward the hello messages (incrementing the distance to leader parameter by one) in order to increase the subnet coverage. A complete description of this procedure is presented in [12]. And an example of the process described above is shown in figure 2.

In the case of a node receiving beacons from two different subnets, the distance to leader parameter is used like the main decision metric, and the distance between the current node and the beacon originator (Rx power) could be used like secondary decision parameter. Other parameters could also be used like a decision parameter.

Subnet ID	Net Hop count	*Next Hop	IP addr. Neigh **Leader	Age
10.152/16	1	10.152.1.10	10.152.1.1	T seg.
10.168/16	2	10.152.1.10	10.168.1.1	T seg.
▬ ▪ ▬ ▪	▬ ▪ ▬ ▪	▬ ▪ ▬ ▪	▬ ▪ ▬ ▪	▬ ▪ ▬ ▪

Fig. 3. Global Routing Table

4.2 Intra-subnet Routing Protocol

The goal of this function is to discover the topology of the subnet. The routing within a subnet can be performed by any topology-based protocol (reactive or proactive), like for example AODV [2] or OLSR [3]. The chosen protocol will maintain the Local Routing Table.

Since some routing protocols (e.g. OLSR) operate with hello transmissions and the Subnet Formation Block also needs of hello transmissions to announce the subnet prefix, the overhead may be reduced sharing the hello protocol. For these propose, the hello messages have to be modified to support the required fields to operate correctly both mechanisms.

If the chosen protocol supports hello transmissions (to discover closed neighbors), this functionality could be performed by the beaconing mechanism (hello messages) used in the Subnet Formation Block (see previous section) to announce the subnet prefix, in order to reduce the overhead generated. This is an optional enhancement to optimize our proposal.

Additionally this function must be capable of sharing information (Access to the Local Routing table) with the Inter-subnet routing mechanism and with other functional blocks for data forwarding and optimization purposes.

4.3 Inter-subnet Routing Protocol

This protocol creates and maintains routes between subnets (leader nodes). All the information obtained by this protocol is stored in the Global Routing Table (figure 3).

All the nodes in the network must be able to receive beacons (listening at layer 3 or higher layers) with an IP prefix different to their current IP address prefix, in order to perform the subnet formation and routing tasks accurately. The nodes that listen (Rx) beacons simultaneously from more than one subnet are called border nodes, and basically they will behave like gateways. These nodes has the following functionalities: i) listen routing packets (inter and intra) transmitted by nodes belonging to other subnets (neighboring subnets), ii) generate inter-subnet routing messages, iii) modify the Global Routing Table, and iv) forward data packets to nodes belonging to other subnets.

Border nodes generate routing packets for inter-subnet routing protocol. However normal nodes are able to receive these messages in order to complete or modify their Global Routing Table. The "Next hop" field of the global routing table (see figure 3), shows the address of a border node (of the same subnet) that will act like a gateway to reach the destination subnet.

Initially, the border nodes fill in their Global Routing Tables with the information obtained from beacons (hello protocol) originated in adjacent subnets, see figure 4. Furthermore, border nodes flood periodically in their subnets inter-subnet routing messages with a list of the best entries per destination stored in their Global Routing Table, figure 5. With the capability of listening routing messages transmitted by nodes belonging to other subnets, the border nodes obtain new routing information (to complete the Global Routing Table) from adjacent border nodes belonging to neighboring subnets. This way, after a period of time the Global Routing information will converge. The routing update (maintenance) due to topology changes is performed following the aforementioned procedure. To summarize, border nodes build and update their global routing table with information provided by the beacons and routing information originated in other subnets. Refer to figures 4 and 5.

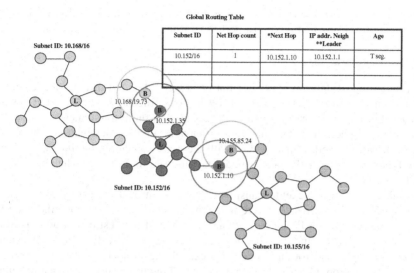

Fig. 4. Example of how the node 10.155.85.24 fills its Global Routing Table. Border nodes obtain information from the beacons transmitted by their neighbors. Node 10.155.85.24 fills the first entry of its table with the route to subnet 10.152/16.

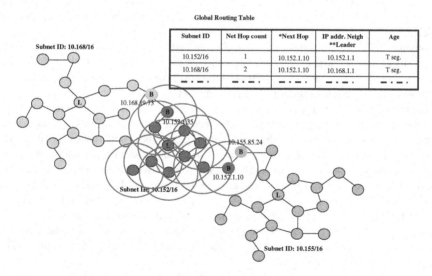

Fig. 5. Example of how the node 10.155.85.24 fills its Global Routing Table. Border nodes flood within their respective subnets their Global Routing tables. With the information transmitted by node 10.152.1.35, node 10.152.1.10 fills the entry to get the subnet 10.168/16, and when this node floods routing information again, the node 10.155.85.24 learns how to get to the subnet 10.168/16.

The hello protocol is also used to detect link failures (to know the link state with the neighbors). For example if after a defined period of time, a node does not receive beacons from its current neighbors, it won't consider these links (or link). This way, the active routes using that link must perform a Route Recovery mechanism.

4.4 Packet Forwarding

The forwarding of data packets does not need to be directed through leader nodes, and they can be forwarded via current, leader, or border nodes alike to the destination. The border and source nodes use the services of the Intra-subnet routing protocol to forward packets to the suitable border node or final destination. During the packet forwarding nodes have to deal with the node hop count and the network hop count fields, where only the border nodes are allowed to decrement the network hop count.

If a node has a data packet to transmit, it requests (through a message exchange) its Leader node the IP address (relative location) of the destination. Once the node has obtained the destination IP address, it can determine if the destination node is in the same subnet or in another. If the destination node is located in the same subnet the node uses its local routing table (or local routing protocol) to obtain a route to reach the destination. Otherwise, it first looks up how to reach the destination subnet (the border node to get other subnets) in its Global Routing Table, and then it uses its local routing table (or local routing protocol) to discover the route (next hop) to the proper border node. Finally the packet is forwarded to the next hop, which performs a look up in its routing tables (global, or local, or both) to find out the next hop to get the destination (destination node or border node). Each intermediate node repeats this process until the data packet reaches its destination.

When a node detects a link failure, it disables all the routes (entries) of its routing tables (local and global), which next hop field uses the broken link. If the intra-subnet routing protocol is proactive, it warns (broadcasts an error message) to the other members of the subnet, in order to update their routing tables.

For the case of a reactive protocol, the node sends an error message to the source of the route through the reverse path, upon the reception of this error message the source of the route updates its routing tables and then it performs a route discovery (using the intra-subnet protocol) to reach the destination or the departure border node, and if this route discovery fails the border node sends a route error to the source of the data packet. We would like to differentiate between the source of the packet and the source of the route. The source of the route is the node that initiates the route discovery (Route Request) for a destination in a subnet (that could be a border node or the final destination of the data packet), while the source node is the node that is the origin of the data packet. Obviously the source of a packet is also the source of the route locally (into its subnet), but abroad it is not.

If a link that connects a border node fails, the detecting node must update its global routing table (disabling the entries which uses that border node), and must inform (via inter-subnet protocol if the detecting node is a border node) to the other members of the subnet with the aim of updating their routing tables. On the other hand, if the detecting node is a border node (located in an adjacent subnet), it updates its Global Routing Table warns the others subnet members using the Inter-subnet routing protocol.

4.5 Mobility Management

To manage the mobility in this proposal there are several alternatives. Here we present some possible candidates that likely will fit into our general scheme.

Mobile IP [27] proposes a network layer solution, which binds a mobile host's permanent IP address from its home network to a temporary care-of address from a foreign network. Then, the home agent tunnels the packets destined to that mobile host to its foreign agent. Various extensions (e.g. [28]) to optimize MIP have been developed. Comparing Mobile IP with our routing scheme, we could consider the Leader node to correspond to the foreign agent. However, a Leader node can carry on the responsibilities of a home agent only, more precisely by the old Leader node. This is not achievable in our proposal, because when a node moves to a new subnet, it acquires a new IP address and it usually loses connection with its old subnet.

The Session Initiation Protocol (SIP [29]) is an application level protocol that provides terminal, personal, session and service mobility. The logical entities that it uses are the following: user agents that initiate and terminate requests; redirect servers, which receive requests and return responses that indicate where the requester should send the request next; proxy servers and registrars. Considering our proposal, a SIP server could correspond to a Leader node and a user agent to a mobile node. When Leader nodes exchange their routing tables, information about a mobile node is propagated throughout the network. Therefore, any Leader node could play the role of the SIP redirect server and SIP could represent a good solution for our proposal, but it still remains unclear how it manages TCP connections.

Host Identity Protocol (HIP) [30] is a key establishment and parameter negotiation protocol, which allows continuous communication across IP address changes. The rendezvous mechanism was introduced in [31] and helps a HIP node to contact a frequently moving HIP node. It involves a Rendezvous Server (RVS), which has HIP nodes as clients. The clients use the HIP Registration Protocol to register their HIT->IP address mappings with the RVS and then, they become reachable at the RVS's IP addresses. With this approach, the RVS could correspond to the Leader node, with the observation that in our proposal, a mobile node can be registered with only one Leader and therefore it can have only one IP address. Other significant differences couldn't be found, so it seems that HIP could perform well with our routing scheme.

Zap [32] is a system for migrating computing environments, which provides transparent migration of legacy and networked applications across machines running independent operating systems without requiring any changes to the operating system. It introduces a thin virtualization layer that decouples applications from host dependencies. The idea is to use an internal address, which remains unchanged and an external one, representing the physical address and which changes with migration, without the transport layer being aware of it. The mechanism that allows Zap to do this is based on the Virtual Network Address Translation (VNAT), and it intercepts packets that leave the transport layer and translate the virtual address into the appropriate physical address before sending them into the network. When receiving packets, their physical address is translated into the virtual address, just before arriving to the transport layer. Zap seems to manage pretty well TCP connections, but further studies are needed to fully understand how it can apply to our scheme.

5 Performance Evaluation

The control packet overhead is a relevant performance metric for scalability in MANETs because the scarce wireless link capacity causes severe performance degradation. This evaluation is based mainly on the preliminary results obtained in [10].

The overhead generated by the proposal results from the following: the Hello Protocol, Subnet Formation and Maintenance, Acquiring Topology data (intra-subnet and inter-subnet), the Link State change, and the Location Registration and Maintenance. The sum of the mentioned factors gives us the total overhead in the network.

5.1 Hello Protocol

The hello protocol allows the subnet formation and maintenance, announcing the subnet prefix and the distance to the leader node. It is also employed by the nodes to learn and verify adjacencies (link state).

The Hello messages are periodically broadcasted to 1-hop neighbors over the shared media, with a frequency h_p. This frequency should be set up according to the mobility rate.

$$h_p = \Theta\left(\frac{v}{R_{Tx}}\right)$$

(1)

Since each node of the network transmits a hello packet per interval, there will be N transmissions per hello interval in the entire network. We could represent the number of packets per second generated by this protocol like

$$\phi_{Hello} = Nh_p$$

(2)

5.2 Subnet Formation and Maintenance

As we mentioned in section 4.1 two parts, the grouping and the address allocation compose the subnet formation. The overhead generated by the former correspond to the overhead calculated in section 5.1, while the overhead generated by the address allocation depends basically on the Duplicated Address Detection (DAD).

The DAD is mainly the exchange of two messages (a DAD, and an address confirmation or deny) between the configuring node and the leader node. Each message must traverse a number of hops equivalent to the distance to the leader announced by the hello message received by the unconfigured node. If d_k is the average diameter of a subnet in terms of the number of nodes (hop count), and these messages are transmitted in unicast packets, we can represent the overhead generated in the entire network by this mechanism with the following expression

$$\phi_{s-f} = 2\frac{d_k}{2}N = d_k N$$

(3)

The parameter d_k is divided by two because we assume the leader node is located in the center of the area formed by the subnet.

However, equation (3) does not consider the packet losses during the procedure. If a packet loss occurs during a message exchange, the DAD procedure must be performed again after timer expiration. We use the parameter p_e to represent the DAD procedure failure probability (due to packet losses or other reasons, such as the requested IP address is already assigned to another node). With this parameter we calculate the average number of packets generated by a node performing the DAD procedure

$$d_k(1-p_e) + 2d_k p_e(1-p_e) + 3d_k p_e^2(1-p_e) + \ldots = d_k(1-p_e)\sum_{i=1}^{\infty} i p_e^{i-1}$$

$$= d_k(1-p_e)\frac{1}{(1-p_e)^2} = \frac{d_k}{(1-p_e)}$$

(4)

Therefore, the number of packets generated by DAD in the entire network could be represented by

$$\phi_{s-f} = N\frac{d_k}{(1-p_e)}$$

(5)

This expression is not relevant to the overhead because it is only incurred at the start up of the network (it is not a rate). Nevertheless, we will use this expression to calculate the overhead generated when a node changes of subnet.

Assuming subnets (area) of fixed size, the change of subnet looks similar to the change of cell paradigm in cellular systems. We are particularly interested in an expression to represent the average subnet crossover rate. In [7] an approximate evaluation for cellular system performance is presented using models based on fluid flow assumptions. We use some of those models to represent the average subnet crossover rate. At this point we present the conditions listed by the authors in [7] to derive a simple expression:

- The nodes and their traffic are uniformly distributed over a given subnet (area or cell).
- The nodes have a mean velocity of v and their directions of movements are uniformly distributed over $[0,2\pi]$

Since our model assumptions meet the aforementioned conditions, we represent the subnet crossover rate η by,

$$\eta = v\frac{P}{\pi S}$$

(6)

Where P corresponds to the perimeter of the subnet, and S is the area of the subnet. Adjusting η to our parameters, and assuming subnets of circular shape we can express it also by

$$\eta = v\frac{2\pi\frac{d_k}{2}}{\pi^2\left(\frac{d_k}{2}\right)^2} = \frac{4v}{d_k}$$

(7)

Each time that a node change of subnet, it has to configure its IP address according to the IP prefix of the new subnet; therefore this node will perform DAD and will generate an overhead equal to (4). The average number of packets generated by the change of subnet in the entire network is given by

$$\phi_{c-s} = N\left(\frac{d_k}{(1-p_e)}\right)\frac{4v}{d_k} = \frac{4Nv}{(1-p_e)} \tag{8}$$

5.3 Acquiring Topology Data

Each node must know the topology of the subnet to which it belongs and the information about how to get the other subnets in the network. The intra-subnet and inter-subnet routing contributes the most of the overhead.

5.3.1 Intra-subnet Overhead

The overhead generated to acquire the topology of the subnet will be influenced by the chosen algorithm (reactive or proactive). Using the models obtained in [6], we can represent the overhead generated by a reactive intra-subnet routing mechanism by

$$\phi_{Acq} = o_r \lambda N_k N \tag{9}$$

Since the route creation in reactive protocols depends mainly of the data traffic creation and diversity, we use the average number of route creation λ by a node during a second to represent it. We take into account the parameters that depend on the protocol, like for example the route request optimization factor o_r, which represents the reduction of the flooding overhead of a protocol. In reactive protocols the average number of emissions for a route request could include the route reply messages. With a pure flooding protocol and route reply from destination, if we relate the number of reply messages with the average size of the subnet d_k (the average number of hops that a route replay must to traverse to get the requesting node), we can express o_r like

$$o_r = 1 + \frac{d_k}{N_k} \approx 1 + \frac{1}{\sqrt{N_k}} \tag{10}$$

This estimation is likely because d_k is proportional to the square root of the number of nodes. See [22].

In a proactive protocol the overhead mainly depends on the regular emission of control packets, having the advantage of not generating any overhead at route creation, because their fixed control traffic overhead includes the cost of the route creation. The parameters concerning to the proactive protocol are, the packets for proactively discovering the local topology (hello packets) emitted by a node per second h_p, and the topology broadcast packets emitted by a node during a second for allowing complete knowledge of the subnet topology t_p. These parameters are expressed in terms of rates. Since proactive protocols can take advantage from their knowledge of the topology in order to optimize broadcasting, a broadcast optimization factor o_p is denoted ($o_p = B_p/N$), where B_p denotes the average number of emissions to achieve a topology broadcast.

In a proactive protocol $h_p N$ hello messages are produced per second in the entire network, initiating $t_p N$ topology emissions, which generate $t_p o_p N N_k$ packets. Since in our proposal we will take advantage of the hello protocol to get topology information, the overhead produced can be represented by

$$\phi_{Acq} = o_p t_p N_k N \tag{11}$$

Independently of the chosen algorithm (reactive or proactive) the overhead will be dominated by

$$\phi_{Acq} = \Theta(N_k N) = \Theta(A_k N) = \Theta(N) \tag{12}$$

5.3.2 Inter-subnet Protocol Overhead

To complete the Global Routing Table the border nodes transmit periodically inter-subnet routing messages to other members within their subnets. Therefore, if we have in average x of border nodes per subnet, that broadcast a message every T seconds (that means N_k packets per subnet), and if we have k subnets, the number of packets generated by the inter-subnet protocol can be expressed by

$$\phi_{LR} = \frac{1}{T} x N_k k \tag{13}$$

We can notice that x is not a relevant factor in the overhead, because, for a constant node density in the network, the number of border nodes will be proportional to $\sqrt{N_k}$ (The proof of this lemma is provided in the Appendix). Additionally, despite k depends on the number of nodes (constant node density) in the network, it is not significant for the overhead, because $k << N$ ($k = \Theta(logN)$).

5.4 Link State Change

The link state changes (creation or breakage) are due entirely to mobility of individual nodes. A link breakage could affect a link between normal nodes that belongs to the same subnet (Intra-subnet link) or a link between two border nodes of different subnets (inter-subnet link). In response to an intra-subnet link state change, a route update must be transmitted (flooded) to the other members of the subnet to which the affected nodes belong via the intra-subnet protocol. The overhead generated in response to this kind of link breakage is defined by

$$\phi_{flood} = o_p \mu N N_k a = \Theta(N) \tag{14}$$

Where a could represent either the average number of active routes per node (activity) in case of a reactive protocol, or the average number of active next hops of a node in case of a proactive protocol. These results are calculated according to [6].

If the breakage affects a link between subnets the overhead generated will be:

$$\phi_{IS} = \mu x k N_k D = \Theta(\sqrt{N}) \tag{15}$$

Like D represents the average degree of a border a node (with respect to other border nodes), this value is not significant to the overhead because is small respect to the other parameters ($D<<k$). The dominant factor is the number of nodes per subnet, and the aforementioned result is obtained from applying the following lemma: For a constant node density the number of border nodes will be proportional to $\sqrt{N}$. The proof of this lemma is provided in the Appendix.

5.5   Location Registration and Maintenance

The location registration and maintenance is the overhead generated by the mobility management function. A location registration occurs when a node arrives to the network for the first time, and the location maintenance occurs periodically and whenever a node migrates from one subnet to another.

Like the location registration is performed simultaneously by the Subnet formation function, and the generated overhead was included in the results presented in section 5.1 and 5.2.

Considering the fact that the location maintenance will be performed only by the leader nodes the overhead incurred by this item would not be relevant, because it only depends on the number of subnets in the network, which is much lower than the number of nodes in the network.

6   Conclusions

We proposed a two level hierarchical routing scheme for MANETs, presented the main challenges for applying such scheme and did a performance evaluation with the scalability with respect to the number of nodes as the relevant metric. Some of the identified challenges were: the address allocation under mobility scenarios, the dynamic creation and removal of subnets, the intra-subnet and the inter-subnet routing, and finally the maintenance of the already established sessions when a node moves from one subnet to another (mobility between subnets).

From the results obtained we can notice the total routing overhead will be dominated by $\Theta(N)$ factor. This result allows us to quantify the scalability of our proposal and provide a quantitative comparison with other routing proposals. If we compare with a flat routing scheme we have that the overhead generated by that kind of schemes is quadratic with respect to number of nodes $\Theta(N^2)$. Such comparison demonstrates that our proposal has a scalability advantage over flat routing, despite the network complexity incurred.

This work exploits the benefits of the hierarchical routing and the flat routing, and provides a good performance under a specific type of scenarios.

The focus of our future work is to solve the mobility of nodes between subnets function and the validation of the model presented in this paper by means of simulations taking into account parameters that our model does not consider.

Acknowledgments. This work has been supported by the Ministry of Education of Spain under grant TEC2004-06437-C05-05, and by the project VI FP project EuroNGI.

References

1. Mobile Ad-hoc Networks working group IETF: http://www.ietf.org/html.charters/manet-charter.html.
2. C. Perkins, E. Belding-Royer, and S. Das. Ad hoc Vector (AODV) Routing. RFC 3561, July 2003.
3. T. Clausen and P. Jacquet, "Optimized Link State Routing Protocol", RFC 3626, October 2003.
4. H. Aiache et al, "WIDENS System Specification", Deliverable 2.2, IST WIDENS, June 2004
5. C. Shiflet, E. M. Belding-Royer and C. E. Perkins. "Address Aggregation in Mobile Ad hoc Networks." Proceedings of the IEEE International Conference on Communications (ICC), Paris, France, June 2004.
6. L. Viennot, P. Jacquet, T. H. Clausen, "Analyzing control traffic overhead versus mobility and data traffic activity in mobile Ad-Hoc network protocols," presented at ACM Wireless Networks journal (Winet), 2004.
7. B. Jabbari, "Teletraffic aspects of evolving and next-generation wireless communication networks," Personal Communications, IEEE [see also IEEE Wireless Communications], vol. 3, pp. 4, 1996.
8. L. Kleinrock, F. Kamoun, "Hierarchical Routing for Large Networks: Performance Evaluation and Optimization," Computer Networks, Vol. 1, pp. 155-174, 1977.
9. K. Weniger, M. Zitterbart, "Address Autoconfiguration in Mobile Ad Hoc Networks: Current Approaches and Future Directions", IEEE Network Magazine Special issue on 'Ad hoc networking: data communications & topology control', Jul 2004.
10. J. López, J. M. Barceló, J. García-Vidal, "Analysing the overhead in Mobile ad-hoc network with a hierarchical Routing structure", International Working Conference Performance Modelling and Evaluation of Heterogeneous Networks' (HET-NETS''05), June 2005.
11. B. Jabbari, "Teletraffic aspects of evolving and next-generation wireless communication networks," Personal Communications, IEEE [see also IEEE Wireless Communications], vol. 3, pp. 4, 1996.
12. J. López, J. M. Barceló, J. García-Vidal, " Subnet Formation and Address Allocation Approach for a Routing with Subnets Scheme in MANETs ", Wireless Syst./Network Architect. LNCS 3883 proceeding, 2005.
13. Z. Haas, "A new routing protocol for the reconfigurable wireless networks," in Proc. IEEE ICUPC, pages 562–566, October 1997.
14. Jinyang Li, John Jannotti, Douglas S. J. De Couto, David Karger, and Robert Morris, "A Scalable Location Service for Geographic Ad-Hoc Routing". In Proceedings of the Sixth Annual ACM/IEEE International Conference on Mobile Computing and Networking (MobiCom), August 2000.
15. Stefano Basagni, Imrich Chlamtac, Violet Syrotiuk, and Barry Woodward, "A Distance Routing Effect Algorithm for Mobility (DREAM)". In Proc. ACM/IEEE MobiCom, pages 76–84, Dallas, Texas, October 1998.
16. Young-Bae Ko and Nitin Vaidya, "Location-Aided Routing (LAR) in mobile ad hoc networks". In Proc. ACM/IEEE MobiCom, pages 66–75, Dallas, Texas, October 1998.
17. G. Pei, M. Gerla, and X. Hong, "Lanmar: Landmark routing for large-scale wireless ad hoc networks with group mobility," in ACM MobiHOC'00, 2000.
18. Guangyu Pei, Mario Gerla, and Tsu-Wei Chen, "Fisheye state routing: A routing scheme for ad hoc wireless networks," in ICC (1), pp.70–74. 2000.

19. Paul F. Tsuchiya, "The landmark hierarchy: A new hierarchy for routing in very large networks," in ACM SIGCOMM. 1988.
20. Benjie Chen and Robert Morris, "L+: Scalable landmark routing and address lookup for multi-hop wireless networks," 2002.
21. Jakob Eriksson, Michalis Faloutsos, Srikanth V. Krishnamurthy: Scalable Ad Hoc Routing: The Case for Dynamic Addressing. INFOCOM 2004.
22. L. Kleinrock and J. Sylvester, "Optimum Transmission Radii for Packet Radio Networks or Why Six Is a Magic Number," Proc. IEEE Nat'l Telecomm. Conf., pp. 4.3.1-4.3.5, Dec. 1978.
23. R. Bruno, M. Conti, E. Gregori, " Mesh Networks: Commodity Multihop Ad Hoc Networks", IEEE Communications Magazine, Vol. 43, No. 3, March 2005, pp. 123-131.
24. I. F. Akyildiz and X. Wang, "A Survey on Wireless Mesh Networks," IEEE Communications Magzine, vol. 43, no. 9, s23-s30, Sept. 2005.
25. X. Hong, M. Gerla, G. Pei, and C.-C. Chiang "A Group Mobility Model for Ad Hoc Wireless Networks", In Proceedings of ACM/IEEE MSWiM'99, Seattle, WA, Aug. 1999, pp.53-60.
26. P. Gupta and P.R. Kumar, "The Capacity of Wireless Networks," IEEE Transactions on Information Theory, vol. 46, no. 2, pp. 388--404, March 2000.
27. C. E. Perkins, K.-Y. Wang, "Optimized Smooth Handoffs in Mobile IP", iscc, p. 340, The Fourth IEEE Symposium on Computers and Communications, 1999.
28. A. Helmy, "A Multicast-based Protocol for IP Mobility Support", Proceedings of NGC 2000 on Networked group communication, Palo Alto, California, United States, p. 49-58, 2000.
29. H. Schulzrinne, E. Wedlund, "Application-Layer Mobility Using SIP", Mobile Comput. Commun. Rev., vol. 4, no. 3, pp. 47-57, July 2001.
30. R. Moskowitz, P. Nikander, P. Jokela (editor), T. Henderson, "Host Identity Protocol", draft-ietf-hip-base-04, Internet-Draft, work in progress, IETF, Oct 2005
31. J. Laganier, L. Eggert, "Host Identity Protocol (HIP) Rendezvous Extension", draft-ietf-hip-rvs-04, October 10, 2005.
32. S. Osman, D. Subhraveti, G. Su, J. Nieh, "The Design and Implementation of Zap: A System for Migrating Computing Environments", In Proc. 5th USENIX Symposium on Operating Systems Design and Implementation, p. 361 – 376, Boston, Massachusetts, December 2002.

Appendix

Following the methodology used in [22], we can demonstrate that x is proportional to $\sqrt{N}$. The nodes of the network are considered uniformly distributed in a two-dimensional space with a node density, and α is defined like the average number of nodes per unit area, and for the scope of this study we considered it constant with respect to the number of nodes increment. Figure A-1 shows the considered situation.

We are particularly interested in an approximation of the average number of nodes (border nodes) that will be in the dark area (green area) and in the transmission radius of about any node located in any other subnet (yellow area). If A represents the area of the ring, we can say

$$x \leq \alpha A \qquad \text{(A-1)}$$

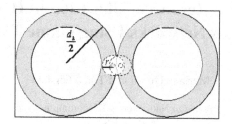

Fig. A-1. Number of border nodes in the network

Since A is equal to the area of big circumference minus the area of the small circumference, therefore

$$A = \pi\left[\left(\frac{d_k}{2}\right)^2 - \left(\frac{d_k}{2} - R_{Tx}\right)^2\right] = \pi R_{Tx}(d_k - R_{Tx}) \approx \pi R_{Tx}d_k \qquad (A-2)$$

Now the result of A-2 in A-1, and expressing α in terms of the average number of nodes in a subnet and the subnet area, we obtain

$$x \approx \frac{N_k}{\pi\left(\frac{d_k}{2}\right)^2}\left(\pi R_{Tx}d_k\right) \approx \frac{4R_{Tx}N_k}{d_k} \approx 4R_{Tx}\sqrt{N_k} \qquad (A-3)$$

Since the R_{tx} is expressed meters and d_k in number of hops, if we express R_{tx} in terms of number of hops, R_{tx} will be equivalent to one hop in the worse of the cases.

$$x \approx \frac{4N_k}{d_k} \qquad (A-4)$$

In [22] is demonstrated that average diameter of a network is proportional to the number of nodes in the network.

Framework for Resource Allocation in Heterogeneous Wireless Networks Using Game Theory

Mariana Dirani and Tijani Chahed

GET/Institut National des Telecommunications
UMR CNRS 5157
9 rue C. Fourier - 91011 EVRY CEDEX - France
{mariana.dirani,tijani.chahed}@int-evry.fr

Abstract. This is a framework for resource allocation in a heterogeneous system composed of various access networks, for instance Third Generation wireless networks (3G) and WLAN, in the presence of multimedia traffic, namely voice and data. Our aim is to present a game theoretical modeling of routing and load-balancing strategies along with admission control and pricing in cooperative and non-cooperative settings.

1 Introduction

In a heterogeneous environment composed of more than one access network, say third generation (3G) [1] [2] and IEEE802.11-based WLAN [3] networks, the question is that of how to allocate resources in a way that is optimal both to the user and operator (see Figure 1).

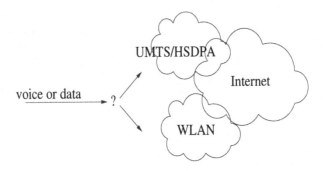

Fig. 1. Reference model

The answer is multi-fold. On the user side, the issue is that of routing. Optimality in this case refers to the best QoS, according to the type of traffic, at the best price. On the operator side, the issue is that of admission control and pricing so as to maximize revenue which is proportional to resource utilization itself subject to granted QoS and the prices assigned to each type of resources as well as their cost.

J. García-Vidal and L. Cerdà-Alabern (Eds.): Wireless and Mobility, LNCS 4396, pp. 144–154, 2007.

Game theory [4] [5] studies interactions and winning strategies for parties involved in situations where their interest conflict with each other. It has applications to real games, economics, commerce, politics and recently telecommunications. The research area of networking games and their application in telecommunications has known rapid developments through the last years [6]. Since optimization theory is unable to take into account interactions between different actors, be they users, protocols, nature or other, game theory has shown to be a useful tool allowing to study behavior and eventual equilibrium of complicated and interacting systems.

Inspired from economical environments, game theoretical modeling proved to be a powerful tool to study resources allocation in homogeneous as well as heterogeneous systems presenting contending users or classes for those resources. More specifically, it has been used in power control [7] and access to a common shared link, but also to study flow control problems and to find structural properties of equilibrias in systems involving routing into links with different capacities ([8], [9]). For a survey on applications but also on methodologies and challenges of networking games in telecommunication, the reader is refered to Reference [6].

Our aim in this work is to model interaction between different, non-homogeneous types of traffic, namely voice and data, with eventually different radio conditions, competing for the use of resources in heterogeneous networks offering different QoS. The dynamic sharing nature of wireless protocols in recent networks, particularly Medium Access Control (MAC) protocols, makes the game theoretical tool suitable to study interaction and resulting strategies of involved players, be they the end users asking for resources and subsequently a QoS level, and the network strategies for admitting those calls and pricing them after admission.

At this point, we have to distinguish between cooperative and non-cooperative settings, both on the user and operator side. On the user side, users may cooperate so as to achieve the best global utility function. This is not very probable. Often, users are non-cooperative wherein only maximizing the individual utility function is at sake.

On the operator side, cooperation is typically given when the heterogeneous access networks belong to one operator and the objective is again to maximize some global utility function. If different players own the different networks, the problem becomes a game where each one tries to maximize its own utility function.

Now, taking the problem as a whole, with both users and operator(s), the resource allocation problem may be solved through some classical Nash equilibrium [5], defined as being the players actions from which no player has an incentive to unilaterally deviate, or may be brought to some optimal operation point through for example incentives by the operator to guide users to choices that simultaneously maximize their utility function as well as his.

The remainder of this work is organized as follows. In section II, we give a basic introduction for the tool of game theory. In Section III, we investigate the routing and show the distinction between cooperative versus the non-cooperative cases. The same distinction pertains for admission control and pricing too and is presented in Section IV. Section V presents a cross-layer modeling of the two systems under consideration. Eventually, Section VI concludes the paper.

2 Game Theory Primer

A strategic game has three components:

- A set of players $\mathbf{Pl}$
- A set of possible actions A_{pl} for each player $pl \in \mathbf{Pl}$
- A set of utilities $\mathbf{U}$, where for each player $pl \in \mathbf{Pl}$, the utility for each player is a function of the action profile $\mathbf{a} = (a_g, a_{-g})$, a_g being the action of player pl and a_{-g} the vector of all other players strategies. An action profile belongs to the set of actions profiles denotes by $\mathbf{A} = \prod_{pl \in \mathbf{Pl}} A_{pl}$. In other words a utility function is a mapping from the set of all actions profiles $\mathbf{A}$ to the set of real numbers $\mathbf{R}$.

Two settings may arise in a system involving several players. Players may cooperate and the problem reduces to an optimization problem where a single player drives the system to a social equilibrium. A standard criterion used in game theor to express efficiency of such equilibrium is Pareto efficiency. A strategy profile $\mathbf{a}$ is called *Pareto efficient* if there is no other strategy $\mathbf{a}'$ for which:

- 1) all users do at least as well
- 2) at least one user does strictly better.

Another important setting is that of non-cooperative players where each decision maker selfishly chooses its strategy. In this case, the equilibrium reached, when it exists, is called a Nash equilibrium and is defined as the point from which no player finds it beneficial to unilaterally deviate.

Pareto efficiency is a desirable operating point for a given system in general, however non-cooperative equilibria are in general Pareto inefficient.An important question that arises is how to drive a system where decision makers have a non-cooperative behavior to the system's optimal point. This question has been addressed in [10].

3 User Side: Routing/Load-Balancing

We consider a QoS-based routing, where each type of traffic, broadly classified into streaming versus elastic and each further decomposed into classes according to various radio conditions, chooses the proportion of flows to be sent to each subnetwork.

At this point, two situations arise. One can imagine some cooperative behavior of different classes, where the routing controller wants to achieve in a social manner, the best global utility, QoS divided by a given price in this case, for different classes in a fair manner. Another case arises when non-cooperative classes behave as selfish players, each player trying to choose individually its routing strategy so as to optimize its individual utility, i.e., its own perceived QoS normalized to the price.

Recall that in the cooperative case, Pareto-optimal points are defined as points corresponding to equilibria from which any deviation will lead to a degradation in the performance of at least one player in the cooperative game. It should be noted that in a multi-class environment, there is an infinite number of solutions, so-called Pareto-optimal strategies. The notion of fairness is then introduced to select a unique operating point. In the theory of cooperative games this is known as the Nash arbitration scheme.

In the non cooperative case, however, every class acts selfishly to optimize its own performance measure regardless of others' performance. Such games are characterized by the Nash equilibrium point, when it exists, defined as the (routing) strategy profile from which no player finds it beneficial to unilaterally deviate. This can arise in situations where a decentralized routing decision is adopted and where end users choose their subnetwork in a selfish manner so as to optimize their individual performance measure.

From an operator point of view, it is more beneficial to operate on Pareto-optimal points since Nash equilibrium points are in some cases inefficient compared to Pareto-optimal solutions.

In what follows, we first present utility functions, the measure that assesses the user degree of satisfaction from a given setting.

3.1 User Utilities

We consider a set of voice and data users, with index $j \in \mathbf{J} = \{v, d\}$ denoting their respective types and an index $k \in \mathbf{K} = \{1, ..., K\}$ denoting each type's radio conditions. Let these users share resources in a set of $n \in \mathbf{N} = \{1, ..., N\}$ possible parallel subnetworks.

We consider probabilistic routing of calls according to their type of traffic and radio conditions. A type-(j, k) selects the n-th subnetwork with a probability $r_n^{j,k}$. Let $\lambda^{j,k} = \sum_{n=1}^{N} \lambda_n^{j,k}$ be the total flow demand of class-(j, k) users, where $\lambda_n^{j,k} = r_n^{j,k} \lambda^{j,k}$ is the mean rate of class-(j, k) flow that is routed through subnetwork n.

The utility function $J^{j,k}$ of class-(j, k) is the utility achieved by that class and depends on its own strategy given by the rate vector $\Lambda^{j,k} = (\lambda_n^{j,k})_{n \in \mathbf{N}}$, but it also depends on other classes routing decisions, denoted by $\Lambda^{-(j,k)}$. Or:

$$J^{j,k} = J^{j,k}(\Lambda^{j,k}, \Lambda^{-(j,k)})$$

For a QoS-based routing, the natural candidate for utility functions is some performance measure seen by the call, blocking probability for voice $B_n^{v,k}$, and the mean transfer time for data $M_n^{d,k}$, normalized to the unitary price p_n of resources of each subnetwork n (p_n corresponds to the price per unit time for the case of voice and to a price per unit volume for the case of data). In this work, we define the utility function of an individual (j, k)-class by :

$$J^{j,k}(\Lambda^{j,k}, \Lambda^{-(j,k)}) = -\sum_{n=1}^{N} \lambda_n^{j,k}(1 - B_n^{j,k})X_n^{j,k} \times p_n$$

where $X_n^{j,k}$ is equal to the blocking probability $B_n^{v,k}$ for voice traffic and mean transfer time $M_n^{d,k}$ for data.

Remark 1. Other utility functions are possible. For instance, the one where a subclass tries to maximize some utility related only to the throughput or mean transfer time, while maintaining its blocking probability below a given acceptable limit. In this case, we are in the presence of a constrained optimization/game problem where the weights on the blocking probabilities are the Lagrange multipliers.

Remark 2. Stability conditions are required in the case where no admission control is implemented in the networks. In this case the admissible region should be specified.

The remainder depends on whether strategies are cooperative or not.

3.2   Non-cooperative Routing

In a non-cooperative setting, different classes are considered as selfish players where each class implements a routing strategy so as to maximize its own net utility function as a response to others' strategies without any concern about others utilities. For a (j, k)-class user, the set of all possible strategies is given by:

$$\mathbf{F}^{j,k} = \{(\Lambda^{j,k}) \in \mathbb{R}^N : \lambda_n^{j,k} \geq 0 \text{ for } n \in \mathbf{N}; \sum_{n=1}^{N} \lambda_n^{j,k} = \lambda^{j,k}\}$$

In this case, optimality cannot be well defined. The Nash equilibrium is considered as a specific form of optimality [5]. When it exists, the Nash equilibrium is a routing strategy profile from which no class finds it beneficial to unilaterally deviate, i.e., no class finds it beneficial for its perceived QoS to unilaterally change the amount of load it is sending to each subnetwork. More precisely, a $(\Lambda^{j,k})$ vector is a Nash equilibrium if for all (j, k), $j \in \mathbf{J}$, $k \in \mathbf{K}$:

$$\Lambda^{j,k} \in \underset{f^{j,k} \in \mathbf{F}^{j,k}}{\operatorname{argmax}} J^{j,k}(f^{j,k}, \Lambda^{-(j,k)})$$

meaning that $\Lambda^{j,k}$ is the best strategy of class-(j, k) player while other players strategies are fixed.

If the above-mentioned utility functions are convex in the routing strategy $\Lambda^{j,k}$, the Kuhn-Tucker optimality conditions are applicable and imply that the response of users of class-(j, k) given by $\Lambda^{j,k}$ is the optimal response to other classes strategies given by $\Lambda^{-(j,k)}$ if and only if there exist Lagrange multipliers $l^{j,k}$ and $(s_n^{j,k})_{n \in N} = (s_1^{j,k}, ..., s_N^{j,k}))$ such that [9][8]

$$\frac{\partial J^{j,k}}{\partial \lambda_n^{j,k}}(\Lambda^{j,k}, \Lambda^{-(j,k)}) - l^{j,k} - s_n^{j,k} = 0 \quad n = 1, ..., N$$

$$\sum_{n=1}^{N} \lambda_n^{j,k} = \lambda^{j,k} \tag{1}$$

$$s_n^{j,k} \lambda_n^{j,k} = 0$$

$$l^{j,k} \geq 0, \quad s_n^{j,k} \geq 0, \quad \lambda_n^{j,k} \geq 0 \quad n = 1, ..., N$$

3.3   Cooperative Routing

We now turn to the cooperative case where for instance a central operator assigns calls to each subnetwork in a probabilistic manner ensuring fairness in terms of the QoS perceived by different classes. In this case, user classes are considered as cooperative players trying to share resources so as to optimize an overall utility function. The JK-dimensioned cooperative game reduces then to an optimization problem where the central decision maker (the router) maximizes a global utility function built of individual ones.

The routing strategy is a routing vector $(\lambda_n^{j,k})_{n\in N, j\in J, k\in K}$. The set of all possible routing vectors is given by:

$$\mathbf{F} = \{ \Lambda = (\lambda_n^{j,k})_{n\in N, j\in J, k\in K} : \lambda_n^{j,k} \geq 0 \text{ for } n \in \mathbf{N}, j \in \mathbf{J}, k \in \mathbf{K}; \sum_{n=1}^{N} \lambda_n^{j,k} = \lambda^{j,k} \}$$

We are interested in Pareto optimality. In this setting, the solution provides that no player can increase its utility without adversely affecting the others [11]. Pareto optimility leads to a set of $P - 1$ equations for P players, therefore an infinite number of operating points called Pareto boundary. To choose one operating point, the notion of fairness is introduced. The cooperative game can be formulated as follows:

$$\max_{\Lambda \in \mathbf{F}} | J(\Lambda) |$$
$$J.J^{-1} = \gamma \tag{2}$$

where γ ($| \gamma | = 1$) is a JK's dimensioned vector defining the direction in which the Pareto point is required. The Pareto boundary can be found by evaluating Pareto points in all possible directions γ, in other words γ refers to the fairness degree that a centralized decision maker might give to different classes.

4 Network Side: Admission Control and Pricing

While end users, if given the right to decide on their routing strategy, are only interested in the QoS they perceive regardless of the good use of resources, the network operator(s) do care about the way resources are utilized. In other words, supposing that a call of type $(j, k) \in \mathbf{J} \otimes \mathbf{K}$ has a revenue p^j, the operator should choose its prices as well as its Call Admission Control (CAC) strategy so as to maximize its total revenues R given by:

$$R(\Lambda, CAC, p) = \sum_{j\in\mathbf{J}, k\in\mathbf{K}} (p - I)\lambda^{j,k}(1 - B^{j,k})$$

where I represents the cost of the investment made by the operator for the given technology.

Please note that in the above expression the revenues of the network are a result of both the offered load, the price and the implemented admission strategy. For every routing strategy, be it cooperative or not, and in order to maximize its revenue, the operator must offer an attractive price and implement some intelligent admission control to make the best profit of his resources given that load is dictated by end users.

Remark 3. If no fairness considerations towards different classes of users are taken into account from the operator side, maximizing revenues only may lead to very unfair situations where for instance users experiencing bad radio conditions are constantly blocked.

We now consider cooperative versus non-cooperative configurations. For the sake of simplicity, we adopt a threshold-based admission control leading to closed-form expressions. Nevertheless, our framework is general and can be used for other families of admission control strategies such as trunk reservation.

4.1   Cooperative Case

To make the best use out of the network resources, the strategy of the operator is to choose a threshold parameter $T_n^{j,k}$ for each class (j, k). The set of all possible strategies for admission control is given by :

$$\mathbf{T} = \underset{n \in \mathbf{N}}{\otimes} \underset{j \in \mathbf{J}}{\otimes} \underset{k \in \mathbf{K}}{\otimes} \mathbf{T}_n^{j,k}$$

where

$$\mathbf{T}_n^{j,k} = \{0, ..., N_n^{j,k}\}$$

and $N_n^{j,k}$ is the maximum number of admitted users of class-(j, k) assuming that this class is the only one served in network n. The dimension of this set is given by $| \mathbf{T} | = \prod_{j \in \mathbf{J}} \prod_{k \in \mathbf{K}} N^{j,k}$.

In the case of a wireless network where capacity is shared in a nonlinear manner, determining the set $\mathbf{T}$ of all possible strategies for admission control is more complex. The set of threshold strategies is a subset of the above-mentioned $\mathbf{T}$ containing elements corresponding to feasible states, i.e., the set of all possible strategies where all admitted users obtain sufficient resources (at the MAC layer) so as to satisfy their QoS.

Similarly, the same analysis holds for the pricing strategy. In the cooperative case, a centralized decision maker chooses a vector of prices $(p)_{n \in \mathbf{N}}$ in a finite set of possible prices $\mathbb{P}$.

In the case of a single operator implementing admission control, the objective function is as follows

$$\underset{T \in \mathbf{T}, p \in \mathbf{P}}{\max} R(\Lambda, T, p) \qquad (3)$$

4.2   Non-cooperative Case

In this case, each network has its own utility function and each network optimizes its CAC parameters and chooses its prices independently of other networks. Formally, each network $n \in \mathbf{N}$ solves selfishly the following maximization problem, considering other network admission strategies fixed to T_{-n} and prices to p_{-n}:

$$\underset{T_n \in \mathbf{T}_n, p_n \in \mathbf{P}_n}{\max} R_n(\Lambda, T_n, T_{-n}, p_n, p_{-n}) \qquad (4)$$

where $(\mathbf{T})_n$ is the set of all possible network n strategies given by:

$$\mathbf{T}_n = \underset{j \in \mathbf{J}}{\otimes} \underset{k \in \mathbf{K}}{\otimes} T_n^{j,k}$$

and each subnetwork chooses its own price p_n from a finite set of possible prices $\mathbf{P}_n$.

4.3 Optimal Strategies

The set of all possible strategies is a finite set limited to the threshold values guaranteeing some QoS to the admitted users as well as prices. An extensive search algorithm is used to find the optimal threshold parameters [12]. Some algorithms accelerating the search for the optimal threshold parameters can be run by ordering traffic classes according to their revenues.

Admission as well as pricing strategies need not be run on the same time scales. The operator may well fix the price first and then optimize according to admission control.

5 Performance Metrics

The above-mentioned utility functions, both for network and user, have been formulated in terms of performance metrics: mean transfer time and blocking probabilities. These performance metrics are derived as follows.

Consider a subnetwork n where the arrival of (j, k)-class users is Poissonian with mean rate $\lambda_n^{j,k}$ for fresh users and $h_n^{j,k}$ for handoff users. The service is exponential with mean rate $\mu_n^{j,k}$. The mean service time of voice users is constant; it depends on the share of resources for data transfers. In what follows, index n will be suppressed for clarity.

In 3G networks, voice calls shall be assigned to constant rate dedicated links whereas data ones shall share the leftover power on shared links implementing High Speed Downlink Packet Access (HSDPA). At the MAC layer, HSDPA implements, among other mechanisms, opportunistic scheduling, typically through the use of the Proportional Fair Scheduling (PFS) algorithm.

The service rate of a class-(k) data call in such a system is given by:

$$\mu^{j,k}(x) = \frac{\psi^k \left(C - \sum_{k=1}^{K} x^{v,k} \phi^{v,k} \right)^k G(x^d)}{\mid x^d \mid}$$

where ψ^k is an attenuation factor related to radio conditions of class-k users, C is the overall system capacity, $\phi^{v,k}$ is the share of resources for voice users out of the total resources and $G(.)$ is the scheduling gain [13].

In IEEE802.11 WLAN, the MAC layer is based on CSMA/CA, and all flows, voice and data, are subject to competition. Voice frames are however severely affected by aggressive data sources as the latter are typically saturated ones, i.e., always with a frame to send. The share of voice and data users in this case is a nonlinear function of the number of users of each type in the system and is explicitly given in References [14] and [15].

The overall system can be described by a Markov process. It is however irreversible which makes product form expressions for the steady-state distribution impossible. As proposed in [16], we consider a quasi-stationary regime, where data calls would reach steady states between voice calls arrivals and departures. Accordingly, the marginal distribution of voice calls in the system is given by an M/M/c/c queueing system with steady state distribution of the number of ongoing voice calls given by [17]:

$$\pi(x^v) = \frac{1}{G} \prod_{k=1}^{K} q^k(x^{v,k}) \tag{5}$$

where

$$q^k(x^{v,k}) = \begin{cases} \dfrac{(\frac{\lambda^{v,k}+h^{v,k}}{\mu^{v,k}})^{x^{v,k}}}{x^{v,k}!} & \text{if } x^{v,k} \leq T^{v,k} \\[2em] \dfrac{(\frac{\lambda^{v,k}+h^{v,k}}{\mu^{v,k}})^{T^{v,k}} (\frac{h^{v,k}}{\mu^{v,k}})^{x^{v,k}-T^{v,k}}}{x^{v,k}!} & \text{if } T^{v,k} < x^{v,k} \leq H^{v,k} \end{cases}$$

and

$$G = \sum_{x^v \in \mathbb{X}^v} \prod_{k=1}^{K} q^k(x^{v,k})$$

is the normalization constant. $\mathbb{X}^v$ is the state space of voice users for which QoS is guaranteed on the packet level, $T^{v,k}$ is the threshold value above which no new voice arrival is admitted and $H^{v,k}$ is the threshold value above which no voice call in handover is admitted.

As of data, it can be modeled as an M/G/1-Processor Sharing (PS) queue with steady-state probabilities given by:

$$\pi(x^d \mid x^v) = \frac{1}{H} \prod_{k=1}^{K} f^k(x^{d,k}) \tag{6}$$

where

$$f^k(x^{d,k} \mid x^v) = \begin{cases} \dfrac{(\frac{\lambda^{d,k}+h^{d,k}}{\mu^{d,k}(x)})^{x^{d,k}}}{x^{d,k}!} & \text{if } x^{d,k} \leq T^{d,k} \\[2em] \dfrac{(\frac{\lambda^{d,k}+h^{d,k}}{\mu^{d,k}(x)})^{T^{d,k}} (\frac{h^{d,k}}{\mu^{d,k}(x)})^{x^{d,k}-T^{d,k}}}{x^{d,k}!} & \text{if } T^{d,k} < x^{d,k} \leq H^{d,k} \end{cases}$$

where H is the normalization constant obtained by setting the sum of all joint probabilities to one, $T^{d,k}$ and $H^{d,k}$ are defined similarly to $T^{v,k}$ and $H^{v,k}$.

These joint steady-state probabilities $\pi(x^v, x^d)$ are given by:

$$\pi(x^v, x^d) = \pi(x^d \mid x^v) \cdot \pi(x^v) \tag{7}$$

Now, the performance measures are given as follows.

The blocking probabilities of a class-k fresh arrival voice or data user is given by:

$$B^{j,k} = \sum_{x^{-(j,k)}} \sum_{x^{j,k}=T^{j,k}}^{H^{j,k}} \pi(x^{-(j,k)}, x^{j,k})$$

and for calls in handover

$$B_h^{j,k} = \sum_{x^{-(j,k)}} \pi(x^{-(j,k)}, H^{j,k})$$

The mean file transfer time W^k of a class-k data call is given by the a phase-2 type distribution taking into account the service received in both subsystems in case of a handover. The sojourn time S in each subsystem is given by the minimum between the dwell time V in the subsystem and W ($\frac{1}{S} = \frac{1}{V} + \frac{1}{W}$) [18]:

$$S^k = \frac{\bar{x}^{d,k}}{\lambda^{d,k}(1 - B^{d,k}) + h^{d,k}(1 - B_h^{d,k})}$$

where $\bar{x}^{d,k}$ is the mean number of data flows of class$-k$ in the subnetwork.

6 Conclusion

We presented in this work a framework for modeling the relationships between users, operators as well as the relationship between them in a heterogeneous environments where several wireless networks share the access of some Internet cloud. We covered the cases of cooperative optimization and non-cooperative games between the different players as these cases arise in real.

Our new step shall be devoted to the numeric analysis of such strategies in an attempt to quantify network-oriented issues, such as what the best options for voice and data users are, whether it is better for network operators to cooperate or not and do users interest correspond to the network's one.

References

1. 3GPP TS 25.855 High Speed Downlink Packet Access (HSDPA); Overall UTRAN description.
2. 3GPP TS 25.856 High Speed Downlink Packet Access (HSDPA); Layer 2 and 3 aspects.
3. IEEE standard for information technology- telecommunications and information exchange between systems- local and metropolitan area networks- specific requirements Part II: wireless LAN medium access control (MAC) and physical layer (PHY) specifications.
4. Drew Fudenberg, Jean Tirole. Game Theory. 1991.
5. T. Basar, G. J. Olsder, Dynamic Noncooperative Game Theory, Academic Press, London/New York, January 1995.
6. E. Altman, T. Boulogne, R. El Azouzi, T. Jimenez and L. Wynter , A survey on networking games , Computers and Operations Research, 2004.
7. T. Alpcan, T. Basar, R. Srikant, and E. Altman, "CDMA uplink power control as a noncooperative game," Wireless Networks, vol. 8, pp. 659–669, November 2002.
8. Y. A. Korilis, A. A. Lazar, and A. Orda, Capacity allocation under non-cooperative routing, IEEE Transactions on Automatic Control, 42(3):309-325, March 1997.
9. E. Altman, R. El-Azouzi, and V. Abramov, Non-Cooperative Routing in Loss Networks, Performance Evaluation 49(1–4), 43-55, 2002.
10. Yannis A. Korilis, Aurel A. Lazar, and Ariel Orda, "Achieving network optima using Stackelberg routing strategies," IEEE/ACM Transactions on Networking, vol. 5, no. 1, pp. 161–173, 1997.
11. Z. Dziong, L. G. Mason, Fair-efficient call admission control policies for broadband networks: a game theoretic framework, IEEE Trans. on Net., February 1996.

12. J. Ni, D. H. K. Tsang, S. Tatikonda, B. Bensaou, Threshold and reservation based call admission control policies for multiservice resource-sharing systems, Infocom'2005.
13. T. Chahed, M. Dirani, Cross-layer modeling of capacity of UMTS/HSDPA networks under a dynamic user setting, VTC-Fall, Montreal, September 2006.
14. M. Dirani, T. Chahed, A MAC/flow level modeling of data and voice intergation in WLANs, Globecom'2006, December 2006.
15. N. Hegde, A. Proutiere, J. Roberts, Evaluating the voice capacity of 802.11 WLAN under distributed control, IEEE LANMAN 2005.
16. N. Benameur, S. Ben Fredj, F. Delcoigne, S. Oueslati-Boulahia and J.W. Roberts, Integrated Admission Control for Streaming and Elastic Traffic, QofIS 2001, Coimbra, September 2001.
17. K. W. Ross, Multiservice Loss Networks for Broadband Telecommunications Networks, Springer-Verlag, 1995.
18. S-E. Elayoubi, T. Chahed, G. Hbuterne, Mobility-aware admission control schemes in the downlink of third generation wireless systems, to appear, IEEE Transactions on Vehicular Technology, January 2007.

On the Performance of Mobile IP in Wireless LAN Environments

Rastin Pries, Andreas Mäder, Dirk Staehle, and Matthias Wiesen

University of Würzburg, Institute of Computer Science, Germany
{pries, maeder, staehle, wiesen}@informatik.uni-wuerzburg.de

Abstract. Wireless Local Area Networks (WLANs) based on the IEEE 802.11 standard have become more and more popular in the last few years. In such networks, a handover has to be performed when moving from one cell to another. When considering small-scale scenarios like an office building, these handovers can be performed on the ISO/OSI layer two solely. However, the size of one subnet is rather restricted. Therefore, the handover has to be lifted to the network layer as well. The performance of this network layer handover will be shown in this paper.

1 Introduction and Related Work

With the increasing number of wireless LAN deployments at universities and companies, one IP subnet is often not sufficient. Therefore, we have to perform the handover on the network layer. Some standards like Cellular IP [1], HAWAII [2], and Mobile IP [3] try to perform the handover on layer three and above. In this paper, we focus on the performance of Mobile IP. IP mobility has been the topic of many researchers for several years. The basic approach by Perkins dates back to the year 1996 [3]. Meanwhile, another two standards [4,5] emerged from this basic approach. All three together are referred to as Mobile IP and they constitute the most promising solution in order to support mobility within the internet protocol. A good overview of Mobile IPv4, Mobile IPv6, and further extensions are given in [6,7].

A large variety of papers have been published which have analyzed the basic Mobile IPv4 handover. Their results show a handover latency of at least 6 seconds which is too high for any type of traffic. In this paper, we want to simulate which parameters cause these long handover delays and will show how to optimize these settings. Furthermore, we do not only look at Mobile IPv4 but also simulate Mobile IPv6 and Fast Mobile IPv6. In the context of Fast Mobile IPv6, we just like to point out two promising approaches. The first one [8] proposes a new mechanism called ARIP (Access Router Information Protocol) to speedup the Fast Mobile IPv6 handover. In their experimental setup, the handover latency of the Fast Mobile IPv6 with ARIP was bounded below 250 ms. With this handover delay it should be possible to support real-time traffic when the mobile user is changing its point of attachment rarely. The second approach, proposed by Sharma et al. [9] introduces a new low latency Mobile IP handover mechanism which they have implemented. They show that they can reduce the handover latency to less than 100 ms which is completely sufficient for real-time traffic. In this study we

J. García-Vidal and L. Cerdà-Alabern (Eds.): Wireless and Mobility, LNCS 4396, pp. 155–170, 2007.

will show how the actual IP connectivity loss and the overall handover delay can be reduced to less than 100 ms with an optimal setting of the layer 2 and layer 3 handover parameters without introducing a new handover mechanism.

The rest of the paper is organized as follows. Section 2 briefly explains the main concept of Mobile IP including Mobile IPv4, Mobile IPv6, and Fast Mobile IPv6. This is followed by Section 3 which describes the simulation model, the used traffic models, and the parameter settings. Section 4 presents our simulation results and finally, Section 5 concludes the paper.

2   Mobility Within the Internet Protocol

The primary goal of Mobile IP's design is to make the network-layer handover transparent to above layers. In order to assure the session continuity, the IP address of a mobile node has to remain the same after a network layer handover. When using Mobile IP, this IP address is called the mobile nodes home address and the subnet this address belongs to is called the home network. A router in this home network is called the *Home Agent* (HA). The network where the *Mobile Node* (MN) is moving to is called the foreign network and the router the *Foreign Agent* (FA).

2.1   Mobile IPv4

"IP Mobility for IPv4" [4] defines a way to always identify a node by its home IP address regardless of its current location. As soon as a mobile node leaves its home network and enters a foreign network, it is not able to receive packets addressed to its home agent anymore. Therefore, Mobile IPv4 describes a mechanism of forwarding data from a MN's home network to its current foreign network. This forwarding mechanism makes use of an IP-in-IP tunnel. The outer datagram of the IP tunnel carries the inner one from the tunnel start point to the tunnel end point. The MN's home address is used as the IP address of the tunnel start point, but the MN still lacks of a temporary foreign network IP address denoting the tunnel end point. This address is called the MN's care-of-address. Mobile IP distinguishes between two care-of-addresses, one is called co-located care-of-address and the other foreign agent care-of-address. When using the co-located care-of-address, the IP tunnel ends at the mobile node and for the foreign agent care-of-address, the foreign agent is the end point of the tunnel. Fig. 1 shows the tunnel after the network layer handover with the end point at the mobile node and Fig. 2 for the tunnel up to the FA.

From the figures you can see the triangular traffic shape. From the mobile node to the *Correspondent Node* (CN), from the CN to the MN's home agent, and from the home agent back to the MN. When a MN enters a FN and obtains a new care-of-address, it has to inform the HA about the new address in order to enable the HA to establish a tunnel to the MN's new location.

The Mobile IPv4 handover starts when the MN recognizes that it has lost the connection to his previous point of attachment. Therefore, Mobile IPv4 introduces *Agent Advertisements* (AAs). These AAs inform about the existence of the HA or a FA and the services it offers. The AAs are broadcasted by the HA and the FAs in periodical

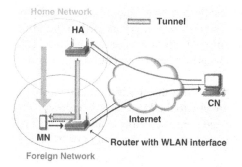

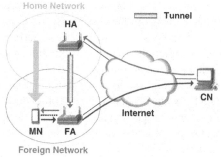

Fig. 1. Co-located care-of-address scenario after the handover

Fig. 2. Foreign agent care-of-address scenario after the handover

intervals. When a MN does not receive any AAs from its agent anymore for a period of time called agent advertisement lifetime, it considers that the connection is lost. The lifetime of an AA is supposed to be as long as at least three times the interval between the transmission of two consecutive agent advertisements. For example, when the HA sends an AA every four seconds, the lifetime field of the AA should be set to at least twelve seconds. Thus, the MN recognizes that a link layer handover has taken place when three consecutive AAs are lost and the MN receives AAs from another mobility agent instead. After analyzing the AAs from the new mobility agent, the MN registers with the agent and the tunnel between the home agent and the new foreign agent or to the MN, depending on the care-of-address, is created. Now, the MN is able to continue with the session. A complete description of the Mobile IPv4 handover procedure can be found in [10].

2.2 Mobile IPv6

Mobility Support in IPv6 [5] is the adaptation of *"IP Mobility Support for IPv4"* [4] to an internet using IP version 6. The design of Mobile IPv6 is very similar to Mobile IPv4 and both standards share the functionality of basic entities like a mobile node, its home agent, and correspondent nodes.

2.3 Bidirectional Tunneling and Route Optimization

In Mobile IPv6, there are two possible modes for communication between a MN and its CNs, namely bidirectional tunneling and route optimization.

The first mode, bidirectional tunneling, does not require Mobile IPv6 support from the CN and is available even if the MN has not registered its current binding with the CN. Packets from the CN are routed to the home agent and then tunneled to the MN. Packets to the CN are tunneled from the MN to the home agent and then routed normally from the MNs home network to the CN. The latter procedure of tunneling packets back to the MNs home address is called reverse tunneling. In this mode, the home address uses proxy neighbor discovery to intercept any IPv6 packets addressed to the MNs home address on the home network. Each intercepted packet is tunneled to the MNs care-of-address. This tunneling is performed using IPv6-in-IPv6 encapsulation [11]. Fig. 3 depicts bidirectional tunneling, which is used when route optimization is not available or intentionally turned off.

The second mode, route optimization, allows to use the shortest communications path between CN and MN by routing packets directly to the MNs care-of-address. This eliminates congestion at the MNs home agent and home network. In addition, the impact of any possible failure of the home agent or networks on the path to or from it is reduced.

In order to do so, route optimization requires the MN to register its current mobility binding at the CN. This means that the MN sends a binding update to every CN, telling it about its current care-of-address. The CNs are then able to create a mobility binding between the MNs home address and the MNs care-of-address in their mobility binding cache. When sending a packet to any IPv6 destination, a CN checks its cached mobility bindings for an entry for the packet's destination IP address. If a cached mobility binding is found, the CN will use a new IPv6 extension header [12] to route the packet to the MN by using the care-of-address indicated in this mobility binding. The main purpose of the extension header is to carry the MNs home address and replace the packet's destination IP address with the home address, once the packet has arrived at the MN. Vice versa, the MN adds a new IPv6 destination option [12] to every packet it sends to a CN. This new option is called the home address option and it is used to inform the CN of the MNs home address. The inclusion of the MNs home address in these packets allows a transparent use of the care-of-address above the network layer.

Fig. 4 depicts the simplification that can be achieved by deploying the route optimization procedure. Please note that the MN has not changed its home address and it still uses the home address of its home network. Furthermore, the arrows symbolize a traffic flow whose IPv6 packets are extended with the extension header. Just as well, the IPv6 packets from the MN to the CN are extended with the home address option.

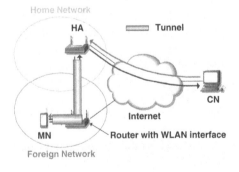

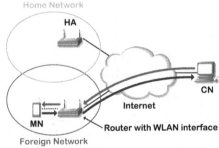

Fig. 3. Bidirectional tunneling in Mobile IPv6

Fig. 4. Mobile IPv6 scenario after network layer handover and route optimization

Route optimization as described so far, has one major weakness. Any node knowing the MNs home address can transmit a binding update to the MNs CN and claim its own source IP address to be the new care-of-address. As a result, the CN stops sending the MNs traffic to the MN and starts delivering it to the malicious node instead. Thus, to assure that only valid MNs are sending binding update messages, route optimization in Mobile IPv6 uses a mechanism called the return routability procedure. It strongly reduces the amount of locations from where potential attackers can transmit malicious binding updates to a CN. A detailed explanation of the return routability procedure is given in [13].

The bidirectional tunneling and route optimization can also be applied for Mobile IPv4. However, there are also some differences between Mobile IPv4 and Mobile IPv6. The agent advertisements from Mobile IPv4 are replaced by router advertisements which can be transmitted with a shorter period. Furthermore, the lifetime of these advertisements is not fixed but can be varied using the so called *Mobility Detection Factor* (MDF). After a MN has detected that it has moved from its home network to a foreign network or from one foreign network to another, the MN generates a care-of-address. Before assigning this new care-of-address to the interface, the MN has to check if the chosen address is not already in use. This is done using a duplicate address detection scheme. To check for duplicates of an IP address, a node sets the neighbor solicitation's target IP address to the address being checked. The source IP address is set to the unspecified address [14] and the destination IP address is set to the solicited-node multicast address of the target IP address. If a node receives a neighbor solicitation message whose target IP address matches the nodes own IP address and whose source address is set to the unspecified address, it will answer by sending a neighbor advertisement. With this method, the MN recognizes that the IP address is already assigned. If there are no duplicates of the target IP address assigned in the local network, the MN performing the duplicate address detection will not receive any responding neighbor advertisements. Thus, it waits for a certain amount of time for responding neighbor advertisements to arrive. However, neighbor discovery for IPv6 recommends a default value of 1000 ms before assuming that the target IP address is unique. Thus, the overall handover is delayed by one second.

2.4   Fast Handovers for Mobile IPv6

Fast handovers for Mobile IPv6 [15] is an optional standard proposed by the IETF to speed up handover times on the network layer when deploying Mobile IPv6. The main goal of Fast Mobile IPv6 is to improve the standard Mobile IPv6 protocol in a way that enables a MN to send IP packets as soon as it detects a new IP subnet and to receive packets as soon as the new access router has detected the MNs attachment. Therefore, Fast Mobile IPv6 defines new IPv6 and neighbor discovery messages, necessary for its operation. However, the protocol is designed to interwork with Mobile IPv6. Once attached to its new access router, the MN engages in Mobile IPv6 operations including the return routability procedure. Furthermore, Fast Mobile IPv6 works without depending on specific link-layer features but it recommends to make use of inter-layer communication between the link layer and the network layer as often as possible. Inter-layer communication is realized via function calls in the MNs link- and network-layer.

They offer a means of event notification between the two layers and are referred to as triggers. In the following paragraphs, we will explain the Fast Mobile IPv6 handover procedure.

Fig. 5 depicts a standard Fast Mobile IPv6 scenario. Since the access routers in both, the MNs old and its new IP subnet, do not necessarily have to be home agents, Fast Mobile IPv6 assigns the new denotions *Previous Access Router* (PAR) and *Next Access Router* (NAR). Accordingly, the IP subnet the MN is leaving is called the previous network and the one it is moving to is called the next network. At the previous network, the MN uses the previous care-of-address, at the next network the next care-of-address.

The main design idea of Fast Mobile IPv6 is to handle as much handover-related IP communication before the actual link layer handover occurs. In order to do so, the MN somehow has to learn, that a link layer handover is forthcoming. The protocol states that this notification may be achieved by conventional router discovery. However the use of a trigger is a more effective solution. A complete description about the exchange between the link layer and the network layer using triggers can be found in [15].

There are two approaches how the Fast Mobile IPv6 handover can be performed, a predictive mode and a reactive mode. In this paper, we focus on the predictive mode which is shown in Fig. 6. The handover starts with the MN asking the PAR about the next network. This is done via the exchange of a router solicitation for proxy advertisement and its response, the proxy router advertisement. Fast Mobile IPv6 does not specify how the PAR obtains the information for according proxy router advertisements. However, the MNs link layer discovered a neighboring AP, by some means. Since every AP provides some kind of identifier, the trigger sends this AP-ID to the network layer, which in turn provides the AP-ID in its router solicitation for proxy advertisement request. If the PAR has subnet-specific information of the discovered AP, it returns an [AP-ID, NAR-Info] tuple back to the MN. The information about the NAR consists of its link layer address, its IP address and the prefixes of the next network. Thus, the MN already possesses all information equivalent to the data stored in a router advertisement of the next access router, while still connected to the previous network.

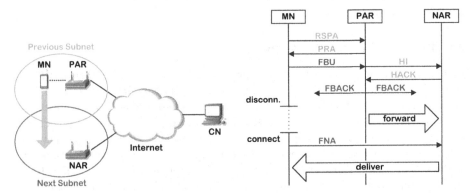

Fig. 5. Reference scenario for Fast Mobile IPv6

Fig. 6. Predictive Fast Mobile IPv6

With the information provided in the proxy router advertisement message, the MN is able to form a prospective next care-of-address, which is sent inside the fast binding update to the previous access router. The sending of the fast binding update may be triggered and its response from the PAR is called a fast binding acknowledgment. However, the main purpose of the fast binding update is to enable the PAR to create a mobility binding between the MNs previous care-of-address and its next care-of-address. Thus, from this time on, the PAR is able to tunnel the MNs packets to the next network. However, before establishing this tunnel, the PAR exchanges a handover initiate message and its according response, the handover acknowledgment with the NAR. The PAR may resolve the NAR's IP address by performing the longest prefix match of the next care-of-address with the prefix list of neighboring access routers. However, the purpose of the handover initiate is to agree upon the prospective next care-of-address with the NAR. If the NAR accepts the prospective next care-of-address, it creates an according proxy neighbor cache entry and starts buffering incoming packets addressed to the next care-of-address. Now, the MN is ready to perform the link layer handover. After the handover, it is recommended that the MN immediately sends a so-called fast neighbor advertisement to the NAR. This is necessary in order to inform the NAR about the MNs successful attachment to the next network. The NAR then turns the MNs proxy cache entry into a standard cache entry and begins to transmit packets forwarded from the PAR and own buffered packets to the MN.

3 Simulation Setup

In order to simulate the Mobile IP handover performance, we have used the OPNET Modeler [16]. The tool already offers the basic Mobile IPv4 and Mobile IPv6 models. Due to the fact that we want to see if it is possible to support QoS even during a network layer handover, first of all we need a fast and reliable handover mechanism on the wireless LAN MAC layer. The performance of the layer 2 handover is studied in [17]. It is shown that only two mechanisms support these demands, the fast active scanning and the active scanning with neighborhood detection. Since only the fast active scanning is included in the standard, we have decided to use this wireless LAN handover mechanism with an average link layer handover time of 34.93 ms. The wireless LAN model was modified in order to implement fast handover for Mobile IPv6. As the FMIPv6 standard suggests, we make use of triggers as often as possible. The first trigger is used after the scanning process is completed. The wireless LAN association process is postponed and the FMIPv6 pre-handover messaging is initiated by a trigger. Afterwards, the wireless LAN association process is started and the link layer again sends a trigger to the network layer to initiate the binding update messages. Fig. 7 depicts the three triggers in the context of the overall handover procedure.

The basic structure of all simulation scenarios is shown in Fig. 8. Three access routers and one correspondent node are interconnected through an IP network. The access routers are connected by a T3 line to the IP core network and the distance between the routers is 200 m. The IP core network, illustrated as an IP cloud in the middle of the scenario can be configured to delay or drop data packets in order to simulate background load. However, we focus in our simulations on the wireless link because

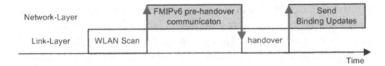

Fig. 7. Triggers used for Fast Mobile IPv6

the major packet delay results on the wireless link and so we have set the background load to zero and do not add any delays on the packets, routed via the IP cloud. The mobile node moves from the previous access router to the next access router with a moving speed of 18 kmph and the handover is initiated at a distance of about 160 m to the PAR based on the SNR. All access routers are configured with the IEEE 802.11g standard and use different, non overlapping channels. The PAR uses channel one, the NAR channel six, and the home agent channel eleven. Hence, fast active scanning and normal association is used on the link layer.

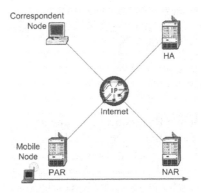

Fig. 8. Typical simulation scenario

For the communication between the MN and the CN, we choose the G.711 [18] voice codec. The codec has a data rate of 64 kbps and the packetization interval is set to 10 ms. For the simulation runs of Fast Mobile IPv6, we want to see the impact of background traffic on the handover performance in the cells and therefore, configure a number of clients within the cells using the same voice traffic profile as the MN. Further parameter settings are shown in Table 1.

4   Simulation Results

4.1   Agent Advertisement Interval of Mobile IPv4

In the first simulation study, the performance of Mobile IPv4 is evaluated. The handover performance mainly depends on the moving speed of the mobile and the interval of the

Table 1. Simulation parameter settings

Parmeter	Value
Data rate	54 Mbps
Channel assignment	Non overlapping channels
Layer 2 scanning	Fast active scanning [17]
Layer 2 authentication	Pre-authentication
Average Layer 2 handover delay	35 ms
Mobility (Mobile Node)	18 kmph
Mobility (Background Nodes)	0 kmph
Distance between the access routers	200 m
Connection of the access router	T3 connection

agent advertisements from either a HA or a FA. If a mobile node does not receive an AA within the lifetime of the last AA, it will know that it has lost its network layer connection. Table 2 gives an overview of the limits, within which the AA sending interval may be configured [10]. This interval has a maximum and a minimum value, which themselves have upper and lower limits.

Table 2. Agent Advertisement interval limits

	Lower bound	Upper bound	Default
Max value	4 s	1800 s	600 s
Min value	3 s	Max value	0.75·Max value

It is easy to see that the minimum interval of 3 s by far exceeds the maximum acceptable one way delay for voice conversations which is according to the ITU-T G.114 specification 400 ms [19]. Furthermore, the corresponding AA lifetime is longer than 9 seconds. This leads to a mean waiting time of more than 7.5 s, for the old AA lifetime to expire after the handover.

Thus, simulations have been made in order to examine, how tweaking Mobile IPv4 AA interval parameters improve the situation. Fig. 9 shows the handover time in dependence on the AA transmitting interval in a foreign agent care-of-address scenario, where a MN moves from its home network to a foreign network. The AA interval is reduced beneath the recommended lower bound of 3 s in steps of 100 ms. Please note that the marked out AA interval applies for both routers, the HA and the FA, equally.

Clearly, the total handover time decreases linearly with decreasing intervals between two consecutive AAs. The step-shaped nature of the graph relies on the fact that the lifetime variable is discrete. The original standard defines the AA lifetime as a 16 Bit unsigned integer, counting the seconds until expiration. If we consider an AA interval of 600 ms with a corresponding AA lifetime of at least 1.8 s, the AA lifetime is truncated to 1 s because only integer values are accepted. This is also the reason why shorter

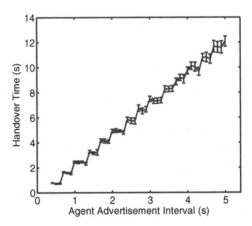

Fig. 9. Mobile IPv4 handover time with reduced AA transmitting intervals

intervals than 400 ms could not be evaluated. An AA interval of 300 ms leads to an AA lifetime of 0.9 seconds, effectively resulting in a lifetime of zero seconds.

The best handover performance can of course be achieved with an AA interval of 400 ms but the average handover time of 750 ms is still not sufficient for real-time traffic if we need to perform a large number of handovers. When using Mobile IPv6 the agent advertisements are replaced by so called router advertisements. The router advertisements are defined in size of milliseconds and the lower bound for these intervals is set to 30 ms. However, such a small router advertisement interval leads to a too large overhead. In our next simulation study, we want to evaluate the impact of the router advertisement interval and the duplicate address detection on the Mobile IPv6 handover performance.

4.2   Duplicate Address Detection

As examined in Section 2, duplicate address detection has a very negative impact on the network layer handover performance. When a MN has formed a new care-of-address using the subnet prefix information it has received with a router advertisement, it has to check whether the generated IP address is already assigned to a node in this subnet. This is done by multicasting a special neighbor solicitation message and actively waiting for a reply. After a configurable timeout, the *Neighbor Solicitation Retransmission Interval* (NSRI), the MN stops waiting for responses and starts sending one or more binding updates.

The impact of the NSRI and the router advertisement interval on the handover performance is shown in Fig. 10. The NSRI is set to 1000 ms and 500 ms. The scenario is a standard Mobile IPv6 scenario without route optimization, where the MN leaves its home network and enters another subnet. The router advertisement interval applies equally to the old and the new access router.

Here, three things can be seen. First, similar to Mobile IPv4, there is a linear behavior between the router advertisement interval and the network layer handover performance.

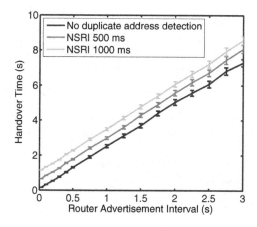

Fig. 10. Impact of different duplicate address detection settings on Mobile IPv6

The smaller the interval, the shorter the handover time. Second, without duplicate address detection, handover latencies in the magnitude of 200 ms seem achievable using extreme router advertisement interval settings. Finally, the value of the NSRI adds a constant delay to the network layer handover. Please note that with a value of 3 seconds, the maximum router advertisement interval in this figure is the minimum router advertisement interval of nodes not supporting Mobile IPv6.

4.3 Mobility Detection Factor

In the previous scenario, the router advertisement lifetime is set to 3 times the router advertisement interval. However, in Mobile IPv6, the lifetime of a router advertisement can be varied and is calculated by multiplying the value contained in the advertisement interval option by the MN specific *Mobility Detection Factor* (MDF). Thus, the time a MN has to wait until old RAs expire, may not only be reduced by increasing the transmitting frequency of the RAs. It may also be shortened, by simply setting the MDF to a lower value.

This is simulated in the next graph. Fig. 11 shows the results of three simulations. Each is based on a standard IPv6 scenario, using the same router advertisement intervals at both routers. The MN moves from its home network to another subnet. Route optimization and duplicate address detection are not supported. The simulations differ only in the value used for the MDF.

The gray curves, plotted beneath the simulation result graphs illustrate the functions: $y = 0.5 \cdot x$, $y = 1.5 \cdot x$, and $y = 2.5 \cdot x$. It can easily be seen that the result graphs are good approximations of those functions. This is because the time, at which a handover occurs, is uniformly distributed between the sending of two router advertisements. Thus, in the average, the handover takes place right in the middle of two RAs. Consequently, when using an MDF of 2 for example, the MN has to wait for another one and a half router advertisement intervals before it may drop its old access router. Of

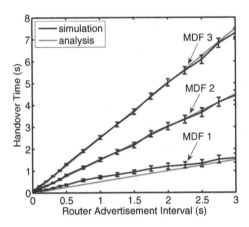

Fig. 11. Effect of the Mobile IPv6 Mobility Detection Factor

course, analog considerations apply for the mobility detection factors 1 and 3. However, although lowering the MDF visibly reduces the network layer handover latency, concurrently the risk increases of disconnecting from the old access point too early. Thus, adjustments to the MDF have to be taken seriously. An MDF of 2 is a good trade off between handover performance and loss probability of router advertisements. However, the MDF might also be adapted according to the network conditions. If we have a high packet loss rate, the MDF has to be increased.

Concluding the results from the duplicate address detection, the router advertisements, and the mobility detection factor, the possibilities to accelerate the network layer handover in Mobile IPv6 are better than the ones in Mobile IPv4. Simulation results show that when using extreme parameter values like a router advertisement interval of 30 ms, network layer handover latencies in the area of 150 ms are not impossible. Thus, fast Mobile IPv6 might be able to support real-time interactive communication in some very special cases. However, it is not designed to do so.

Furthermore, we strongly recommend to deploy some means of overcoming the extreme delay caused by duplicate address detection. Such a means may be *"Optimistic Duplicate Address Detection for IPv6"* [20]. If no such mechanism is used, the standard Mobile IPv6 network layer handover takes at least one second because the default value for the neighbor solicitation retransmission interval is one second.

4.4 Fast Mobile IPv6

Especially designed for reducing network layer handover latencies, Fast Mobile IPv6 constitutes a very promising solution if we want to support real-time traffic. In our implementation, we use three triggers to further accelerate the protocol operation. For the next simulation scenarios, we turned the duplicate address detection off, since the amount of MNs in the subnet is quite manageable.

The goal of the Fast Mobile IPv6 scenarios is not only to see the performance gain compared to the normal Mobile IPv6 scenarios, but also to see the impact of background traffic on the handover latency. Therefore, we use an increasing number of VoIP clients. We discovered that a wireless LAN cell using the IEEE 802.11g standard is able to manage 22 VoIP clients that are all communicating with respective VoIP correspondents using the traffic model described in Section 3. Those 22 clients include the moving MN.

We simulate all three possible movements with up to 21 clients generating background traffic. Those three movements are from the home network to a foreign network, from one foreign network to another, and from a foreign network back to the home network. Thereby, we do not measure the duration of the previous wireless LAN scan for two reasons. First, the scan takes longer then the whole Fast Mobile IPv6 protocol operation. Second, in Fast Mobile IPv6, the wireless LAN scan does not extend the duration of the IP connectivity loss. This is because after the scan, the MN has connectivity again in order to handle the pre-handover communication. Thus, the network layer handover related IP connectivity loss begins with the initialization of the actual link layer handover.

Fig. 12, Fig. 13, and Fig. 14 respectively illustrate two parts of a Fast Mobile IPv6 handover. The IP connection loss is the time in which the MN can not send nor receive IP packets and knows that it has no connection. The overall protocol activity time without route optimization begins as soon as the wireless LAN module tells Fast Mobile IPv6 about the forthcoming handover. Thus, it includes all pre-handover protocol operations and ends when the binding acknowledgment message from the MNs home agent is received. On the x-axis, the number of wireless LAN clients generating real-time VoIP traffic in the background is applied. The y-axis measures the time in milliseconds.

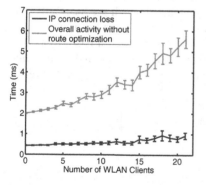

Fig. 12. Fast Mobile IPv6 moving from the home network to a foreign network

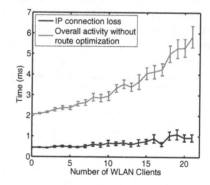

Fig. 13. Fast Mobile IPv6 moving from one foreign network to another

The three handover behaviors are almost identical which is different to normal Mobile IPv4 or Mobile IPv6 scenarios where the handover delay differs caused by tunneling redirections or tunnel removals. The time of the IP connection loss is quite independent of the amount of clients in the cell. It has the magnitude of 1 ms and thus, it is not much longer than the wireless LAN reassociation procedure. However, the overall protocol activity may take up to 6 ms when many clients are present.

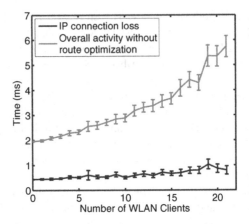

Fig. 14. Fast Mobile IPv6 moving from a foreign network back to the home network

4.5   Fast Mobile IPv6 with Route Optimization

Finally, we want to take a look at the overhead of route optimization. As described in Section 2, route optimization reduces the traffic which is normally routed over the home network by using mobility binding caches at the correspondent nodes. For this simulation scenario, we take a look at the handover delay when traversing from one foreign agent to another foreign agent. Fig. 15 shows the results of this simulation setup. In order to compare the handover latency using route optimization with the original handover latency, we also plotted the delay without route optimization. The x-axis shows again the number of VoIP wireless LAN clients at each cell which produce background traffic and the y-axis shows the handover latency. The IP connection loss is the same for both scenarios, with and without route optimization, but the overall Fast Mobile IPv6 latency differs. The overall activity with route optimization takes around 1.5 ms longer but is with less than 10 ms still faster than the scanning procedure on the link layer.

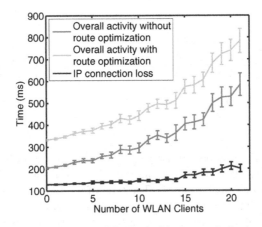

Fig. 15. Fast Mobile IPv6 with route optimization

The results of Fast Mobile IPv6 have shown that it is possible to support real-time traffic even when a network layer handover has to be performed. The overall handover latency consisting of link layer scanning, the Fast Mobile IPv6 messages and the reassociation on the link layer has been less than 50 ms for all simulation settings. However, a communication between the link layer and the network layer has to be managed.

5   Conclusion

In this paper we have shown the performance of different Mobile IP versions and their extensions. The Mobile IP handover process can be subdivided into three phases. Those are the movement detection phase, the care-of-address configuration phase, and the registration phase. Mobile IPv4 suffers from a too long movement detection latency that prevents the protocol from achieving overall handover delays smaller than six seconds. One method to reduce the movement detection latency is to reduce the agent advertisement interval to a value smaller than the one specified in the RFC. However, real-time applications requiring a specific QoS level can still not be supported.

Mobile IPv6 on the other hand has a much better design in terms of feature integration and security. However, as an extension to version 6 of the internet protocol, it inherits a major drawback. This is the duplicate address detection, which ensures that an IPv6 address is not already assigned to another node on the same subnet. Our results have shown that with the duplicate address detection turned on, real-time traffic can not be supported even if we reduce the mobility detection factor because an additional second is needed to identify the uniqueness of the IP address.

In principle, Fast Mobile IPv6 also suffers from the drawback of the duplicate address detection latency, which is surely a knockout criteria. However, the specification shows a way of how to avoid the duplicate address detection. The results of the simulation studies of Fast Mobile IPv6 without duplicate address detection have shown that the network layer handover can be performed in less than 10 ms. If we add the time needed for scanning on the link layer, the complete handover is, with less than 50 ms, still fast enough to support real-time traffic. However, the communication between the link and the network layer has to be implemented.

Finally, with route optimization, the traffic which is normally routed over the home network can be minimized with only a little overhead on the handover latency. In future work, we will take a look on the performance of Hierarchical Mobile IPv6 [21] and evaluate if the handover performance can further be increased.

References

1. Valkó, A.G.: Cellular ip: A new approach to internet host mobility. SIGCOMM Comput. Commun. Rev. **29** (1999) 50–65
2. Ramjee, R., Varadhan, K., Salgarelli, L., Thuel, S.R., Wang, S.Y., Porta, T.L.: HAWAII: a domain-based approach for supporting mobility in wide-area wireless networks. IEEE/ACM Transactions on Networking (TON) **10**(3) (2002) 396–410
3. Perkins, C.E.: IP Mobility Support. RFC 2002, http://www.ietf.org/rfc/rfc2002.txt (1996)
4. Perkins, C.E.: IP Mobility Support for IPv4. RFC 3344, http://www.ietf.org/rfc/rfc3344.txt (2002)

5. Johnson, D., Perkins, C.E., Arkko, J.:   Mobility Support in IPv6.   RFC 3775, http://www.ietf.org/rfc/rfc3775.txt (2004)
6. Akyildiz, I.F., Xie, J., Mohanty, S.: A Survey of Mobility Management in Next-Generation All-IP-Based Wireless Systems. IEEE Wireless Communications 11 (2004) 16–28
7. Li, J., Chen, H.H.: Mobility Support for IP-Based Networks. IEEE Communications Magazine 43 (2005) 127–132
8. Kwon, D.H., Kim, Y.S., Bae, K.J., Suh, Y.J.:   Access router information protocol with FMIPv6 for efficient handovers and their implementations. In: GLOBECOM 2005 - IEEE Global Telecommunications Conference, St.Louis, MO, USA (2005) 3812–3817
9. Sharma, S., Zhu, N., Chiueh, T.: Low-Latency Mobile IP Handoff for Infrastructure-Mode Wireless LANs. IEEE Journal on Selected Areas in Communications 22(4) (2004) 643–652
10. E-Perkins, C.: Mobile IP Design Principles and Practices. Prentice Hall PTR (1998)
11. Conta, A., Deering, S.:   Generic Packet Tunneling in IPv6 Specification.   RFC 2473, http://www.ietf.org/rfc/rfc2473.txt (1998)
12. Deering, S., Hinden, R.:   Internet Protocol Version 6 (IPv6) Specification.   RFC 2460, http://www.ietf.org/rfc/rfc2460.txt (1998)
13. Johnson, D.B., Perkins, C.E.: Route Optimization in Mobile IP. Internet Draft draft-ietf-mobileip-optim-11.txt (work in progress) (2001)
14. Deering, S., Hinden, R.: Internet Protocol Version 6 Addressing Architecture. RFC 3513, http://www.ietf.org/rfc/rfc3513.txt (2003)
15. Koodli, R.: Fast Handovers for Mobile IPv6. RFC 4068, http://www.ietf.org/rfc/rfc4068.txt (2005)
16. (OPNET Modeler, OPNET University Program: http://www.opnet.com/services/university/)
17. Pries, R., Heck, K.: Simulative Study of the WLAN Handover Performance. In: OPNET-WORK 2005, Washington D.C., USA (2005)
18. ITU-T Recommendation G.711: Pulse Code Modulation (PCM) of Voice Frequencies. International Telecommunication Union (1998)
19. ITU-T Recommendation G.114: One Way Transmission Time (2000)
20. Moore, N.: Optimistic Duplicate Address Detection for IPv6. Internet Draft (2005)
21. Soliman, H., Castelluccia, C., Malki, K.E., Bellier, L.: Hierarchical Mobile IPv6 Mobility Management (HMIPv6). RFC 4140, http://www.ietf.org/rfc/rfc4140.txt (2005)

Network Selection Box: An Implementation of Seamless Communication

Stefan Chevul[1], Lennart Isaksson[1], Markus Fiedler[1],
Peter Lindberg[2], and Roland Waltersson[2]

[1] Dept. of Telecommunication Systems
School of Engineering
Blekinge Institute of Technology
371 79 Karlskrona, Sweden
{stefan.chevul, lennart.isaksson, markus.fiedler}@bth.se
[2] Saab Communication,
SE-351 80 Växjö, Sweden
{peter.lindberg, roland.waltersson}@saabgroup.com

Abstract. During recent years, it has become evident that mobility functions will have a profound impact on current and future wireless networks. Users expect service connectivity anywhere and anytime without having to think about the underlying communication systems used at that particular moment in time.

On this background, this paper presents a ready-to-deploy implementation of a mobility framework that supports seamless communication and represents an important enabler for adaptive applications through its simple QoS feedback mechanism. The framework selects the best available network through a decision algorithm that takes advantage of both experience with different network types for certain types of services and a link performance monitoring concept. The impact of the proposed framework on performance in terms of processing and throughput overhead is also discussed.

1 Introduction

The emergence of mobile networks has led to mobile end-users who expect access to information sources from anywhere at anytime. Such access should preferably be implemented in a seamless way: the user should be able to use a service without even having to think about which network technology is used at the moment. If a change of network technology is necessary, for instance due to the fact that a user leaves the coverage area of a Wireless Local Area Network (WLAN) hot spot and has to be connected via General Packet Radio Service (GPRS) instead, that change should happen more or less "on the fly", *i.e.* during ongoing communication without breaking the session. Thus, with *seamless communication*, we mean roaming between different types of networks or network operators in a handover-fashion, preserving connectivity to the selected service as far as possible and minimizing the performance degradation perceived by the application.

J. García-Vidal and L. Cerdà-Alabern (Eds.): Wireless and Mobility, LNCS 4396, pp. 171–185, 2007.
© Springer-Verlag Berlin Heidelberg 2007

The main goal is to be Always Best Connected (ABC). This is defined as always connected according to a decision based on different static and dynamic criteria aiming at optimizing the perception of a certain type of service.

Unfortunately, the Internet Protocol (IP) is not designed to deal gracefully with mobility. In IP, the point-of-attachment to the Internet is uniquely identified by the node's IP address. Thus, the IP address is tied tightly to the network where the device is located. In order to keep the Internet connectivity, the mobile device has to change its IP address every time its point-of-attachment to the Internet changes. This makes it impossible for the node to maintain transport layer connection during a location change. In other words, the connectivity breaks and the corresponding data transmission has to be re-initiated.

The Internet Engineering Task Force (IETF) has proposed Mobile IP (MIP) [1] as a solution for mobility in the future all-IP networks [2]. Although MIP has been standardized, it is hardly implemented in the Internet. The main reasons are the limited number of IPv4 addresses and MIP mechanism issues such as the triangular routing, frequent and long distant registration updates, and single-point of failures [3]. MIP also requires additional network elements to be introduced in the network, *e.g.* Foreign Agent and Home Agent *etc.* This has a direct impact on the cost of deploying a MIP enabled network. Floroiu *et al.* [4] reports of a case study of seamless handover in MIP for WLAN/GPRS. The results show that the Round Trip Time (RTT) is one of the important parameters indicating performance degradation. Seamless handover was only considered between two different types of wireless technologies.

In this paper, we present an implementation and evalutation of a new mobility management concept that supports seamless communication independetly of MIP. The concept is called Network Selection Box (NSB). Ideally, a NSB has several networks to select from *e.g.* General Packet Radio Service (GPRS), Universal Mobile Telecommunications System (UMTS), Wireless Local Area Network (WLAN), Digital Audio Broadcast (DAB), *etc.* Based on knowledge of the requirements of an application in terms of performance and cost and accessibility, the NSB will choose an appropriate network that fulfills these requisites at the lowest possible expense. In case an available network cannot meet the requirements but still provides connectivity, it is considered as as limited appropriate. Such a limitation might be known beforehand [5] – the service needs more than the network in question can offer – but it might also arise during operation, *e.g.* due to bad transmission conditions. The latter is revealed by more or less continuous monitoring of the different network paths. The NSB achieves seamless communication by hiding the change of current point-of-attachment to the Internet from the application through a virtual network interface (TAP), thus making the handover transparent for the application. Furthermore, through control messages to the application, the NSB provides a simple Quality of Service (QoS) feedback mechanism. One of the side effects of the NSB is the overhead in terms of more data to be sent and more processing to be performed. In some way this can be considered as the price of achieving seamless communication in the existing access networks without needing to make any changes in these networks.

The remainder of the paper is organized as follows. In Section 2 foundation of mobility issues are described together with a proposed solution. The architecture of the proposed mobility framework is described in detail in Section 3, while Section 4 presents a performance assessment of the NSB implementation in order to reveal its impact on the data streams as such. Finally Section 5 presents conclusion and outlook.

2   Foundations of Mobility and Seamless Communication

The main challenge when it comes to mobility is the fact that IP protocol does not support any mobility by itself. This is reflected in the way IP addresses are used, mainly as topological locators and network interface identities. Thus, every time a mobile node changes the point of attachment to the Internet, it changes its IP address. *E.g.*, a switch from WLAN to any cellular network, such as GPRS or UMTS, results in a change of IP address. Most transport protocols, *e.g.* Transmission Control Protocol (TCP), can not handle IP address changes without breaking the communication session.

In order to attain seamless communication, the communication session must be maintained as far as possible to ensure minimal packet loss and performance degradation perceived by the application. This can be achieved by hiding the change of the IP address from the application, *i.e.* making the handovers transparent to the application. The NSB adopts a virtual network interface (TAP) for this purpose, see Figure 1. The TAP device consists of a driver running in kernel mode and origins from the open source VPN project OpenVPN [6]. In

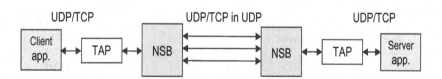

Fig. 1. Virtual Network Interface in the NSB

most respects, the TAP device works as any network interface; it will show up in Microsoft Windows XP as just another network connection, to which an IP address may be assigned. By allocating a low metric to the TAP device, we ensure that any application will bind its sockets to the TAP, unless if the application specifically states another network interface. At the sender, the original packet is encapsulated in a new User Datagram Protocol (UDP) datagram or Transmission Control Protocol (TCP) segment before sending it through the physical network interface to the Internet, as depicted in Figure 2. Thus, with the aid of the TAP device, a tunnel is implemented and the change of IP address is hidden from the application. On the receiver side, the outer header (by default a UDP header) is removed, and the original datagram sent by the application

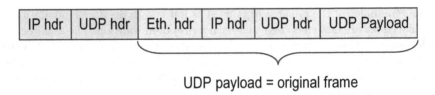

UDP payload = original frame

Fig. 2. Encapsulated packet for tunnelling purpose

is recovered. The application socket bound to the TAP device will receive the datagram seamlessly.

3   Network Selection Box (NSB) Architecture

The NSB is implemented as client-server architecture; the building blocks are shown in Figure 3. The NSB consists of the following building blocks: TAP device, NSB Controller, Network Selector, Link Monitor, Link Parameter database and Roaming Policy.

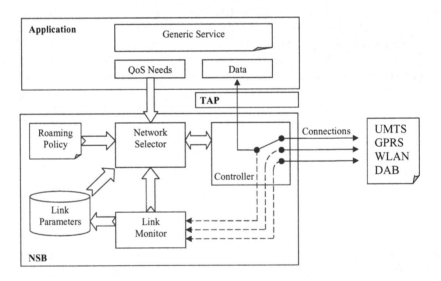

Fig. 3. Building blocks of the NSB

The *Controller* is responsible for sending packets, receiving packets, sending and reacting to control messages, and executing handovers between the different available wireless networks. The Controller on the server side is also responsible for allocating virtual IP addresses to clients and, for each client, it keeps a list with available networks (and their perceived quality) that packets may be sent over. This database is updated by control messages sent from clients.

The *Network Selector* determines the best network to use at the moment. For this purpose, a simple decision algorithm is implemented. The decision algorithm decides for each packet to be sent which network to choose. This decision is based upon recent measurements of link performance in terms of RTT, packet loss and time-outs. This task is carried out by the *Link Monitor*. These values are stored in the *Link Parameter database* on the server and in a separate database on the client. Based on own measurements [7,8], an a-priory network selection is derived [5].

The *Roaming Policy* depends on general scanning and predefined priorities depending on the service selected. The predefined priorities are also based on current status of the connection. The general scanning also depends on distinction of rank, which means choosing the best technology in advance. For example, an a-priory for streaming service is associated with the following list of priorities: WLAN (1), UMTS (2), and GPRS (3). Now let us imagine that there is no WLAN connectivity, and that GPRS experiences a high RTT. In this case the network selector decides that UMTS is currently the best link to send packets over, although UMTS initially had a lower priority than the WLAN network.

3.1   Implementation and Communication Management

Both NSB Client and Server were implemented on desktop computers, running the popular Microsoft Windows XP. C# .NET was used as the programming language.

The NSB uses blocking, synchronous send and receive operations, running in different threads. On the client, one socket is created for each network. All sockets are UDP sockets. UDP is better suited for encapsulation of IP since UDP provides a connectionless transmission medium for IP, thus avoiding nesting one reliability layer into another *i.e.* TCP over TCP that essentially produces a whole level of redundancy.

To assure that packets are sent on the intended interface, a route is created in the routing table for each added network, with the same metric value as the other networks. In this way, Windows will not route packets in an undesirable way.

Prior to sending each packets, the NSB server refers to the tables in the Controler and the `evaluateSend()` method in the Network Selector to find the best network to use. The NSB client uses a similar table and the `evaluateSend()` method. In this way, the NSB can be seen as a multiplexer.

The NSB uses control messages for communication management between NSB client and server. Furthermore, the control messages are also used to monitor network performance. All control messages use the same UDP sockets as the data traffic with the exception of the `APPPREF` message, which uses a separate port. Table 1 lists the control messages.

The two control messages `REGISTER` and `ACKREGISTER` are used for address allocation. The client sends a `REGISTER` request together with information about his first network. The server answers with an `ACKREGISTER` message containing the virtual IP. In this sense the server operates much like a Dynamic Host Configuration Protocol (DHCP) server, although the address lease times are

Table 1. NSB control messages

Message	Direction	Interface	Explanation
REGISTER	Client – Server	NSB – NSB	Register with server and get a virtual IP.
ACKREGISTER	Server – Client	NSB – NSB	Response to register request.
ADDNET	Client – Server	NSB – NSB	A new network is available.
REMOVENET	Client – Server	NSB – NSB	A network was lost.
IAMALIVE	Client – Server	NSB – NSB	Client is alive and wants to keep his virtual IP.
BYE	Client – Server	NSB – NSB	Client logging of, release virtual IP.
NETSTAT	Both ways	NSB – NSB	Network statistics.
ACKNETSTAT	Both ways	NSB – NSB	Response to NETSTAT message.
APPPREF	App.	App. – NSB	For controlling NSB settings and QoS feedback.

generally infinite. The client will keep this address until it disconnects with the control message BYE.

ADDNET and REMOVENET are sent by the client when a new network is connected or when a connection is lost. ADDNET contains the virtual IP of the client, and information about the new network. The REMOVENET message is not that critical, as the server's monitor will discover a network loss anyway within time. It is sent to speed up the server's adoption to the new situation.

IAMALIVE is used by the client to hold on to a virtual IP address. The server expects all clients to send this message periodically, otherwise it assumes that the client has crashed without notification and releases the client's virtual IP so that others can use it. When the client NSB shuts down normally, it sends a BYE message to tell the server that it does not need its virtual IP anymore.

Applications have that possibility to control the NSB by using the APPPREF control message. The message contains information about the requirements of the application in terms of e.g. performance and cost. This information is used by the Network Selector to find the most suitable network to use. Applications do not need to control the NSB as the NSB implements automatic network selection. APPPREF are also used by the application in order to enquire QoS status of the network connection used at the moment.

Through control messages NETSTAT (issued by the sender and includes a time stamp) and ACKNETSTAT (issued by the receiver upon reception of a NETSTAT message) the application-level RTT is measured. If no ACKNETSTAT message has been received for a predefined period of time, it is considered lost. A specific network is classified as unavailable when a predefined number of ACKNETSTAT are lost. According to our experience, this value is set to five. However, the value might be further tuned for special network and application scenarios.

In addition, the NETSTAT and ACKNETSTAT packets contain information about how many packets that were sent by the sender and received at the receiver side in the last time period. In this way, packet loss can be measured.

4 Performance Evalutation of the NSB

The NSB can be viewed as a middleware, therefore its impact on the network performance as perceived by the application must be evaluated. We investigate whether the NSB is transparent from a performance viewpoint or it is a bottleneck that introduces loss and throughput reductions. To this end measurement of streaming traffic is considered. The measurements are produced by using a cooperative UDP tool, consisting of a traffic generator and a receiver. Both generator and receiver have to run simultaneously at each end in order to implement coordinated and comparative measurements. The generator, developed in C#, is trying to send UDP datagrams of constant length as regularly as possible with a sequence number inside each datagram. The datagrams are not sent *back-to-back*, but spaced in order to yield a certain load, hence exact timing on the sender side is important. The minimal time the packets are spaced is hereafter called *inter-packet delay*. The software tries to keep this value as closely as possible. Since the original *C#* time stamp resolution is limited to 10 milliseconds, specific coding was necessary to improve the time stamp resolution to one thousand of a millisecond. This was achieved by using *performance counters* in conjunction with the system time to provide smaller time increments. To this aim the kernel32.dll functions QueryPerformanceCounter and QueryPerformanceFrequency were used. References [9] and [10] discuss the time stamping issue in detail.

4.1 Measurement Setup

For the measurements, two scenarios were considered: the first is called the *downlink scenario* (*cf.* Figure 4), in which the client is connected to a base station (BS) and the server to the Internet via 100 Mbps Ethernet. The second one is called the *uplink scenario* (*cf.* Figure 4), in which the server is connected to a BS and the client to the Internet via 100 Mbps Ethernet. The scenario names are based on the direction of the data traffic in reference to the BS. The encapsulation used by the TAP device, *cf.* Figure 2, leads to an overhead of 42

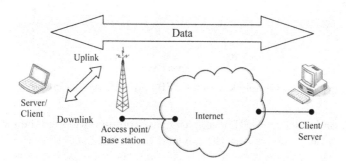

Fig. 4. Uplink and downlink scenario

bytes that potentially can lead to undesirable fragmentation. Hence, the tool takes as a parameter the desired packet length in order to yield comparable load on the link.

4.2   Measurements and Results

The first case presented is a modestly loaded UMTS uplink measurement where the NSB is not used. By choosing a payload size of 158 bytes and a nominal inter-packet delay of 100 ms, the server transmission rate was set to 12.64 kbps which is matched by the averaged throughput at the application for both server and client. The plots from the time domain are displayed in Figure 5. Jitter at the senders sleep function is hardly visible, cf. Figure 5 (top). Figure 5 (second from top) shows very small jitter in the senders send function, three orders of magnitude smaller as compared to the jitter at senders sleep function. The inter-packet delay at the client side, cf. Figure 5 (bottom), displays distinct burst deviations that seem to originate from the UMTS channel itself. The client does not indicate any packet loss.

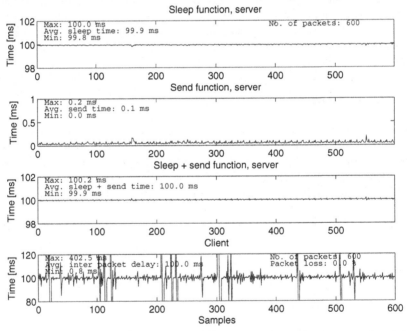

Fig. 5. Timeplot UMTS uplink without NSB and with 100 ms inter-packet delay

In the second case, the NSB is activated and compensation for the introduced overhead is done by decreasing the payload by the size of the overhead, i.e. 42 bytes. Thus, the payload is set to 116 bytes and the frame size on the link layer is kept the same, i.e. 200 bytes. The nominal inter-packet delay is also maintained at 100 ms. Figure 6 indicates a rather small jitter at the client side. Distinct burst deviations are identified. As in the previous case, these bursts seem to originate from the UMTS channel itself, rather than from the NSB. Still the client does not indicate any packet loss. Table 3 summarizes the statistical results from all measurements, including the uplink measurements.

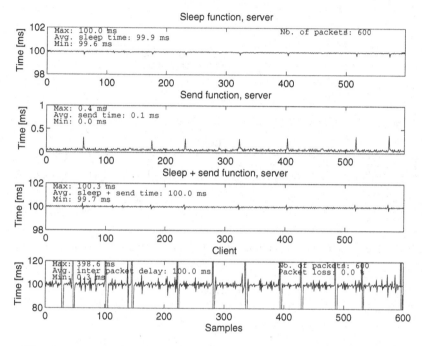

Fig. 6. Timeplot UMTS uplink with NSB and 100 ms inter-packet delay

The UMTS downlink case without NSB is depicted in Figure 7. Here the payload size is set to 1158 bytes and a nominal inter-packet delay to 100 ms. The server transmission rate was set to 92.64 kbps, which is matched by the averaged throughput at the application for both server and client. Figure 7 shows that the mean inter-packet delay at the client side is slightly smaller than the mean inter-packet delay at the server, displaying distinct burst deviations. The client does not experience any packet loss. Figure 8, shows the UMTS downlink case when the NSB is activated. The payload is set 1116 bytes in order to compensate for the overhead introduced by the NSB. The frame size of the link layer amounts to 1200 bytes. The nominal inter-packet delay is also maintained at 100 ms. No packet loss is perceived by the client. However, Figure 8 (bottom) displays several distinct burst deviations indicating that more jitter is perceived by the client. Table 3 summarizes the statistical results of the downlink measurements.

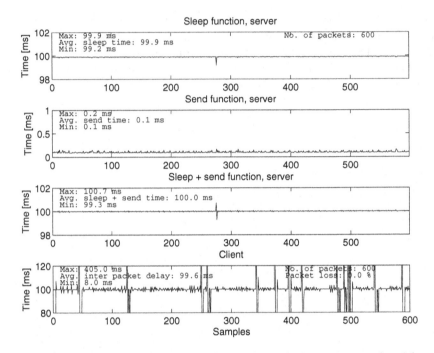

Fig. 7. Timeplot UMTS downlink without NSB and 100 ms inter-packet delay

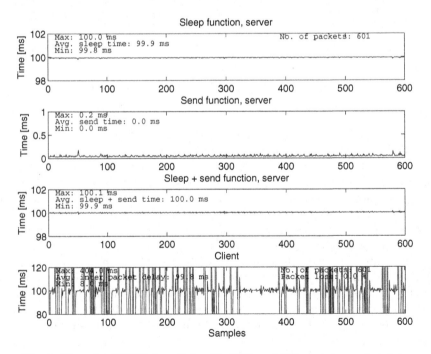

Fig. 8. Timeplot UMTS downlink with NSB and 100 ms inter-packet delay

The next case is a stress test of the NSB. To this aim, the UMTS network is replaced with a Local Area Network (LAN) 10 Mbps link. The payload size is set to 1458 bytes with no NSB used and 1416 bytes with NSB activated. Thus, the frame size at the link layer is kept at 1500 bytes. When the NSB is not used, the jitter perceived by the client is rather high together with some moderate amount of packet loss, *cf.* Figure 9. On the other hand, when NSB is activated, the client still perceives rather high jitter while there is no packet loss, *cf.* Figure 10. Table 3 summarizes the statistical results from all measurements.

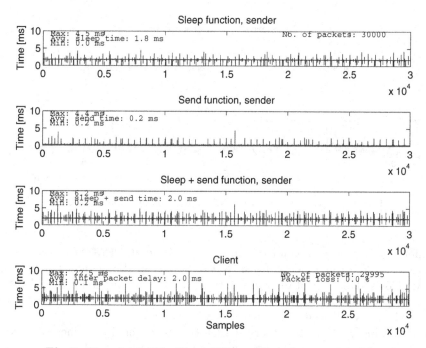

Fig. 9. Timeplot LAN without NSB and 2 ms inter-packet delay

4.3   Handover Delays

Handover delays between WLAN and UMTS were investigated. Two scenarios were considered: the first addresses handover without backup network, in which the client first has to detect the network loss, then make a decision regarding which network to connect to, and finally establish the connection. This means that when connecting to the UMTS network, the time for dialling is included in the delay. In the second scenario, handover with a backup network is considered. In this scenario the UMTS network is already connected, thus the delay does not include time for dialling although it includes the time to detect loss of network connection. Network loss can be detected either by the loss of ACKNETSTAT control messages or through the socket API reporting failed a send. Hence, choosing

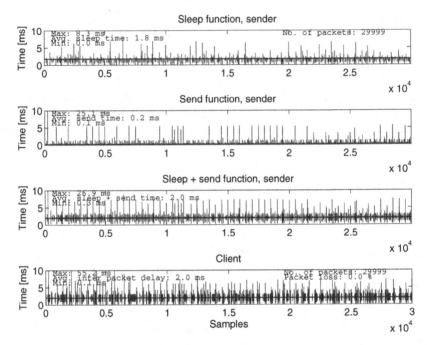

Fig. 10. Timeplot LAN with NSB and 2 ms inter-packet delay

a different parameter value for the number of missed ACKNETSTAT might reduce the time for detecting a network loss. Network loss can also be detected through the Windows Management Instrumentation (WMI). This method was used in the early stage of the NSB development but was abandoned due to severe memory leakage in the WMI that was not resolved by Microsoft.

From Table 2 it can be observed that the handover delay when a backup UMTS network exists is considerably shorter as compared to the case when no backup network exists. The longer delay partly arises from the additional time it take to connect to the UMTS, *i.e.* the time it takes for the modem to dial the UMTS connection.

The handover delay can be further reduced by decreasing the times for detecting network loss, which can be achieved by choosing different parameter values for the number of missing ACKNETSTAT control message.

Table 2. NSB handover delay between WLAN and UMTS networks

	min [s]	mean [s]	max [s]
without backup network	6.98	9.13	10.26
with backup network	2.18	3.10	4.00

4.4   Relative Overhead vs. Frame Size Ration

The encapsulation used by the TAP device, *cf.* Figure 2, implies an overhead of 42 bytes. This has a minor impact on the application-perceived throughput hence the MTU of application is reduced in order to avoid fragmentation on the link layer. The overhead also results in larger frame size on the link layer. On the other hand, large frames at the link layer have a positive effect on the efficiency.

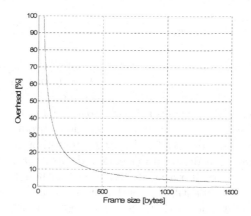

Fig. 11. Relative overhead vs. frame size ration

Table 3. Overview of the NSB performance assessment

		UMTS				LAN	
		uplink		downlink			
		IPD 100 ms		IPD 100 ms		IPD 2 ms	
		excl. NSB	incl. NSB	excl. NSB	incl. NSB	excl. NSB	incl. NSB
sleep function, server [ms]	min	98.8	99.6	99.2	99.8	0.0	0.00
	mean	99.9	99.9	99.9	99.9	1.8	1.8
	max	100.0	100.0	99.9	100.0	4.5	8.3
	stddev	0.0	0.0	0.0	0.0	0.1	0.2
send function, server [ms]	min	0.0	0.0	0.1	0.0	0.2	0.1
	mean	0.1	0.1	0.1	0.0	0.2	0.2
	max	0.2	0.4	0.2	0.2	4.4	25.1
	stddev	0.0	0.0	0.0	0.0	0.1	0.3
sleep + send function, server [ms]	min	98.9	99.7	99.3	99.9	0.2	0.3
	mean	100.0	100.0	100.0	100.0	2.0	2.0
	max	100.2	100.3	100.7	100.1	6.2	26.9
	stddev	0.0	0.0	0.0	0.0	0.2	0.3
client [ms]	min	0.8	0.3	8.0	8.0	0.0	0.0
	mean	100.0	100.0	99.6	99.8	2.00	2.0
	max	402.5	398.6	405.0	404.0	22.5	55.2
	stddev	32.1	37.1	34.9	82.2	0.3	0.5

In Figure 11 the ratio between the overhead and frame size is plotted. When using frames larger than 450 byte the overhead is less than 10 % of the frame size.

Table 3 summarizes the statistical results from the measurements. We recognize that the client perceives more jitter than the server. This behaviour has also been observed in [7,8,5]. However, the jitter seems to originate from the physical layer rather than from the NSB. In fact even when considering different load scenarios, we have not seen any considerable differences between using the NSB or not doing so.

5   Conclusion and Outlook

We have described and evaluated a ready-to-deploy mobility framework that supports seamless communication and represents an important enabler for adaptive applications through a simple QoS feedback mechanism. The framework is called NSB, and ideally has several networks to select from *e.g.* GPRS, UMTS, WLAN, *etc.* The design of the NSB has been described in detail, where the network selection is based on measured network performance.

Performance evaluation of the framework indicates that the NSB is transparent to the upper layers, in terms of throughput, although rather small jitter at the receiver has been identified. The fact that no loss occurred during the measurements is partly due to that the server uses a blocking send function. Hence, in case the server transmits datagrams too fast, the send function itself holds packets until they can be sent, which can be considered as some kind of force feed-back. No performance implication was found besides the tunnel-typical overhead of 42 bytes.

Furthermore, measurements of handover delays between WLAN and UMTS networks indicate that rather short handover delays can be achieved when a backup network such as UMTS was available. The handover delays are highly dependent on how fast a network loss can be detected and whether there exists backup network connectivity.

Future work includes a refined roaming strategy that will take advanced performance monitoring into account and faster handover by optimizing the corresponding parameter setting. Also additional measurements of one-way delays and TCP goodput are considered.

References

1. C. Perkins. IP Mobility Support for IPv4. Technical Report IETF RFC 3344, August 2002.
2. L. Morand and S. Tessier. Global Mobility Approach with Mobile IP in All IP Networks. In *IEEE International Conf. on Communications (ICC)*, pages 2075–2079, May 2002.
3. J-.W. Lin and J. Arul. An efficient fault-tolerant approach for Mobile IP in wireless systems. In *IEEE Trans. on Mobile Computing*, volume 2, pages 207–220, July-Sept. 2003.

4. J.W. Floroiu, R. Ruppelt, D. Sisalem, and J. Voglimacci. Seamless handover in terrestrial radio access networks: a case study. *IEEE Communications Magazine*, 41(11):110–116, Nov. 2003.
5. M. Fiedler, L. Isaksson, S. Chevul, P. Lindberg, and J. Karlsson. Measurements and Analysis of Application-Perceived Throughput via Mobile Links. In *Proceedings of the 2005 3rd Performance Modeling and Evaluation of Heterogeneous Networks (HET-NETs)*, July 2005.
6. OpenVPN. URL: http://openvpn.net/.
7. S. Chevul, J. Karlsson, L. Isaksson, M. Fiedler, P. Lindberg, and L. Strandén. Measurements of application-perceived throughput in DAB, GPRS, UMTS and WLAN Environments. In *Proceedings of RVK'05*, Linköping, Sweden, June 2005.
8. L. Isaksson, S. Chevul, M. Fiedler, J. Karlsson, and P. Lindberg. Application-Perceived Throughput Process in Wireless Systems. In *Proceedings of ICMCS'05*, Montreal, Canada, August 2005.
9. S. Chevul. *On Application-Perceived Quality of Service in Wireless Networks*. Licentiate Dissertation Series No. 2006:11. Blekinge Institute of Technology, 2006.
10. S. Chevul, L. Isaksson, M. Fiedler, and P. Lindberg. Measurement of Application-Perceived Throughput of an E2E VPN Connection Using a GPRS Network. In *Wireless Systems and Network Architectures in Next Generation Internet, Second International Workshop of the EURO-NGI Network of Excellence*, pages 255–268, Villa Vigoni, Italy, 2005.

Joint Connection and Packet Level Analysis in W-CDMA Radio Interface

Vilius Benetis[1], Larissa Popova[2], and Villy Bæk Iversen[1]

[1] COM·DTU
Technical University of Denmark,
Kongens Lyngby, Denmark
{vb,vbi}@com.dtu.dk
[2] Lehrstuhl für Mobilkommunikation,
Universität Erlangen-Nürnberg, Germany
popova@LNT.de

Abstract. This work introduces a new analytical method for performance evaluation of wireless packet-oriented networks. Unlike traditional call admission control procedures commonly used for performance evaluation of wireless networks, this paper deals with the problem of coupling connection and packet level QoS characteristics by analysis. At connection level we use the Blocked-Calls-Cleared (BCC) model, whereas at packet level we use the Blocked-Call-Interfered (BCI) model which has no immediate feedback from packet level to connection level about lost data. At connection level we use the convolution algorithm which defines the feasible state space at packet level. At packet level we take into consideration wireless interference (soft blocking). The traffic is modeled as multi-rate Binomial-Poisson-Pascal (BPP-) traffic at connection level and *on-off* traffic at packet level. We obtain individual performance measures for each service, both at connection level and at packet level. By case studies we investigate the trade-off between the two levels to meet Grade of Service (GoS) requirements for cellular networks with WCDMA radio interface.

Keywords: Two-level analysis, WCDMA, multi-service wireless network, connection level, packet level, soft blocking, teletraffic, Blocked-Calls-Cleared, Blocked-Calls-Held, Blocked-Calls-Interfered models.

1 Introduction

Rapid growth of wireless multimedia services and their demand for high data rates put a considerable load onto the valuable and limited resources of radio networks. The third generation of wireless networks employs packet-switching technology to gain higher efficiency and better utilization of scarce radio resources to serve multimedia.

In general, applications and services can be divided in two groups: real-time demanding and non-real time demanding. The main distinguishing factor between these service classes is the delay sensitivity; streaming traffic is highly delay sensitive, while non-real time applications such as ftp and e-mail are delay

J. García-Vidal and L. Cerdà-Alabern (Eds.): Wireless and Mobility, LNCS 4396, pp. 186–199, 2007.

insensitive and can tolerate delay variations. Most multimedia applications from the last group do not require dedicated circuits for the entire duration of connection. They have variable bit rate (VBR) with packet transmission at peak rates. Thus connections have average rates less than peak rates, and we may overbook the system and admit new calls even if their peak rates cannot be continuously accommodated. We may still maintain an acceptable performance level of the system due to statistical multiplexing among services. However such flexibility makes the call admission control (CAC) procedure more complex.

To address this problem and to ensure a sufficient quality-of-service (QoS) level for the end-to-end packet-users, performance metrics must be considered at both connection and packet levels. Traffic sources at connection level are characterized by *arrival process* and *service process*. At packet level a connection is characterized by *activity factor* (percentage of time in *on* state) and bandwidth requirement during *on* periods. The model is insensitive to connection duration, and only the activity factor a is of importance for the *on-off* statistical multiplexing.

QoS parameters at connection-level are *blocking probability*, which measures service connectivity, and *handover dropping probability* (beyond the scope of this work). At this level, new connections will experience a blocking level which depend on both the bandwidth required and the state (load) of the system. A new call attempt is blocked if the actual load of the system surpasses a certain level. A congestion at this level may be denoted as a hard blocking.

QoS measures at packet level are *packet loss probability* and *packet delay*. At packet level each connection is accepted with a certain peak rate, and will become an *on-off* sources transmitting at peak rate during *on* periods and at zero or a constant lower rate during *off* periods (for example web browsing or VoIP). At packet level there is no feedback to the user and thus a packet will be transmitted independently of whether it is delayed or (partly) lost. This leads to degradation of service quality perceived by the users. In this context packet-level and connection-level QoS becomes a trade-off and their joint optimization should be considered.

The actual load of the existing 3G packet-oriented networks is still not sufficiently researched to observe and analyze the system behavior during the busy hour, but two possible ways of predicting the performance of 3G networks are feasible: analytical modeling and simulations.

Most CAC algorithms only deal with connection level performance measure [14,12]. These approaches are correct and sufficient as long as performance of circuit-switched services is analyzed. Optimization problems of QoS in wireless networks accommodating constant bit rate (CBR) services has been extensively studied [15,13]. In this case, the packet-level QoS is assured as long as the required bandwidth is guaranteed, and the problem becomes the same as for connection-oriented circuit-switched services. Thus, the joint optimization two-level QoS problem can be reduced to analyzing the system behavior at connection-level. On the other hand in works addressing packet-level QoS aspects, algorithms for applying appropriate traffic performance relation to attain

QoS targets for a given population of the specified kind of users are typically not considered. In [1,3,6] considerable efforts are spent on the design of a variety of QoS strategies and mechanisms.

Currently, there are only a few proposals addressing connection and packet-level QoS metrics simultaneously. New-call blocking probabilities, handover-call dropping probabilities, and packet losses are calculated in [5] based on a joint connection and packet-level QoS. However a key feature of wireless networks, such as the interference limited soft capacity, has so far not been included into the model.

In all studies mentioned above system performance was analyzed using suitable simulation tools. An analytical approach for performance estimation in packet-oriented networks with *on-off* traffic sources is proposed in [11]. Connections arrivals are modeled by batch Poisson processes and at packet level the classical blocked packets (calls) cleared model (BCC) is assumed. However, the model is analyzed for two levels in a separate manner and assuming a product form, i.e. service independence. The reduced load due to lost packets, i.e. reduction of connection time, is not taken into account at connection level, and thus the model is an approximation.

The motivation behind our work is to investigate the QoS provisioning problem in wireless packet-oriented cellular networks by taking the interaction between the two service levels (admission control procedure and call handling process) into account. Although we focus our research on UMTS Radio Access Network (UTRAN) and consider *on-off* variable bit rate traffic (VBR) the principle can also be applied to the other systems such as ATM, MPLS.

The blocking probability of a new connection and the probability of packet loss are our primary QoS metrics for connection level and packet level, respectively. Blocked Calls Held model is used for packet level analysis.

The work presented is based on analysis and differs from other analytical solutions for QoS estimation of packet-oriented networks in the way performance results are evaluated, taking into account both the specifics of UTRAN, e.g. joint behaviour of two QoS provisioning levels, as well as wireless interference, etc. The analytical method demonstrates the flexibility and accuracy of our approach.

Numerical results indicate that the user admission control procedure and call handling process are not independent and that their interaction has a significant effect on the QoS.

The paper is organized as follows. Section 2 presents an analytical model applied for estimation of joint connection-level and packet-level QoS for VBR traffic in UMTS networks. In Section 3, the proposed algorithm is presented. Numerical results are given in Section 4, where the performance of the proposed scheme is evaluated for realistic UMTS scenario. Finally, we summarize the key issues in Section 5.

2   System and Traffic Models

In this section we describe the system considered and the traffic model.

2.1   UMTS Capacity: Basic Relations and Definitions

The system considered is a cellular UMTS network. We examine the performance of one single cell within a multi-cell environment. We assume that the overall system is homogeneous in traffic patterns and load, and that it is in statistical equilibrium.

We concentrate our research on UTRAN, where all users served by a given cell make use of the same frequency channel. Differentiation of the transmitted signals is possible by application of orthogonal codes [10].

Knowledge about idle spreading codes in the cell is not sufficient to determine the maximum number of simultaneous users a UMTS system can support while maintaining QoS requirements. The self-induced interference occurring due to multi-path propagation in a radio channel restrict the capacity of the UTRAN, as capacity of UMTS systems tends to be limited in the coverage before they run out of available codes. Normally it is estimated that maximal usage of radio interface resources without violating the QoS agreement will be at 50-80 %.

The analysis of the UTRAN system capacity is performed using two-step top-down analytical model: a connection level and a packet level.

The pole capacity of the system (cell) is n bandwidth units to be referred to as channels. We choose the bandwidth unit so that all services use an integral number of channels. We assume a fully accessible group which is offered multi-service traffic streams, none of the service class have a priority over other classes. The conversion from power-interference-based capacity into channel-based capacity is done as in [7].

2.2   Traffic Model

At connection level the network serves N independent classes of Binomial-Poisson-Pascal (BPP) traffic streams with traffic intensities $\lambda_i(j)$, where j i number of connections of traffic stream class i in the system. The peakedness is Z_i $(i = 1, \ldots, N)$ [2]. Streams of service class i have resource requirement d_i channels, where $i = 1, \ldots, N$.

A stream of type i requires d_i channels. The mean service time for stream of type i is μ_i^{-1}. Traffic stream i is characterized by mean offered traffic A_i and peakedness Z_i. For a Poisson arrival process, $A_i = \lambda_i/\mu_i$ is the offered traffic measured in number of connections, and the peakedness is one. For the Binomial (Engset) case we have a positive number of sources and the arrival rate when x_i sources are busy is $(S_i - x_i)\gamma_i$. For the Pascal case the arrival rate is $(S_i + x_i)\gamma_i$ when x_i sources are busy. For a linear state-dependent Poisson arrival process the offered traffic is $A_i = S(1 - Z_i)$, where S_i is the number of traffic sources. The peakedness is $Z_i = 1/(1 + \beta_i)$, where $\beta_i = \gamma_i/\mu_i$, and γ_i is the arrival rate of an idle source. Mathematically, we can deal with Pascal traffic using the same formulæ as for Engset by letting S_i and β_i be negative. For Engset traffic peakedness is less than one (smooth traffic), whereas for Pascal traffic peakedness is greater than one (bursty traffic). We have the following relations between the two representations:

$$A = S \cdot \frac{\beta}{1+\beta}, \qquad Z = \frac{1}{1+\beta},$$
$$\beta = \frac{1-Z}{Z}, \qquad S = \frac{A}{1-Z}. \tag{1}$$

For each service class, a two-state *on-off* model is used to describe the traffic stream at packet level. The user of service class i can alternate between the active *on*-mode, requiring the data rate d_i or the inactive *off*-mode, using no resources. An activity factor a_i defines the proportion of time stream i spends in *on*-mode.

The service time for the packet calls (packet data session) is composed of multiple packet data calls with periods of inactivity in between. Service time distributions are assumed to be any general time distribution with a mean of μ_i^{-1}, independent of the arrival process.

We denote the traffic load, which reflects the load of all users, which are in *on*--mode, as the effective system load. The effective system load depends on the activity factor of each particular stream class.

3   Mathematical Model and Algorithms

3.1   Connection Level

At this level new connections will experience blocking, with a probability which depends on both the bandwidth required and the state of the system. A new call attempt is blocked if the actual load of the system surpasses a certain level. At this level we use the Blocked-Calls-Cleared (BCC) model (Fig. 1). This system may be evaluated for *BPP* multi-rate traffic streams using either the convolution algorithm allowing for minimum and maximum allocation for each stream [9], or the generalized state-based algorithm allowing for trunk reservation [8,16]. Poisson batch arrivals as well can be dealt with but are not considered in this paper. For each service we may evaluate time congestion E, call congestion B, and traffic congestion C. [9]. These congestion measures are identical for Poisson arrival processes (*PASTA*-property), but for Engset and Pascal traffic the relevant measure is the traffic congestion C, i.e. the proportion of offered traffic which is lost. Congestion at this level may be denoted as hard blocking.

3.2   Packet Level

At packet level each connection is accepted with a certain peak rate d_i channels. It will be *on–off* sources transmitting at peak rate during *on* periods and with zero rate during *off* periods. The proportion of time stream i is on s called the activity factor $a_i, 0 < a_i \leq 1$. Thus the actual average transmission rate $(a_i\, d_i)$ will be lower than the peak rate and due to statistical multiplexing advantages we may overbook the system at connection level admission control. At packet level there is no feedback to the user, and thus a packet will be transmitted independently of whether it is (partly) lost. This is modeled by Fry-Molina's Blocked-Calls-Held (BCH) model where call means packet [4]. In our models we use a modified version, Blocked-Calls-Interfered (BCI), where in case of overload all the packets which are blocked due to the wireless interference will be lost (Fig. 1). At packet level we have loss due to overload in multiplexing streams (other users in own cell) and because of interference from neighboring cells. This neighbor cell interference is modeled as a Log-Normal distributed random variable described in [7]. For a given number of accepted heterogeneous connections we evaluate the loss due to interference at packet level using multi-rate Engset BCI models and incorporating other cell interference. Blocking at packet level is called soft blocking and depends on both the state of the system and the bandwidth of the source as described in [7]. The main performance measure for the BCI–model is the system throughput, which can be directly derived from the rate of successful packet transmissions.

This loss should be below a certain level to ensure the QoS, and thus we may by averaging the loss at packet level give feedback to the connection level. The blocking at connection level should not depend on fluctuations of interference at packet-time scale, but upon the blocking at a time scale of same order as connections mean holding times.

The principles of Blocked-Calls-Cleared (BCC) and Blocked-Calls-Held (BCH) and Blocked-Calls-Interfered (BCI) models are illustrated in Fig. 1.

The numerical evaluation of the model is rather demanding. At connection level we apply the convolution algorithm to calculate the normalization constant and the individual state probabilities. For each state at connection level we have a fixed number of on-off sources which offer traffic at packet level. By finding the performance at packet level for each state at connection level and summing over all states, we find the performance of the system at both levels.

4   Analysis of Results

In the following some numerical examples of the proposed method for performance estimation in wireless packet-oriented networks are presented. First case shows how performance measures for a particular traffic mix are obtained, the second one demonstrates effects of changing offered traffic load. The two last examples investigates the quality of service level by changing the packet drop level and the activity factor, respectively.

4.1   Performance of a Traffic Mix

Performance measures of a particular traffic mix are presented below. Our calculations are based on system and traffic parameters defined in Table 1. The service mix data was selected in the following way. Three services ($N = 3$) were defined being

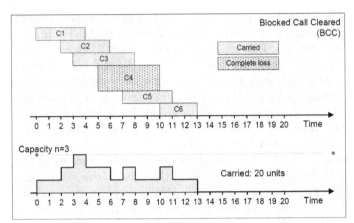

(a) Blocked-Calls-Cleared (BCC) model

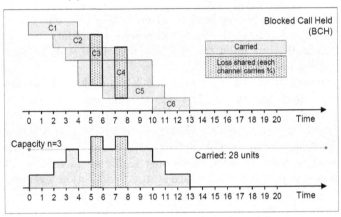

(b) Blocked-Calls-Held (BCH) model

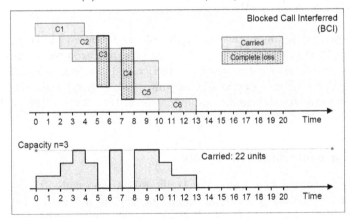

(c) Blocked-Calls-Held (BCI) model with Interference

Fig. 1. Blocked-Call models

- voice (regular narrow-band: $Z_1 = 1, d_1 = 1, a_1 = 0.5$),
- web browsing (quite regular broadband: $Z_2 = 0.2, d_2 = 10, a_2 = 0.3$),
- e-mail (bursty narrow-band: $Z_3 = 1.5, d_3 = 2, a_3 = 0.7$).

The service definitions are given in Table 1.

We denote the cell capacity unit as *a channel*, which equals to the amount of resources needed to carry one voice call. The maximum cell capacity is $n = 128$ channels (which is the pole capacity of the cell). The more elaborate derivation can be done as described in [7].

In the example we show the system behavior in case when the offered load is close to full cell capacity (127.5 erlang), where each service class contributes with approximately the same amount of traffic.

Table 1. Service traffic description. Cell parameters are: other-to-own-cell interference ratio is $i = 0.55$, and maximum number of channels in the system $n = 128$.

Stream	$i=1$: Poisson (voice)	$i=2$: Binomial (web browsing)	$i=3$: Pascal (e-mail)	Total
λ_i	1	–	–	
S_i	∞	5	-37	
γ_i	0	4	$-\frac{1}{3}$	
μ_i	1	1	1	
$Z_i = \frac{1}{1+\frac{\gamma}{\mu}}$	1	0.2	1.5	
d_i	1	10	2	
$A_i = S(1-Z)d$	50.5	40	37	127.5
a_i	0.5	0.3	0.7	
$A_{c_p} = A_i\, a_i$	25.25	12	25.9	63.15

The other cell interference b_x is modeled by a log-normal distribution as described in [7]. The mean value of the other cell interference is chosen equal to variance to indicate the other cell load is of medium level with average fluctuations. Calculations were done as well for the case with small fluctuations (the variance equals $1/10$ of the mean value) and for the large fluctuations of interference (the variance is two times bigger than the mean value). Graphs of factor b_x for all three cases is presented in Fig. 2. All further calculations are only presented by the case with mean value equal to the variance.

Performance results of defined setup are presented in the Table 2 and should be read as follows.

E_i, C_i and B_i denotes time, traffic and call congestion at connection level, respectively (see definition of congestions in [9]). Y_i is carried traffic at connection

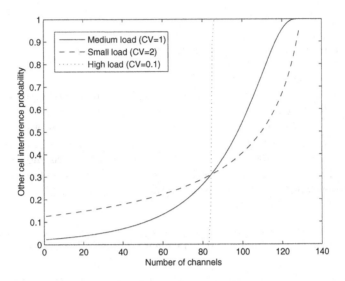

Fig. 2. Other-cell-interference contribution b_x

level, $A_i^p = Y_i \cdot a_i$ is traffic accepted at packet level (carried traffic at connection level scaled down by activity factor). Y_i^p is carried traffic at packet level. $C_i^p =)A_i^p - Y_i^p)/A_i^p$ is traffic congestion at packet level.

$Y_i^{p_{th}}$ is the carried traffic for BCH model, where loss level is identified by threshold and without neighbor cell interference, see Fig. 1. BCH should be used in non-wireless environments like MPLS. $C_i^{p_{th}} = (A_i^p - Y_i^{p_{th}})/A_i^p$ is proportion of lost traffic at packet level. Traffic congestion expresses the proportion of information lost at packet level.

4.2   Analyzing Trends by Load Change

A goal of this analysis is to study how system performance changes when the load is altered. System load is changed by keeping offered load from two service classes fixed and varying the 3rd traffic class. In figures presented below, web browsing and email traffic are fixed and voice traffic load (A_1) is increased from 8 till 48 erlang, while the other two services have the same load as shown in Table 1. Similar calculations for other services were performed as well.

The graph (a) of Fig. 3 presents the change of carried traffic for each service at connection level. The results are as expected and may also be obtained either by convolution algorithm or by generalized algorithm [8]. It is included for scenario visualization purposes.

The graph (b) of Fig. 3 shows the change of carried traffic at packet level for each service. Increasing load at connection level reduces the carried traffic on packet level due to increased interference. At packet level, usually applications can tolerate a particular amount of lost traffic (protection by FEC or ARQ mechanisms either at physical level or at application level – like TCP segment

Table 2. Performance results of the traffic scenario described in Table 1

Stream	$i=1$: Poisson (voice)	$i=2$: Engset (web browsing)	$i=3$: Pascal (e-mail)	Total
Connection level results				
E_i	0.049	0.467	0.098	
C_i	0.049	0.096	0.146	
B_i	0.049	0.348	0.102	
Y_i	48.02	36.14	31.59	115.75
Packet level results				
$A_i^p = Y_i \cdot a_i$	24.008	10.843	22.111	56.962
Y_i^p	20.699	9.012	18.964	48.676
$C_i^p = \frac{A_i^p - Y_i^p}{A_i^p}$	0.138	0.169	0.142	
Y_i^{Pth}	23.643	10.496	21.73	55.869
$C_i^{Pth} = \frac{A_i^p - Y_i^{Pth}}{A_i^p}$	0.015	0.032	0.017	

retransmission, or MPEG frame interpolation). If this level is exceeded, most probably session will be terminated either by network for not satisfying the QoS requirements, or packets will become extensively delayed.

Graph (c) shows the dependence of the carried traffic for each service at packet level from the accepted traffic on connection level. It is the same picture as graph (b) just the x-axis is transformed. In (b) the x-axis shows the accepted load for voice service, while in (c) each curve follows its own accepted load at packet level.

Graph (c) should be read as follows. The load of voice service is increasing, so accepted traffic at packet level is increasing (from left to right), and at the same time the probability of packet loss increases. In the meanwhile web traffic and email services have the same offered load at connection level, but because of higher blocking probabilities, the accepted load at packet level is reduced (curves move from right to left) and at the same time less traffic is carried at packet level (curves go downwards).

Finally, graph (d) shows the achieved average throughput for each service. It is lower than requested (10, 2 and 1 channels) because of lost traffic at packet level.

4.3   Adjustment of Loss Rates at Packet Level

As mentioned above, there is a motivation to improve the success rate at packet level, as it directly results in higher user satisfaction. Technically, it means that the graph in Fig 3 (d) should be closer to the target values.

The way to do such an adjustment is to accept less traffic at connection level. In the previous scenario users were allowed to load network up to the pole

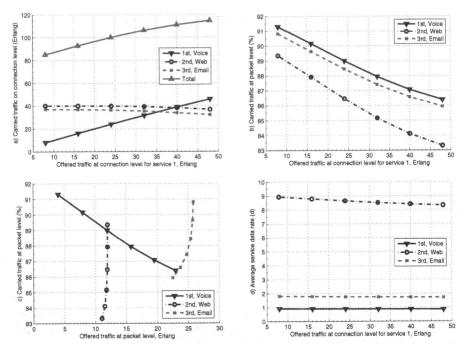

Fig. 3. Carried traffic at connection/packet level as a function of offered traffic at connection/packet level, respectively (total number of channels 128.)

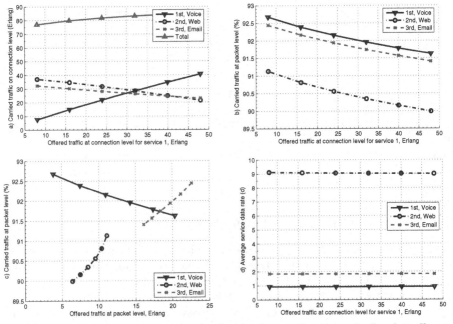

Fig. 4. Carried traffic at connection/packet level as a function of offered traffic at connection/packet level, respectively (total number of channels 128)

capacity (128 channels) (because of the activity factor, network at packet level is never loaded to pole capacity). Fig. 4 presents results when connection admission level is reduced to 90 channels (or, cell load is up to 70 % of pole capacity), while keeping the same offered traffic.

After such adjustment, the total carried traffic by all 3 service classes at connection level at offered load for voice service of 48 erlang (heavy load) is reduced from 115 to 85 erlang (compare graph (a) of Fig.4 with graph (a) of Fig. 3), while packet level performance improves from 86.5% to 91.5% for voice service, and from 83% to 90% for bursty email service (graphs (b)).

If services are able to tolerate up to 10% of packet loss such adjustment would ensure that sessions are not dropped (or delayed) at the expense of reducing the total accepted traffic by 20 erlang .

4.4 Behavior Analysis When Changing Activity Factor

Modeling of the system performance at connection and packet level allows to assess the benefit of multiplexing gain and evaluate the impact of neighbor cell interference. The multiplexing gain is achieved by interleaving on-off traffic sources, which is represented in our models by activity factor a_i.

Fig. 5 shows how the traffic performance changes when the activity factor of the second service (broadband web browsing) is 0.6 instead of 0.3, and the bursty third service is reduces its activity factor from 0.7 to 0.3. At the same time, the

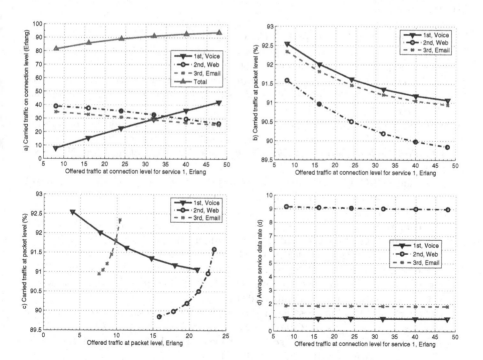

Fig. 5. Impact of activity factors on the system throughput

system capacity is limited to 78% (100 channels). The resulting performance is presented in Fig. 5.

5   Conclusions

Our work introduce a new analytical method for performance evaluation of wireless packet-oriented networks. The method is based on a combined analysis of connection and packet levels which are evaluated by Blocked-Call-Cleared (BCC) and Blocked-Calls-Interfered (BCI) strategies. The models are insensitive to the service time distribution at packet level and to both the *on* and *off* time distributions at packet level. The advantage of using the BCI model at packet level is that the load of the system only depends on the blocking at connection level, not upon the blocking at packet level. Thus we may calculate the performance measures in one step. In other works as [11] the BCC model is used both at connection level and at packet level. Then the model becomes approximate as the reduced load due to lost packets is not taken into account at connection level. The BCI model is more realistic at packet level. Previously developed algorithms [8] and [7] were used to apply the methodology to WCDMA radio interface transmission technology. Four examples are presented to show how to apply the proposed methodology for traffic engineering.

References

1. J.M. Capone and I. Stavrakakis. Delivering QoS requirements to traffic with diverse delay tolerances in a TDMA environment. *IEEE/ACM Transactions on Networking*, 7(1):55–87, September 1999.
2. L.E.N. Delbrouck. On the steady-state distribution in a service facility carrying mixtures of traffic with different peakedness factor and capacity requirements. *IEEE Trans. Commun.*, 11:1209–1211, 1983.
3. N. R. Figueira and J. Pasquale. Providing QoS for wireless links: wireless/wired networks. *IEEE Pers. Communications*, 6(5):42–51, October 1998.
4. T.C. Fry. *Probability and Its Engineering Uses*. D. van Nostrand Co., New York, 1928.
5. L. Huang and C.-C. Jay Kuo. Joint connection-level and packet-level quality-of-service support for VBR traffic in wireless multimedia networks. *IEEE Journal on Selected Areas in Communications*, 23(6), June 2005.
6. J.Y. Hui, M.B. Gursoy, N. Moayeri, and R.D. Yates. A layered broadband switching architecture with physical or virtual path configurations. *IEEE Journal on Selected Areas in Communications*, 9(9):1416–1426, December 1991.
7. V. Iversen, V. Benetis, N. Ha, and S. Stepanov. Evaluation of multi-service CDMA networks with soft blocking. In *Proc. of 16th ITC Specialist Seminar*, pages 212–216, Antwerp, Belgium, September 2004.
8. V.B. Iversen. Modelling restricted accessibility for wireless multi-service system. *Springer Lecture Notes on Computer Science*, 3883:93–102, July 2005.
9. V.B. Iversen. *Teletraffic Engineering Handbook*. ITU-D Study Group 2, Question 16/2, http://www.com.dtu.dk/teletraffic, January 2005.
10. K. Kim and I.S. Koo. *CDMA Systems Capacity Engineering*. Artech House, 2005.

11. I.D. Moscholios and M. Logothetis. Call-level blocking of on-off traffic sources in a shared resource environment with batched Poisson arrival processes. In *Proc. International Teletraffic Congress, ITC-19*, pages 143–152, Beijing, China, September 2005.
12. M. Naghshineh and S. Schwartz. Distributed call admission control in mobile/ wireless networks. *IEEE Journal on Selected Areas in Communications*, 14(4):711–717, May 1996.
13. J. M. Peha and A. Sutivong. Admission control algorithms for cellular systems. *Wireless Networks*, 7(2):117–126, April 2001.
14. R. Ramjee, D. Towsley, and R. Nagarajan. On optimal call admission control in cellular systems. *Wireless Networks*, 3(1):29–41, May 1997.
15. S. Wu, K.Y.M. Wong, and B. Li. A new distributed and dynamic call admission policy for mobile wireless networks with QoS guarantee. In *Proc. of Ninth IEEE International Symposium on Personal, Indoor, and Mobile Radio Communication (PIMRC)*, pages 260–264, Boston, USA, September 1998.
16. H. Zheng, Q. Zhang, and V.B. Iversen. Trunk reservation in multiservice networks with BPP traffic. *Springer Lecture Notes on Computer Science, this volume*, 2007.

Trunk Reservation in Multi-service Networks with BPP Traffic

Zheng He, Qi Zhang, and Villy Bæk Iversen

COM · DTU, Technical University of Denmark,
DK-2800 Kgs. Lyngby, Denmark
{s041436, qz, vbi}@com.dtu.dk

Abstract. In this paper we develop approximate models for trunk reservation in multi-service systems with BPP (Binomial–Poisson–Pascal) multi-rate traffic streams. The approximation is a generalization of previous work by Tran-Gia & Hübner who assumed Poisson arrival processes. It is based on a generalized algorithm which allows for calculation of individual performance measures for each service, in particular the traffic congestion. The algorithm is numerically robust and requires a minimum of computer memory and computing time. The approximation is good when the services have equal mean service times.

Keywords: trunk reservation, BPP traffic, multi-rate traffic, wireless systems.

1   Introduction

Trunk reservation is a call admission control policy widely used in communication systems. For instance, it is used in wireless cellular networks to give priority to hand-over calls by reserving capacity (guard channels) for these calls. It is also used in multi-service broadband networks to equalize blocking probabilities to guarantee same QoS (Quality-of-Service) for services with different bandwidth demands, or to give priority to some services.

In the past decades trunk reservation has been studied by many researchers in order to differentiate admission policies for different services. It is shown that trunk reservation is an effective way to equalize time congestion probabilities, to implement priority policy, to ensure QoS for different services, and to obtain optimal network resource utilization. It is applicable to both loss and delay systems. Tran-Gia & Hübner [1] use trunk reservation to balance the grade of service, i.e. equalize the time congestion probability, based on a approximative solution. But only Poisson traffic is investigated. Lindberger [2] consider bursty (overflow) arrival traffic in addition to Poisson arrival traffic and both types of traffic are multi-slot traffic streams. The results are approximations based on heuristics which works well for systems with more than 30 channels. Vázquez-Ávila & al. [3] discuss a recursive formula for fractional guard channel (trunk reservation) policies, but it is only studied for single slot traffic. Brandt & Brandt [4] model trunk reservation system by an overflow system, but they

J. García-Vidal and L. Cerdà-Alabern (Eds.): Wireless and Mobility, LNCS 4396, pp. 200–212, 2007.
© Springer-Verlag Berlin Heidelberg 2007

only deal with single slot traffic only. Pla & al. [5] study admission control policy issues using an inverse approach. With known arrival rate, occupied channels, system capacity and blocking probability, they find the optimal upper limit for achieving maximum carried traffic. But they also only deal with Poisson traffic.

In current broadband networks, multi-service traffic streams do not only have different data rates but also different arrival processes. Therefore, it is important to develop more general recursive approximation algorithms for different traffic models. So far, no one has tackled the trunk reservation problem in multi-rate system with BPP traffic which we consider in this paper. We develop approximate models for trunk reservation in multi-service systems with BPP (Binomial–Poisson–Pascal) multi-rate calls.

2   Traffic Model

We consider a system with N traffic streams and n channels with blocked calls cleared. For traffic stream i, the arrival rate is $\lambda_i(j)$, where j is the number of connections of type i. One connection of type i requires d_i channels. The mean service time for stream i is μ_i^{-1}. In the following we restrict ourselves to Binomial–Poisson–Pascal (BPP) traffic, where $\lambda_i(j)$ is a linear function of j. Traffic stream i is characterized by mean offered traffic A_i and peakedness Z_i. The peakedness is the variance–mean ratio of the state probabilities. For a Poisson arrival process $\lambda_i(j) = \lambda_i$ is independent of the state of the stream. $A_i = \lambda_i/\mu_i$ is the offered traffic measured in number of connections, and the peakedness is one. For the Binomial (Engset) case we have a positive number of sources and the arrival rate when x_i sources are busy is $(S_i - x_i)\,\gamma_i$. For the Pascal case the arrival rate is $(S_i + x_i)\,\gamma_i$ when x_i sources are busy. For a linear state-dependent Poisson arrival process the offered traffic is $A_i = S(1 - Z_i)$, where S_i is the number of traffic sources. The peakedness is $Z_i = 1/(1 + \beta_i)$, where $\beta_i = \gamma_i/\mu_i$, and γ_i is the arrival rate of an idle source. Mathematically, we can deal with Pascal traffic using the same formulæ as for Engset by letting S_i and β_i be negative. For Engset traffic peakedness is less than one (smooth traffic), whereas for Pascal traffic peakedness is greater than one (bursty traffic). Finite source traffic is characterized by number of sources S and offered traffic per idle source β. Alternatively, we often use the offered traffic A and the peakedness Z. We have the following relations between the two representations:

$$A = S \cdot \frac{\beta}{1 + \beta},$$
(1)

$$Z = \frac{1}{1 + \beta},$$
(2)

$$\beta = \frac{1 - Z}{Z},$$
(3)

$$S = \frac{A}{1 - Z}.$$
(4)

3   Algorithm for Multi-rate Systems

Algorithms for evaluating multi-rate systems may be divided into two classes:

- Convolution algorithms aggregate the state space by aggregating the individual services. This allows for access control based on number of channels occupied by each service, for example minimum and maximum allocation of bandwidth for each service. But it does not allow for access control based on global state probabilities.
- State-based algorithms aggregate the state space and allow for access control based on the global state probabilities, but they do not keep account of resources used by the individual traffic stream.

A new state-based algorithm for BPP–traffic [6] keeps record of the contribution of each traffic stream to the global state probabilities. If we denote the global state probability in state x by $p(x)$ and the contribution to this probability from stream i by $p_i(j)$ (due to arrivals of type i in state $(x-d_i)$ bringing the system into state x), then we have:

$$p(x) = \begin{cases} 0 & x < 0 \\ 1 & x = 0 \\ \displaystyle\sum_{i=1}^{N} p_i(x) & x = 1, 2, \ldots, n \end{cases} \tag{5}$$

where

$$p_i(x) = \begin{cases} 0 & x \le 0 \\ \dfrac{d_i}{x} \cdot \dfrac{S_i\,\gamma_i}{\mu_i} \cdot p(x - d_i) - \dfrac{x - d_i}{x} \cdot \dfrac{\gamma_i}{\mu_i} \cdot p_i(x - d_i) & x = 1, 2, \ldots n \end{cases} \tag{6}$$

The algorithm is initiated by letting number of channels $n = 0$ and $p(0) = 1$. We denote the non-normalized state probabilities of $p_i(x)$ and $p(x)$ by $q_i(x)$ and $q(x)$, respectively. Then in each recursion we increase number of channels n by one, calculate the relative state probabilities $q_i(n)$ and $q(n)$, normalize all state probabilities $q_i(j)$ by the normalization factor $1 + q(n)$ and thus get the true probabilities $p_i(j)$ and $p(j)$ $(j = 0, 1, \ldots n)$. This is a stable algorithm as we divide with a term always bigger than one. Memory requirements of the algorithm is of the order of size:

$$m_m = O\left\{ \sum_{j=1}^{N} d_j \right\}. \tag{7}$$

The number of operations is of the order of size:

$$m_c = O\{n \cdot (m_m + N)\} \tag{8}$$

as we for a given number of channels need to calculate N new terms from $\max\{d_j\}$ previous global states and normalize m_m terms. Thus the complexity of the algorithm is linear in both number of traffic streams and number of states.

3.1   Trunk Reservation

We introduce trunk reservation so that call attempts from traffic stream i observe a system with r_i channels. Thus a call attempt of type i will be blocked in states

$$r_i - d_i + 1, r_i - d_i + 2, \ldots, n \,.$$

If a stream has full accessibility, then $r_i = n$. An obvious modification of the above algorithm is to let

$$q_i(x) = 0 \,, \qquad x > r_i \tag{9}$$

so that also $p_i(x) = 0 \,, x > r_i$ because we don't enter these states due to an arrival of type i.

Introducing trunk reservation implies that the process looses the reversibility property, and the system is no more insensitive the the holding time distribution. For single-rate calls all having the same mean holding time the above modification will give the exact state probabilities when all arrival processes are Poisson processes. For multi-rate traffic and individual mean holding times the above modification is an approximation to the exact solution. The exact solution is only obtainable by solving the node balance equations. In the following we will look at the accuracy of this approximation, comparing results obtained by the new algorithm with exact results obtained by solving the node balance equations.

4   Performance Measures

The above generalized algorithm allows for calculation of individual performance measures for each traffic stream. For BPP–loss systems we have three measures, the most important one being the traffic congestion:

Time congestion is the proportion of time a traffic stream is blocked. For traffic stream j it becomes:

$$E_i = \sum_{j=r_i-d_i+1}^{n} p(j) \,. \tag{10}$$

Traffic congestion is the proportion of offered traffic blocked. The carried traffic is obtained from the general algorithm by:

$$Y_i = \sum_{j=0}^{r_i-d_i} j \cdot p_i(j) \,. \tag{11}$$

Thus the traffic congestion becomes:

$$C_i = \frac{A_i - Y_i}{A_i} \,. \tag{12}$$

The call congestion B can be obtained as the time congestion by one source less. It may also be obtained from the the state probabilities $p_i(j)$. It is emphasized that the most important performance measure is the traffic congestion. For a given peakedness it yields congestion values similar to the methods of the classical overflow theory. For Poisson arrival processes the time, call and traffic congestion are equal. In all other cases the time congestion has no importance. For renewal arrival processes the call congestion is equal to the traffic congestion.

5   Examples and Comparisons

In this section, three numerical examples are presented to show the results of the new algorithm in dealing with trunk reservation scheme for BPP traffic. The related notations employed are given as follows: offered traffic A_i, peakedness Z_i, and number of slots required per call d_i.

5.1   Multi-slot Poisson Traffic

In the first example, we consider a multi-service systems with 48 channels which are offered three traffic streams specified in Table 1. The trunk reservation parameters are specified in Table 2. The total offered traffic to the system ranges from 12 erlang to 84 erlang (measured in channels), while offered traffic of each stream has an increasing step of 1 erlang. Each stream offer the same traffic when measured in channels.

The blocking probabilities of different traffic streams calculated by the new algorithm are compared with the exact values shown in Figure 1. As all traffic stream are Poisson type arrival the PASTA theorem is valid, and time congestion of each stream equals both call congestion and traffic congestion. So we use one figure to illustrate the results. Because we implement *equalization* policy in the system, the three traffic streams experience the same time congestion E, call congestion B and traffic congestion C. Consequently the three lines overlap each other. There is a very small gap between the exact value and the approximate ones (order of size 0.005) when the total offered traffic is 48 erlang (channels) is equal to number of channels (fully loaded system). Some typical values are given in Table 2.

5.2   Single-Slot BPP Traffic

In the second example, we consider a multi-service system with 30 channels which is offered single slot BPP traffic. The parameters of BPP traffic are defined in Table 3. As they are single slot traffic, they experience the same time congestion in a full accessible system. We implement *priority services* policy instead of

Table 1. Traffic parameters of multi-slot Poisson streams in the first example. Total system capacity = 48 channels. The offered traffic is in connections.

Stream 1 Poisson traffic	Stream 2 Poisson traffic	Stream 3 Poisson traffic
$A_{1,start}=$ 4	$A_{2,start}=$ 2	$A_{3,start}=$ 1
$A_{1,end}$ = 28	$A_{2,end}$ = 14	$A_{3,end}$ = 7
$d_1=$ 1	$d_2=$ 2	$d_3=$ 4

Table 2. Comparison of exact and new generalized algorithm with all Poisson traffic streams input

Trunk Reservation Threshold $r_i=$ 45 46 48 channels						
	A_{total} = 24 erlang		A_{total} = 48 erlang		A_{total} = 72 erlang	
Stream i	Exact	New_alg	Exact	New_alg	Exact	New_alg
E_1	0.004051	0.003941	0.18689	0.18319	0.40721	0.40243
E_2	0.004051	0.003941	0.18689	0.18319	0.40721	0.40243
E_3	0.004051	0.003941	0.18689	0.18319	0.40721	0.40243

the former *equalization policy*. The third traffic stream (Pascal arrival type) is assumed to have highest priority. One guard channel is retained in the system, which ensures Pascal traffic experience lower blocking probability. From Figure 2 we see that the protected stream experiences lower time congestion, as it has access to the last idle channel in the system. The other two traffic streams experience the same time congestion.

The approximation errors by the new algorithm are amplified when we calculate traffic congestion and call congestion as compared with the exact solution. Thus, the results become less accurate by the new method, especially the call congestion of single slot traffic which can be considered as a rough estimate.

Detailed numerical results are listed in Table 4. We notice that the traffic congestion by the new algorithm is too low for Poisson traffic, but on the safe side for Engset and Pascal traffic streams.

Table 3. Second example. Traffic parameters of BPP streams with single slot and a total system capacity = 30 channels.

Stream 1 Engset traffic	Stream 2 Poisson traffic	Stream 3 Pascal traffic
$A_{1,start}=$ 5	$A_{2,start}=$ 5	$A_{3,start}=$ 5
$A_{1,end}$ = 15	$A_{2,end}$ = 15	$A_{3,end}$ = 15
$d_1=$ 1	$d_2=$ 1	$d_3=$ 1
$Z_1=$ 0.5	$Z_2=$ 1	$Z_3=$ 2

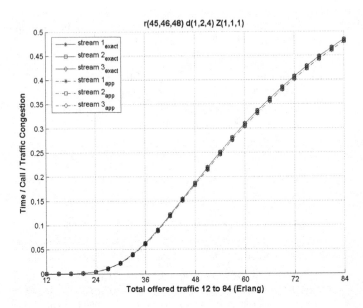

Fig. 1. Comparison of exact solution and new generalized algorithm for equalized blocking probability with all Poisson traffic streams

Table 4. Blocking probability for single slot BPP traffic in a multi-service system with trunk reservation scheme

Trunk Reservation Threshold $r_i=$ 29, 29, 30 channels and $A_{total}=27$ erlang					
	Time Cong		Call Cong		Traffic Cong
Stream i	Exact	New_alg	Exact	New_alg	Exact	New_alg
1	0.13281	0.11677	0.12179	0.10740	0.06807	0.07032
2	0.13281	0.11677	0.13281	0.11677	0.13281	0.11677
3	0.03365	0.02794	0.04267	0.03121	0.08185	0.12107

5.3 Multi-slot BPP Traffic

In the third example, we consider a multi-rate multi-service system with 48 channels. The parameters of multi slots BPP traffic streams are listed in Table 5. In order to equalize time congestion of all streams, we choose trunk reservation thresholds $r_i=$ 45, 46, 48. The calculated time congestion, traffic congestion and call congestion, both by exact solution and algorithm proposed, are illustrated in Figure 5, 6 and 7, respectively. Results when the system is fully loaded (48 erlang channels traffic offered to 48 channels) are presented in Table 6.

The results in Figure 5 are self-evident, as the system with equalization policy block the arrivals from all three streams at the global state 44, regardless of how many slots they need. Hence, the sum of probabilities of upper four states (states

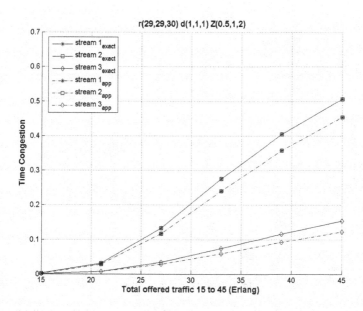

Fig. 2. Time congestion comparison of exact and new generalized algorithm for single slot BPP traffic streams

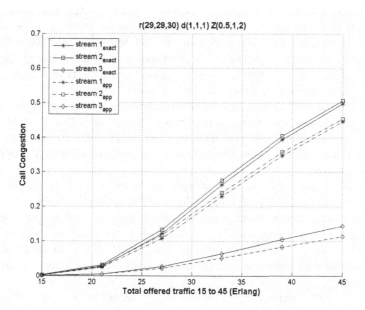

Fig. 3. Call congestion comparison of exact and new generalized algorithm for single slot BPP traffic streams

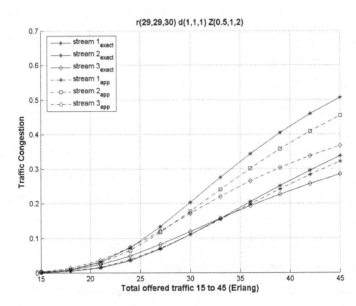

Fig. 4. Traffic congestion comparison of exact and new generalized algorithm for single slot BPP traffic streams

45, 46, 47, 48) is the time congestion experienced by the three streams. There is still a gap between exact values and results obtained by the new generalized algorithm. In case of fully loaded system, the difference is about 0.02 (10%). It is not as accurate as the results in the first example because the traffic types are more general (BPP). But it is still a good approximation considering its complexity and time costs, which will be discussed below.

The traffic congestion and call congestion experienced by the three streams are different because of different arrival types (Engset and Pascal). The values of traffic congestion and call congestion by the second traffic stream is the same as its time congestion, because of Poisson type arrival and PASTA property as mentioned before.

The performance results in more details are listed in Table 6 for the case of fully loaded system $n = 48$ channels and $A = 48$ erlang (channels).

The difference between exact values of time congestion and approximate values of time congestion from algorithm is 0.022. It is the same for all three traffic streams which experience the same time congestion. The deviations of traffic congestion from exact solution and the approximate approach are as follows: for Poisson traffic C_{ex} is larger than C_{apx} by 0.02; for Engset traffic C_{ex} is smaller than C_{apx} by 0.02; and for Pascal traffic C_{ex} is larger than C_{apx} by 0.02. Although the absolute differences are the same for all three streams, the traffic congestions experienced by three streams are different. For instance, the largest traffic congestion C of Pascal traffic stream is $C_{ex} = 0.34111$ and $C_{apx} = 0.36307$, and the smallest traffic congestion of Engset traffic is $C_{ex} = 0.093255$ and $C_{apx} = 0.1117$.

All the above indicates that the new algorithm effectively equalizes the time congestion of BPP traffic by trunk reservation. But the values of the more important traffic congestion cannot be equalized in a simple way.

Table 5. Third example. Traffic parameters of BPP streams with single slot. Total system capacity = 48 channels.

Stream 1	Stream 2	Stream 3
Engset traffic	Poisson traffic	Pascal traffic
$A_{1,start}= 4$	$A_{2,start}= 2$	$A_{3,start}= 1$
$A_{1,end} = 28$	$A_{2,end} = 14$	$A_{3,end} = 7$
$d_1= 1$	$d_2= 2$	$d_3= 4$
$Z_1= 0.5$	$Z_2= 1$	$Z_3= 2$

Table 6. Blocking probability for BPP traffic streams with multi-slot in multi-service system with trunk reservation Scheme

Trunk Reservation Threshold r_i= 45 46 48 channels and A_{total}=48 erlang					
	Time Cong		Call Cong		Traffic Cong	
Stream i	Exact	New_alg	Exact	New_alg	Exact	New_alg
1	0.16659	0.14423	0.16153	0.14006	0.093255	0.1117
2	0.16659	0.14423	0.16659	0.16659	0.16659	0.14423
3	0.16659	0.14423	0.20221	0.16015	0.34111	0.36307

5.4 Complexity

Finally, we compare the execution time of calculating blocking probability by exact solution (solving node balance equation) and the generalized algorithm. The results are shown in Table 7. The used computer has a CPU of Pentium IV 2.8 GHz and 512 MB memory. In the example, we have BPP multi-slot traffic in a trunk reservation system with equalization policy. It means that the trunk reservation factor for each traffic changes when the system capacity n increases. The total offered traffic A is also enlarged in this case.

As the exact solution needs to solve the node equations for all system states, it evidently suffers the dimension problem. When the system capacity $n = 70$ (not listed in the Table 7) and the number of states in the example would be about 42875 (70/4*70/2*70). The exact solution program took more than 3000 seconds and the Windows operating system shows warning of running out of memory. But our generalized algorithm works still very well and fast (only 0.016 second needed). Even if the system capacity $n = 10000$ which results in a number of states of the order 10^{10}, it only took 30 seconds to do the calculations. Hence, it clearly shows that our algorithm is stabler and much faster.

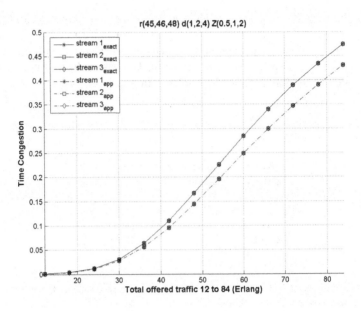

Fig. 5. Time congestion comparison of exact and new generalized algorithm for multi-slot BPP traffic streams

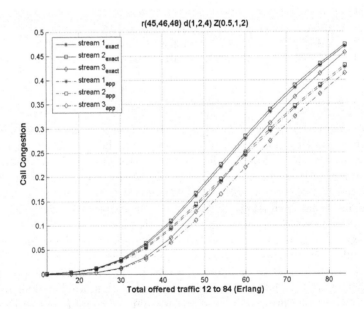

Fig. 6. Call congestion comparison of exact and new generalized algorithm for multi-slot BPP traffic streams

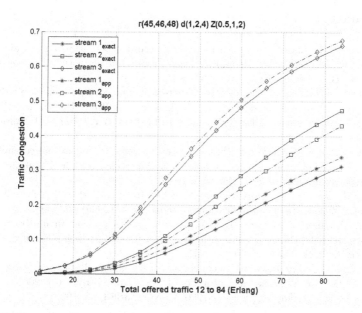

Fig. 7. Traffic congestion comparison of exact and new generalized algorithm for multi-slot BPP traffic streams

Table 7. Comparison of execution time of exact solution and new generalized algorithm

$d_i=$ 1, 2, 4 and $Z_i=$0.5, 1, 2					
n (channel)/ A_{total}(erlang)	20/15	30/ 22.5	40/30	50/37.5	60/45
Exact solution (second)	0.281	1.2	6.5	28	120
generalized algorithm(second)	0.015	0.016	0.016	0.016	0.016

6   Conclusions

In this paper, we propose a new algorithm to calculate time congestion, call congestion, traffic congestion individually in a multi-rate multi-service system with trunk reservation. This approximate recursive algorithm for trunk reservation not only avoids numerical problems with a large number of different multi-rate traffic streams, but can also be used in system with different traffic models.

Although trunk reservation is very efficient to guarantee Quality of Service for multi-rate multi-services, it is a static connection admission control policy. It reduces the utilization of the system, compared with that of complete sharing system. Therefore, dynamic or adaptive scheme can be investigated as extension of this algorithm to increase the system utilization. Future investigations will study the influence of mean holding times.

References

1. Tran-Gia, P., Hübner, F. In: An analysis of trunk reservation and grade of service balancing mechanisms in multi-service broadband networks. Elsevier Science Publishers B.V. (North-Holland) (1993) 83–97.
2. Lindberger, K.: Blocking for multi-slot heterogeneous traffic streams offered to a trunk group with reservation. Traffic Engineering for ISDN Design and Plannng, ITC Specialist Seminar, Elsevier Science Publishers B.V. (North-Holland)(1988) 151–160.
3. Vázquez-Ávila, J., Cruz-Perez, F., Ortigoza-Guerrero, L.: Performance analysis of fractional guard channel policies in mobile cellular networks. IEEE Transactions on Wireless Communications5(2) (2006) 301–305.
4. Brandt, M., Brandt, A.: Individual overflow and freed carried traffics for a link with trunk reservation. Telecommunication Systems **29**(4) (2005) 283–308.
5. Pla, V., Martínez, J., García, D.: Admission control policies in multiservice cellular networks: Optimum configuration and sensitivity. Springer Lecture Notes in Computer Science **3427** (2005) 121–135.
6. Iversen, V.: Modelling restricted accessibility for wireless multi-service system, Euro-NGI workhop on Wireless and Mobility, Lake Como, Italy, July 2005. Springer Lecture Notes in Computer Science (2005) LNCS, **3883**, 93–102.

Feasible Load Regions for Different RRM Strategies for the Enhanced Uplink in UMTS Networks

Andreas Mäder[1], Dirk Staehle[1], Tuo Liu[2], and Hans Barth[3]

[1] University of Würzburg, Department of Distributed Systems
Am Hubland, D-97074 Würzburg
{maeder,staehle}@informatik.uni-wuerzburg.de
[2] University of Sydney, School of Information Technologies, Australia
tliu@it.usyd.edu.au
[3] T-Systems Enterprise Services GmbH
hans.barth@t-systems.com

Abstract. The UMTS enhanced uplink or high speed uplink packet access (HSUPA) provides efficient mechanisms for the radio resource management of radio bearers for best effort traffic. The resources available for the enhanced uplink users depend on several factors like the spatial configuration of the mobiles in the cells, the number of QoS users and the implemented RRM strategy. In this work, we provide a model for the calculation of the resources assigned to the enhanced uplink users which also allows the inclusion of the maximum transmit power and downgrants for the reduction of the other-cell interference. We further show the impact of centralized and de-centralized radio resource management strategies on the feasible load region.

1 Introduction

The UMTS enhanced uplink or high speed uplink packet access (HSUPA) is a set of new transport and signaling bearers as well as functional entities which had been introduced in release 6 of the 3GPP UMTS standard [1]. The purpose of the enhanced uplink is to overcome certain limitations of the existing dedicated channel (DCH) transport bearers if used in conjunction with packet switched data. Packet switched data traffic can be roughly categorized in elastic traffic like web or p2p traffic, i.e. traffic originating from typical best-effort applications and traffic which requires certain quality of service guarantees like voice over IP (VoIP), video streaming or gaming. While DCH bearers are suitable for the transport of QoS traffic, the characteristics of elastic traffic require transport bearers which adapt to the traffic demand to avoid waste of resources. In the same time, elastic traffic also permits the downgrading of existing connections, since the don't have hard QoS requirements which have to be fulfilled.

The enhanced uplink meets these requirements by introducing two new main features: Shorter transport time intervals (TTI) of 2ms and a flexible resource

J. García-Vidal and L. Cerdà-Alabern (Eds.): Wireless and Mobility, LNCS 4396, pp. 213–228, 2007.
© Springer-Verlag Berlin Heidelberg 2007

allocation mechanism which is located mainly in the NodeB. Additional features are Hybrid ARQ and multi-code transmissions. An overview of the changes and additional features of the enhanced uplink is provided e.g. in [2]. The short TTIs and the fast rate control enables fast reactions on variations in traffic demand or resource availability and thus leads to a more efficient resource allocation than in Rel. 5 or Rel. 99. In contrast, the rate control mechanism in UMTS Rel. 99 and 5 which is responsible for the resource allocation is located in the RNC. This leads to long signaling delays and consequently to reaction times which are too long to adapt to fast channel condition fluctuations. Measurements have shown that in some imlementations changes of the radio bearer bit rate are a matter of at least seconds in Rel. 99 [3].

Additionally, the E-DCH standardization documents define a fine granularized set of possible bit rates or *transport block sizes* (TBS), which are the number of bits which can be transported within one TTI [4]. This and the fast allocation of these TBS enables theoretically to implement a Radio Resource Management (RRM) strategy which globally (in the sense of network-wide) tries to optimize the system for a certain utility function.

The fast rate control feature of the enhanced uplink is implemented by moving parts of the RRM entity from the RNC to the NodeB, which reduces signaling delay. However, the drawback is that the now distributed RRM has to work with ony local knowledge (i.e. local with respect to the NodeB) about the interference situation, since NodeBs do not know anything about the load in neighboring NodeBs. This make the implementation of an RRM strategy which avoids load overshoots significantly more complex.

In this paper we want to investigate the influence of different RRM strategies on the so called feasible load region, which describes the region in which the resource assignments for the E-DCH users must be in order to meet the RRM constraints.

In the next section, an overview of related work is given, followed by Sec. 3, which gives a short introduction to the principles of the enhanced uplink. In Sec. 4, the RRM for the enhanced uplink is introduced. In 5, we propose an interference and load model, and in Sec. 6, a model for the resource assignment is proposed. In Sec. 7 we present some numerical examples and finally we conclude our work with Sec. 8.

2   Related Work

In [5], the authors propose an analytical single cell model for the enhanced uplink, which is based on the assumption that the RRM always try to maximize the resource utilization by concurrently obeying a certain maximum load (or target load) and interference, resp. This *greedy* RRM strategy can be seen as the uplink equivalent of downlink best-effort bearers like the HSDPA or 1xEV-DO, since it allocates as much resources as possible to the users which are currently needing them, thus supporting the elastic nature of best-effort traffic (which one this could be in the uplink is beyond the scope of this paper, but one hint is the expansion of peer-to-peer file sharing networks into the mobile domain [6]).

In the literature, several works exist which investigate the optimality and feasibility of centralized and decentralized RRM strategies. One of the first is [7], in which the author proposes a centralized optimizing RRM strategy to maximize the system utilization and minimize the outage probability, which is defined as the probability that the required minimum signal-to-noise-ratio (SNR) of a mobile cannot be reached. In [8], some resource allocation algorithms are described with different degrees of knowledge about the total interference in the network. The system throughput for the different algorithms is calculated by solving the corresponding optimization problem. In [9], some important results on the feasibility region of the CDMA uplink power assignment problem have been found. The authors show that the solution set of the problem is *log-convex* if the QoS-requirements for the link are convex in the log domain itself. This makes the problem solvable within reasonable time with standard algorithms like line search. In [10], the authors use the results of the previous mentioned work for an optimization framework. Additionally, they propose a distributed RRM algorithm which is based on load factors at the base stations. Similar approaches exist in the context of the uplink of CDMA 2000, one example is [11]. Here, the non-linear optimization problem is converted to linear optimization problem by restricting the feasibility region.

3 Introduction to the Enhanced Uplink

The enhanced uplink was officially as final specification introduced with Rel. 6 into the 3GPP standard suite. It introduces the Enhanced dedicated channel (E-DCH), which is designed to provide the users with a higher bandwidth and lower packet delay than with the conventional dedicated channel (DCH) radio bearers. The first goal is reached by introducing multi-code transmissions with up to 4 parallel orthogonal codes, which enables a maximum bit rate of around 5.7 Mbps. For reduced packet delays, the transport time interval (TT) between (sub)frames has been reduced to 2ms. Additionally, Hybrid ARQ (HARQ) has been introduced similar like for the high speed downlink packet access (HSDPA) for an increased link efficiency.

For the operator, the most important feature is probably the distributed RRM mechanism. In order to avoid long signaling delays, the majority of the RRM functionality has been moved from the RNC to the NodeB. This allows the rapid reaction on varying load conditions, decreasing the probability of load-overshoots and increasing resource utilization.

Figure 1 shows a graphical overview of the E-DCH RRM. The RRM entity of the radio network controller (RNC) defines the radio resource policy which should be enforced by the NodeBs. This is done in two ways: First, the RNC restricts the set of possible transport format combinations (TFC) for the UEs. Second, the RNS sets the maximum tolerable interference (or received wideband

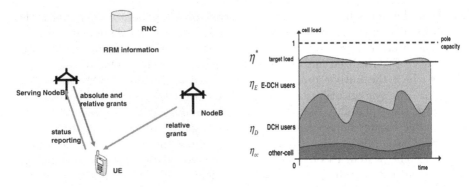

Fig. 1. Overview of the rate control functionality of the E-DCH

Fig. 2. Load at a NodeB

transmission power, RWTP) and the maximum other-cell interference to own-cell interference ratio at the NodeBs.

The serving NodeB has the possibility to set the maximum transmit power of the E-DPDCH relative to the DPCCH on a 2ms basis via scheduling grants. Two kinds of scheduling grants are defined: Absolute grants and relative grants. While absolute grants set the absolute power of the E-DPDCH, relative grants of type UP, DOWN or HOLD increase, decrease or keep the current transmit power. According to that and to the current buffer status, the UE may then select a transport format combination (TFC) with a corresponding transport block size (TBS). The TBS defines the number of information bits which can be transmitted within one TTI. So if we assume that the UEs have always buffered data, the UEs will always choose the maximum TBS. Additionally, the non-serving NodeBs may send DOWN or HOLD relative grants to the UE if the ratio between own- and other-cell interferences is below a certain threshold [1]. This is done to avoid the flooding of cells with other-cell interference, however, these DOWN-grants are restricted to UEs which are in the soft-handover area of the flooded NodeB. The UE may send information over its current power consumption, power headroom (defined as maximum minus current power) and buffer occupancy back to the NodeB, which may use it for its scheduling and RRM decisions.

4   Radio Resource Management for the E-DCH Best Effort Service

How much resources resources are available for the enhanced uplink is in the hand of the operators, which can define a certain target load for their network corresponding to the maximum RWTP. The basic idea is to keep the uplink load in all cells as close as possible but below this target load, which we denote with η^*, c.f. Fig. 2. A higher target load means more resources and higher bit rates for the enhanced uplink users, but also increases the probability of load overshoots which may lead to outage events in the worst case. A lower target load leads to a more stable system, but may also lead to insufficient resources for the best-effort users. The uplink load consists of several parts, which reflect the different possible interference sources. We define the load at a NodeB x as

$$\eta_x = \eta_{x,D}^{own} + \eta_{x,E}^{own} + \eta_{x,D}^{oc} + \eta_{x,E}^{oc}. \tag{1}$$

In this equation, $\eta_{x,D}^{own}$ is the own-cell dedicated channel load generated by mobiles with DCH radio bearers which are power controlled by NodeB x, $\eta_{x,E}^{own}$ is the own-cell load coming from enhanced uplink best-effort users, $\eta_{x,D}^{oc}$ is the other-cell load originating from DCH users in surrounding cells and $\eta_{x,E}^{oc}$ is the other-cell load from enhanced uplink users in surrounding cells. The different loads are related to the interference by the common load definition as defined e.g. in [12], such that we can write

$$\eta_x = \frac{\hat{I}_{x,D}^{own} + \hat{I}_{x,E}^{own} + \hat{I}_{x,D}^{oc} + \hat{I}_{x,E}^{oc}}{\hat{I}_x + W \hat{N}_0}. \tag{2}$$

In this equation, the meaning of the different interferences $\hat{I}$ correspond to their counterparts in Eq. (1). The interference $\hat{I}_x$ in the denominator is the sum of all interferences in the nominator. The load which is available for the enhanced uplink users is then simply the difference between the target load and the remaining loads:

$$\eta_{x,E}^{own} = \eta_x^* - \eta_{x,D}^{own} - \eta_{x,D}^{oc} - \eta_{x,E}^{oc}. \tag{3}$$

5   Interference and Load Model

We consider a UMTS network with a set of NodeBs $\mathcal{L}$ and a set of user equipments (UEs) $\mathcal{M}$. Each UE is connected via a DCH or E-DCH radio bearer and controlled by one NodeB. So, corresponding to each NodeB x two sets $\mathcal{E}_x$ and $\mathcal{D}_x$ exist, the first containing the controlled E-DCH users and the second the DCH users. We write $k \in x$ with $x \in \mathcal{L}$ to denote a UE controlled by NodeB x, regardless of its bearer.

The received power $\hat{S}_{k,x}$ of a mobile k at it's controlling NodeB x depends on the target-E_b/N_0 requirement and the bit rate of the mobile. If we assume perfect fast power control it must hold:

$$\hat{\varepsilon}_k^* = \frac{W}{R_k} \frac{\hat{S}_{k,x}}{W \hat{N}_0 + \sum_{j \in \mathcal{M} \setminus k} \hat{S}_{j,y}}, \tag{4}$$

where $\hat{\varepsilon}_k^*$ is the target-E_b/N_0-values, W is the system chiprate (3.84 Mcps in UMTS FDD), R_k is the instantaneous bit rate and $\hat{N}_0$ is the one-sided thermal power density. Solving for the received power $\hat{S}_{k,x}$ yields

$$\hat{S}_{k,x} = \omega_k \cdot \left(W \hat{N}_0 + \sum_{j \in \mathcal{M}} \hat{S}_{j,y} \right). \tag{5}$$

The term ω_k is an effective bandwidth measure of the load this mobile generates at its controlling NodeB. We will denote it as *service load factor* in the rest of the paper. It is defined as

$$\omega_k = \frac{\hat{\varepsilon}_k^* R_k}{\hat{\varepsilon}_k^* R_k + W} \tag{6}$$

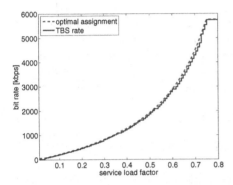

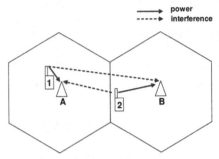

Fig. 3. The service load factors and the corresponding bit rates

Fig. 4. Simple example scenario with two mobiles and two NodeBs

and depends only on the target-E_b/N_0-value and the bit rate. Fig. 3 shows the the bit rate as function of the SLF. The solid line corresponds to the SLFs calculated form the TBS table in [4]. The dashed line is directly calculated from the SLFs as $R = \frac{\omega \cdot W}{\hat{\varepsilon}^* \cdot (1-\omega)}$. We see that both lines are very close to each other due to the fine granularity of the possible bit rates. In the rest of the paper we therefore use the direct relation between bit rate and SLF.

The sector interference in a unsynchronized CDMA system depends generally not only on the number of transmitting mobiles in the own sector, but also on the interference generated in surrounding cells and sectors, respectively. This interference is called other-cell (or inter-cell) interference, since it originates from cells other than the cell we are currently looking on. With the same argument, the interference which is generated in other cells also depends on the interference of the own-cell. Fig. 4 shows an example with two mobiles. The first one is close to its controlling NodeB and thus requires only a low transmit power to reach its target-E_b/N_0. The second mobile, controlled by NodeB B, is close to the cell edge such that both NodeB A and NodeB B nearly receive the same power from this mobile. The interference power $\hat{S}_{k,y}$ from one mobile to an none-controlling NodeB is given by the ratio between the link gains between the mobile and the two NodeBs:

$$\hat{S}_{k,y} = \frac{\hat{d}_{k,y}}{\hat{d}_{k,x}} \hat{S}_{k,x} = \hat{\Delta}_{k,y}^x \hat{S}_{k,x}, \tag{7}$$

where x is the controlling NodeB, y is a non-controlling NodeB, $\hat{d}_{k,x}$ is the link gain between mobile k and NodeB x, and $S_{k,x}$ is the received power at NodeB x. Note that the link gain ratio $\hat{\Delta}_{k,y}^x = 1$ if $x = y$.

We define the interference at a NodeB x as the sum of all received signal powers from all mobiles in the network. The interference is then from Eq. (7) given by

$$\hat{I}_x = \sum_{l \in \mathcal{L}} \sum_{k \in l} \Delta_{k,l}^x \cdot \omega_k \cdot \left(W \bar{N}_0 + \hat{I}_l \right). \tag{8}$$

With matrices, we formulate this equation as

$$\bar{I} = \widetilde{G} \cdot \left(\bar{N}_0 + \bar{I} \right), \tag{9}$$

where $\bar{I}$ is the $|\mathcal{L}| \times 1$-vector of interferences, $\bar{N}_0$ is a $|\mathcal{L}| \times 1$-vector with $(\bar{N}_0)_j = W N_0$, and $\widetilde{G}$ is an $|\mathcal{L}| \times |\mathcal{L}|$ matrix with the sum of the link-gain ratios multiplied with the corresponding SLF as elements, such that

$$(\widetilde{G})_{ij} = \sum_{k \in j} \Delta_{k,j}^i \cdot \omega_k. \tag{10}$$

Note that in our notation j is the set of mobiles which are connected to NodeB j. The interference at each NodeB is than the result of solving Eq. (9) for $\bar{I}$:

$$\bar{I} = \left(\widetilde{E} - \widetilde{G} \right)^{-1} \cdot \left(\bar{N}_0 \cdot \widetilde{G} \right), \tag{11}$$

where $\widetilde{E}$ is the identity matrix.

Up to now, our model does not make any distinction between DCH and E-DCH users. Both user types are characterized through their service load factor ω. However, in Sec. 4 we defined an RRM strategy for the E-DCH users which tries to maximize the resource utilization in each cell. Since the resource in our case is the interference and corresponding to that, the cell load, the remaining resources are distributed to the E-DCH users as in Eq. (3). Essentially this means that DCH users have fixed SLFs, while E-DCH users get the remaining load in a typical best-effort manner. We can express this by splitting the interference equation further up after the signal source:

$$\hat{I}_x = \hat{I}_{x,D}^{own} + \hat{I}_{x,D}^{oc} + \hat{I}_{x,E}^{own} + \hat{I}_{x,E}^{oc}, \tag{12}$$

which corresponds to the matrix form

$$\begin{aligned} \bar{I} = {} & \tilde{G}_D^{own}(\bar{N}_0 + \bar{I}) + \tilde{G}_D^{oc}(\bar{N}_0 + \bar{I}) \\ & + \tilde{G}_E^{own}(\bar{N}_0 + \bar{I}) + \tilde{G}_E^{oc}(\bar{N}_0 + \bar{I}). \end{aligned} \tag{13}$$

Here, the elements of the load matrices correspond to the set of users which generate interference. The matrices $\tilde{G}_D^{own}$ and G_E^{own} are diagonal matrices with elements $(\tilde{G}_D^{own})_{ii} = \sum_{k \in \mathcal{D}_x} \omega_k$ and $(\tilde{G}_E^{own})_{ii} = \sum_{k \in \mathcal{E}_x} \omega_k$. The matrizes for the other-cell interference contain zeros at the diagonal, and on the remaing entries the sum of SLFs multiplied with their link gain ratios, i.e. $(\widetilde{G}_D^{oc})_{ii} = 0$ and $(\widetilde{G}_D^{oc})_{ij} = \sum_{k \in \mathcal{D}_j} \hat{\Delta}_{k,j}^x \cdot \omega_k$ for all $i \neq j$.

6   Resource Assignment to E-DCH Users

In the previous section, we defined a general framework for the calculation of the interferences and loads at a NodeB. We now want to use this framework for obtaining the actual resources, which can be assigned to an E-DCH user. Let us for this reason first define some common constraints, within the assignment takes place.

1. The maximum load or interference should not be exceeded. The purpose is to guarantee a stable system, since if the cell loads get too high, the required transmit powers for the mobiles tend to infinity, which makes it impossible for them to reach their required target-E_b/N_0. Hence we define the constraint

$$C_{load} : \quad \eta_x \leq \eta_x^*. \tag{14}$$

2. All E-DCH users have a certain minimum bandwidth guarantee, which corresponds to a minimum TBS and thus to a minimum SLF ω_{min}. This condition avoids quasi-outage of users. Further, the maximum SLF ω_{max} is defined by the highest TBS, which corresponds to 5.74 Mbps. So it is mandatory that

$$C_{SLF} : \quad \omega_{min} \leq \omega \leq \omega_{max}. \tag{15}$$

3. The mobiles have a maximum transmit power $\hat{T}_{max}$, which is normally either 21 dBm or 24 dBm, so

$$C_{pow} : \quad \hat{T}_m \leq \hat{T}_{max}. \tag{16}$$

Note that transmit powers can be easily calculated from the interference at the serving NodeB x and the pathloss as

$$\hat{T}_m = \hat{d}_{m,x}^{-1} \cdot \omega_m \cdot (W \hat{N}_0 + \hat{I}_x). \tag{17}$$

4. In [1] it is stated that DOWN grants are sent to mobiles in adjacent cells if the ratio between the E-DCH other-cell interference and the total interference from E-DCH users exceeds a certain, operator-defined threshold. This reduces flooding of cells from adjacent sites due to high-bitrate mobiles near the cell borders. Let $\mathcal{H}_x$ the set of UEs which are in the soft handover area but not controlled by NodeB x. The condition can then be expressed as

$$C_{grant} : \quad \frac{\sum_{h \in \mathcal{H}_x} \hat{S}_{h,x}}{\hat{I}_E} \leq t_{SHO}, \tag{18}$$

where t_{SHO} is an operator-defined threshold.

The goal of the resource assignment procedure is that all this conditions are fulfilled. Under certain circumstances, this may not always be possible, which may lead to a load overshoot event. A load overshoot does not necessarily mean that a UE experiences outage, however it may affect the connection or system stability negatively, so it should be avoided if possible.

In our model, load overshoots corresponds to a resource assignment which is not in the feasibility region, which is defined by the constraints above. Depending on the RRM strategy and the degree of knowledge that the executing entity on the global load situation has, the feasibility regions significantly differ from each other. We distinguish between three kinds of RRM implementations: One with global knowledge of the system load, which constitutes the optimal case, one with global knowledge but with a distributed implementation such that it has a reduced feasibility region and a totally decentralized one with only local knowledge of the load, which corresponds to the single cell resource assignment scheme. Generally, load overshoots can occur because of two reasons: First, the load generated by the DCH users is so high, that the target load is exceeded. Normally, the admission control prevents such events. The second case is, that the RRM implementation is such that cells may be flooded with interference from adjacent cells. This may occur with the local RRM implementation. Besides of load overshoots, it may also happen that the target load is not reached. This occurs if the RRM implementation decides to lower the load in some cells to prevent load overshoots, i.e. for the global RRM implementation.

Global Resource Assignments. From Eq. (8) we see that the SLF and interference calculation can be interpreted as a non-linear optimization problem. In our model we try to optimize the cell load with a utility function $U(\cdot)$. In the literature, several options are mentioned to optimize for different fairness goals. The most straightforward utility function is to sum over all individual loads of the E-DCH users. However, this approach leads to unfair assignments in the sense that UEs close to the NodeB get as much load as possible, while the more distant UEs may only get the minimum SLF. An often mentioned generic fairness criterion is that of α-fairness, where the optimization converges to different fairness goals according to the setting of a parameter α, [13]:

$$U(\omega_m) = \frac{\omega_m^{1-\alpha}}{1-\alpha} \tag{19}$$

With this utility function, proportional fairness [14] can be achieved with $\alpha \to 1$ and max-min-fairness can be achieved in the limit $\alpha \to \infty$. The optimization problem, formulated as a non-linear program, is then:

$$\text{OPT}_{\text{nlin}}: \quad \max. \quad \sum_{m \in \mathcal{M}} U(\omega_m) \tag{20}$$

$$\text{s.t.} \quad \text{C}_{\text{load}}: \quad \eta_x \le \eta_x^* \tag{21}$$

$$\text{C}_{\text{SLF}}: \quad \omega_{min} \le \omega_m \le \omega_{max} \tag{22}$$

We consider the load and SLF as the basic set of constraints. Later throughout the paper we additionally take the power and the DOWN-grant constraints into account.

Linearized Feasibility Region. The non-linear constraint on the load lead to optimal assignments if the RRM entity has knowledge of the load situation in all cells. In practice, however, this is very difficult to implement since it would need a very high amount of signaling to a central point, which should be avoided. In [11] and [8] the authors therefore propose a RRM implementation which can be implemented in a distributed way. These proposals are based on the assumption that the feasibility region is linear, such that the distributed algorithm converges to a global optimum. The optimization problem is therefore in our model complemented with a linear constraint on the row sums of system matrix $\tilde{G}$:

$$\text{OPT}_{\text{lin}} : \quad \max. \quad \sum_{m \in \mathcal{M}} U(\omega_m) \tag{23}$$

$$\text{s.t.} \quad \text{C}_{\text{lin}} : \quad \sum_{x} \sum_{k \in x} \Delta_{k,j}^i \cdot \omega_k \leq \eta_x^* \tag{24}$$

$$\text{C}_{\text{SLF}} : \quad \omega_{min} \leq \omega_m \leq \omega_{max} \tag{25}$$

Note that with condition C_{lin} also condition C_{load} is fulfilled, see e.g. [11].

Constant Load Assumption with a Static Assignment Policy. In Sec. 4, we introduced a RRM strategy for the E-DCH which always tries to maximize the resource utilization up to a certain threshold, which we call the target load η^*. The target load relates to an equivalent target interference by $\hat{I}^* = \frac{\eta^*}{1-\eta^*}(W\hat{N}_0)$.

Let us now assume, that the target interference is reached in all cells, i.e. $\hat{I}_x = \hat{I}_x^*$ for all NodeBs. The total interference term in Eq. (8) is then independent of the actual spatial user configuration. If we divide by the constant term $(WN_0 + \hat{I}_x)$, the left hand side is per definition the target load, and the rhight hand side are the sums of all SLFs times their link gain ratios, if we assume that $\hat{I}_x^* = \hat{I}_y^*$ for all $x, y \in \mathcal{L}$:

$$\eta_x^* = \sum_{l \in \mathcal{L}} \sum_{k \in l} \Delta_{k,l}^x \omega_k. \tag{26}$$

So under this assumption, we can calculate with the load factors only. If we split up the total load after the sources, Eq. (26) becomes

$$\eta_x^* = \eta_{x,D} + \eta_{x,E}^{own} + \sum_{y \in \mathcal{L} \setminus x} \sum_{j \in \mathcal{E}_y} \Delta_{j,y}^x \omega_j \tag{27}$$

The most straightforward way to calculate the SLFs for the E-DCH users is to solve the load equation system for the E-DCH own cell load η_E^{own}. This means, we assume that the load at each NodeB is constant and corresponds to the target load and solve for the own-cell load for the E-DCH users. This requires that, if we have more than one user per cell[1], we have to fix the partitioning of the E-DCH load to the individual SLFs with a *policy* factor g, such that

$$\sum_{j \in \mathcal{E}_x} g_j \cdot \eta_{x,E}^{own} = 1. \tag{28}$$

---

[1] Note that we assume that at least one E-DCH user is in each cell.

The policy factor can rely just on the number of E-DCH mobiles, such that $g_j = \frac{1}{|\mathcal{E}_x|}$ or can include distances or path gains to prioritize mobiles which are close to the NodeB. Following Eq. (3), we can now calculate the own-cell E-DCH load directly in matrix formulation:

$$\bar{\eta}_E^{own} = \bar{\eta}^* - \bar{\eta}_D - \tilde{F}_E'^{oc} \cdot \bar{\eta}_E^{own}, \tag{29}$$

where $\tilde{F}_E'^{oc}$ contains the link gain ratios as well as the policy factor g_j:

$$(\tilde{F}_E'^{oc})_{ij} = \begin{cases} \sum_{k \in \mathcal{E}_j} \Delta_{k,j}^i \cdot g_k, & \text{if } i \neq j \\ 0 & \text{else} \end{cases} \tag{30}$$

Solving for $\bar{\eta}_E^{own}$ yields the own-cell E-DCH load at each NodeB and with the policy factor also the resource assignment for each individual E-DCH user:

$$\bar{\eta}_E^{own} = (\tilde{E} + \tilde{F}_E'^{oc})^{-1} \cdot (\bar{\eta}^* - \bar{\eta}_D). \tag{31}$$

This approach, which we will call "local" or "direct" in the reminder, leads to negative results for $\bar{\eta}_E^{own}$ if either $\bar{\eta}_D > \bar{\eta}^*$ for one element, which means that the DCH load is higher than the target load, or if the spatial configuration is such that the other-cell E-DCH load is higher than $\eta^* - \eta_D$. In this case, we assume that the SLFs for the E-DCH users in the specific cell is set to the minimum, which leads to a load overshoot.

6.1   Feasible Load Region and Boundaries

Let us now consider a simple example with two cells, two E-DCH users (one per cell) and two DCH users. The values for Δ correspond to the path gain ratio between the non-serving and the serving NodeB. The first E-DCH user is close to the cell edge, which leads to an high Δ of 0.9. The second E-DCH user in the second cell is close to it's serving NodeB. The DCH user in the first cell has moderate distance to NodeB A. As fairness criterion for the global RRM schemes we chose max-min-fairness, since it is closest to the behavior of the local RRM scheme with equal load assignments for all E-DCH users in a cell.

Table 1. Example scenario

	E-DCH 1	E-DCH 2	DCH 1	DCH 2
S-NodeB	A	B	A	B
ω			0.1	0.05
Δ	0.9	$6 \cdot 10^{-4}$	$3 \cdot 10^{-4}$	$1 \cdot 10^{-4}$

The resulting feasible SLF regions for the two E-DCH users are shown in Fig. 5. For the global RRM strategies, we considered the power, the linear and

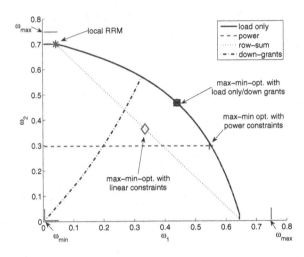

Fig. 5. Feasible SLF region for the two-cell scenario

the DOWN-grants constraints individually, i.e. we considered only one constraint additionally to the load and SLF constraint, which are always considered. The max-min-optimal points for the global RRM differ significantly from the direct approach, which yields a very unbalanced result between the two E-DCH users but still lies within the feasible region. The power constraints in this scenario leads to a SLF configuration which favors the first E-DCH user, while for the load-only and the DOWN-grant constraint as well as for the linear constraint the SLF values are balanced. The direct approach for the local RRM corresponds to the linear constrained RRM with sum-optimal utility function. The feasible region does not reach the maximum possible SLF ω_{max} due to the load from the DCH users. The optimal solution for the DOWN-grant constraint correspond in this case to the solution with load constraints only, however this would change if the maximum allowed ration between own-cell to total E-EDCH load is set to a lower value.

The corresponding load η_A at the first NodeB is shown in Fig. 6. The loads for the non-linear and linear case begin to diverge on the solution point for the direct approach. The effect of the linear constraint on the load is that the target load is not reached for a large range of the feasible SLF region. Further, the max-min-optimal point in this case is significantly lower than for the non-linear case. The direct approach naturally reaches the target load at both NodeBs, but at the expense of a very low SLF for the first E-DCH UE. It should be mentioned that this scenario is quite extreme, which is the reason for the different results of the approaches. As we will see in the next section, with more users the results get more close to each other.

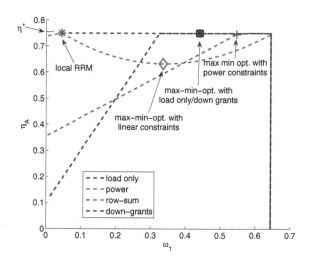

Fig. 6. Cell loads at NodeB A

7   Numerical Example

In order to get a better idea of the impact of the RRM strategies on the resource assignments, we simulated a example scenario with a Monte-Carlo simulation. To see the influence of the power and DOWN-grant constraints better, we chose a layout with seven cells and a large distance between the NodeBs, 2 km. The layout follows a hexagonal 7 cell scheme. For the results we consider only the cell in the center. The pathloss is calculated from the COST-231 small urban Hata model, and the target load is set to $\eta^* = 0.75$, which corresponds to a target interference of $-103\,\mathrm{dBm}$. For each run, the simulation generates the position of each UE new and then calculates the loads and interferences according to the RRM implementation. To see the influence of the number of E-DCH and DCH users, the total number of the users in each cell is fixed to 10, while the fraction of E-DCH user grows from 2 users to 8 users. The rest are DCH users with a bit rate of 64,kbps. For the local RRM we consider an equal-rate scheme, i.e. all E-DCH users in a cell get the same SLF. The users' locations follow a spatial Poisson process. Since it is not practical to let go $\alpha \to \infty$ in Eq. (19), the utility function for the optimization problem is defined as $U(\omega_m) = \sum_m \omega_m^{-1}$, which corresponds approximately to a max-min-fair resource assignment [15].

In Fig. 7 the load overshoot probability for the local RRM is shown. For one E-DCH user in each cell the overshoot probability is around 7%, but with an increasing number of E-DCH users the overshoot probability falls to nearly zero. Remember that a load overshoot occurs if the E-DCH SLFs in a cell are set to ω_{min}, but the target load is nevertheless exceeded because of a high other-cell load. This explains why the load overshoot probability decreases with an increasing number of E-DCH users: Although the probability that some UEs are close to the cell border is higher with more users, the fact that the E-DCH UEs

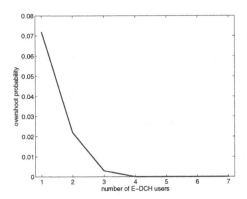

Fig. 7. Probability of load overshoot with local resource management

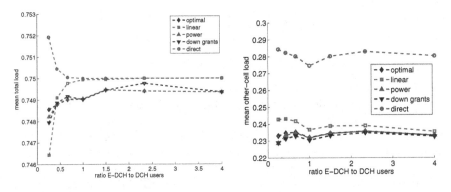

Fig. 8. Mean total load η **Fig. 9.** Mean other-cell load η^{other}

may get very high SLFs for a lower number of users outweights this effect. With a higher number of E-DCH users some UEs must have locations close to each other on the cell border to act as an "equivalent" E-DCH user with a high SLF.

The total loads, shown in Fig. 8, reflect the load overshoot probabilities for the local RRM. With an increasing number of E-DCH users, the mean total load decreases from 0.752 to the target load of 0.75. Correspondingly, the the loads for linear (or distributed) RRM increase until the target load is reached. The total loads for the global RRM with different constraints stay all below the target load but are close to each other. Only in the case of two E-DCH users it can be observed that the DOWN-grants and the power constraints lead to a lower load than with load and SLF constraints only.

In Fig. 9, the other-cell load for the local RRM is significantly higher than the loads for the global approaches, and the distance between the curves is more or less constant for all considered E-DCH to DCH ratios. As expected, the linear RRM as the highest other-cell loads for the global RRM implementations, and the DOWN-grant constrained RRM has the lowest, although the difference to

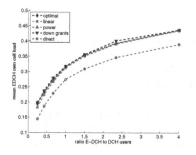 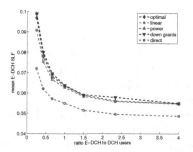

Fig. 10. Mean E-DCH own cell load   **Fig. 11.** Mean E-DCH SLFs

the other non-linear approaches is not very high. This is leads also the highest own-cell E-DCH load as shown in Fig. 10, although the difference is even smaller between the different global RRM approaches. The local RRM yields, corresponding to the highest other-cell load, the lowest E-DCH loads with a nearly constant difference to the global RRM strategies of 5%. Note that the own cell E-DCH grows linear with the number of E-DCH users. Corresponding to the E-DCH own cell load the mean assigned SLFs are shown in Fig. 11. The highest SLF is 0.1 for the global RRM, which corresponds to a bit rate of approximately 220 kbps. For two E-DCH users the SLFs for the local RRM are around 0.07, which corresponds to a bitrate of 150 kbps.

8   Conclusion and Outlook

The goal of this paper was to show the influence of different radio resource management strategies on joint power and rate controlled CDMA systems like the UMTS Enhanced Uplink. We considered three kinds of strategies: Global with knowledge of the whole load situation in the network, global with linear constrained feasibility region and a local with knowledge about the load in the local cell only. We further investigated the impact of several constraints like transmit power and DOWN grants from non-serving NodeBs. The results show that the local RRM strategy, which allows a direct calculation of the assigned resources to the users, lies on the boundary of the feasibility region of the global approach with linear constraints. Accordingly, the results for the total load of both approaches converge to each other if the probability for load overshoots decreases. The resource assignments, however, tend more to the results for the global approach, which yields the best results. Generally, we have seen that there is a significant difference between the global and local approaches in terms of resource efficiency. In this work we did only consider static or instantaneous scenarios, but not the influence of flow sizes or mobility on the system. So a next step would be to extend this work in that direction.

References

1. 3GPP: 3GPP TS 25.309 V6.4.0 FDD enhanced uplink; Overall description; Stage 2. Technical report, 3GPP (2005)
2. Parkvall, S., Peisa, J., Torsner, J., Sågfors, M., Malm, P.: WCDMA Enhanced Uplink – Principles and Basic Operation. In: Proc. of VTC Spring '05, Stockholm, Sweden (2005)
3. Mäder, A., Wagner, B., Hoßfeld, T., Staehle, D., Barth, H.: Measurements in a Laboratory UMTS Network with time-varying Loads and different Admission Control Strategies. In: 4th International Workshop on Internet Performance, Simulation, Monitoring and Measurement, Salzburg, Austria (2006)
4. 3GPP: 3gpp ts 25.321 v6.6.0 medium access control (mac) protocol specification. Technical report, 3GPP (2005)
5. Mäder, A., Staehle, D.: An Analytical Model for Best-Effort Traffic over the UMTS Enhanced Uplink. In: Proc. of IEEE VTC Fall '06. (2006)
6. Hoßfeld, T., Tutschku, K., Andersen, F.U., de Meer, H., Oberender, J.: Simulative performance evaluation of a mobile peer-to-peer file-sharing system. (2005)
7. Zander, J.: Performance of Optimum Transmitter Power Control in Cellular Radio Systems. IEEE Trans. on Vehicular Technologies **41** (1992)
8. Lundin, E.G., Gunnarsson, F., Gustafsson, F.: Robust Uplink Resource Allocation in CDMA Cellular Radio Systems. In: Proc. of Joint IEEE Conference on decision and control (CDC) and European Control Conference (ECC), Sevilla, Spain (2005)
9. Boche, H., Stanczak, S.: Optimal QoS Tradeoff and Power Control in CDMA Systems. In: Proc. of INFOCOM '04. (2004)
10. Hande, P., Rangan, S., Chiang, M.: Distributed Uplink Power Control for Optimal SIR Assignment in Cellular Data Networks. In: Proc. of INFOCOM '06, Barcelona, Spain (2006)
11. Price, J., Javidi, T.: Decentralized rate assignments in a multi-sector CDMA network. In: Proc. of IEEE GLOBECOM '03. Volume 1. (2003) 65–69
12. Holma, H., (Eds.), A.T.: WCDMA for UMTS. John Wiley & Sons, Ltd. (2001)
13. Mo, J., Walrand, J.: Fair end-to-end window-based congestion control. IEEE/ACM Trans. Netw. **8** (2000) 556–567
14. Kelly, F., Maulloo, A., Tan, D.: Rate control in communication networks: shadow prices, proportional fairness and stability. Journal of the Operational Research Society **49** (1998)
15. Boche, H., Schubert, M.: Resource Allocation in Multi-Antenna Systems – Achieving Max-Min Fairness by Optimizing a Sum of Inverse SIR. IEEE Trans. Signal Processing **54** (2006)

On the Interactions Between TCP Westwood and the AODV Routing Protocol

Rosario G. Garroppo, Luca Tavanti, Stefano Giordano, and Stefano Lucetti

Dip. Ingegneria dell'Informazione – Università di Pisa
Via Caruso, 16 – Pisa, I-56122 – Italy
luca.tavanti@iet.unipi.it
http://netgroup.iet.unipi.it

Abstract. The paper presents an experimental analysis of the performance of TCP Westwood in AODV-routed ad hoc networks. Several tests have been carried out in both emulated and real environments, with varying network topologies, routing protocol settings and channel quality levels. As expected, TCP is deeply influenced by the settings of the routing protocol and the fluctuations in the signal to noise ratio. However, the results also reveal a quite novel aspect: AODV and TCP perceive the radio link quality in different ways and this effect is further enhanced by the presence of network interface cards based on the IEEE 802.11 standard. This aspect leads to some performance anomalies that are shown in the paper.

1 Introduction

Performance evaluation of ad hoc networks has by now become a vastly researched area. However, most papers report on simulative or theoretical findings, whereas much less work deals with experimental evaluation. Still among these works, the interactions between medium access, routing and data plane transport layers have been scarcely investigated. For instance, [1] presents measurements of TCP throughput with a modified version of AODV (signal strength aware AODV), but only average figures are given and insights into protocol behaviour are rather superficial. Moreover, though designed to choose more stable routes, the employed protocol is experimental and not publicly available.

A more detailed analysis has been performed by [2], which reports communication throughput, end-to-end delay, packet loss, and route discovery time under the impact of various beaconing intervals, packet sizes, and route lengths in both static and mobile scenarios. However, the authors relied on ABR (Associativity-Based Routing), which is a non-standard routing protocol. Finally, [3] compared two AODV implementations with respect to their effect on the performance of transport layer protocols (UDP and TCP). The main shortcoming of this work is in the network configuration: since all the links are assumed to be good and the nodes do not move, only the static behaviour of the protocols is analyzed.

The work we present is targeted at filling the gap in this area. We look into the details of the behaviour of TCP under different patterns of propagation

J. García-Vidal and L. Cerdà-Alabern (Eds.): Wireless and Mobility, LNCS 4396, pp. 229–240, 2007.

conditions and settings of the routing protocol. Our goal is to identify which factors at the link and routing layers influence the performance of the data plane transport layer, and in what measure they do it.

The evaluation has been led on an experimental testbed. To make our results immediately portable to practical implementations, we have decided to use the most widely available technologies. Hence, we employed the AODV routing protocol, which is a IETF ratified (RFC 3561) and well accepted protocol, and IEEE 802.11b cards. Several quality levels of the radio links have been accurately emulated and practically realized.

2   Description of the Testbed

The nodes realizing our testbed were laptop PCs equipped with IEEE 802.11b cards and running the Linux OS. As for 802.11 settings, all parameters were left at their default, except for the RTS/CTS mechanism, which was disabled. The laptops were set up with AODV version 0.9.1 from the Uppsala University [4] and with the Westwood enhancement of the TCP protocol [5].

We decided to use TCP Westwood (in short, TCPW) as it already embeds some enhancements designed to tackle the typical troubles that TCP encounters in wireless communications. By the way, we also carried out some preliminary tests (not reported in here) in which TCPW effectively showed some improvements over the default TCP implementation of the Linux OS. A short overview of AODV and TCPW is in Sections 2.1 and 2.2.

TCP traffic was generated with netperf [6], which allowed a fine tuning of some TCP parameters. Traffic statistics were collected through the Magnet toolkit [7], which has been extended to generate a few figures about the MAC and physical layers as well.

The connection scenarios were realized through the netfilter framework [8]. By filtering out (at MAC layer) a predefined amount of the packets received from certain nodes, we could emulate a wide range of link conditions.

2.1   Overview of AODV

The Ad Hoc On Demand Distance Vector (AODV) routing protocol is a reactive protocol that creates routes only when some data transferral is requested. The routes are kept into a node cache just for the time necessary to deliver the data, and deleted afterwards. A route is discovered via broadcasting of a Route Request control message, which is re-broadcast until it reaches the destination node (or a node that knows how to reach it). This node replies with a Route Reply message, which is back-propagated to the source node in a unicast manner. The source node can now start delivering data along the discovered route. If any of the links along the path fails, a Route Error message is sent to the source node, which must restart the route discovery procedure.

AODV also provides each node to optionally broadcast Hello messages. These are periodic control messages, which are never forwarded, that allow nodes to have knowledge of their one-hop neighbours. Since the goal of Hello messages is to permit faster route discovery and fault detection, this feature is usually enabled.

2.2   Overview of TCP Westwood

TCP Westwood (TCPW) is a sender-side modification of the TCP congestion window algorithm. By monitoring the rate of returning ACKs, it estimates the bandwidth used by the connection. More in detail, the bandwidth estimate is obtained via low-pass filtering of the measured samples. Each bandwidth sample is given by:

$$b_k = \frac{d_k}{t_k - t_{k-1}},$$

where b_k is the instantaneous bandwidth, t_k is the time of reception of the kth ACK and d_k is the amount of data which the ACK refers to. The filter, whose (rather complex) expression is in [5], produces the low-frequency components of the available bandwidth $\hat{b}_k$.

After a congestion episode, the new congestion window and slow start threshold are computed using the bandwidth estimate. Basically, after three duplicate ACKs, the congestion window is set in order to approach $\hat{b}_k$, which is recognized to be a feasible bandwidth. TCPW thus introduces a recovery mechanism that avoids over-shrinking the congestion window. This mechanism should be particularly effective over wireless links where sporadic losses occur due to radio channel problems.

2.3   Parameters of the Routing Protocol

AODV allows to tune several parameters, but the most interesting are those regarding the periodic Hello messages: Hello Interval (HI), Allowed Hello Loss (AHL) and Hello Timeout (HTO). Given that HI and AHL are self-explaining, HTO determines how long the neighbours are kept in the node table after hearing the last Hello message. Consequently it controls the stability and reactivity of the protocol (see [4] for more details on ADOV). In particular, HTO is bound to HI and AHL through the expression:

$$HTO = HI \cdot AHL$$

The goal is to find out the combined effect of these parameters on data traffic and which configuration of the three gives the best results. To accomplish this task we have varied HI, AHL, and HTO along some lines in the HI-AHL plane (see Figure 1). More in the detail, each line keeps one of the three parameters constant. Particularly interesting are the lines at constant HTO, since along these AODV maintains the same degree of reactivity.

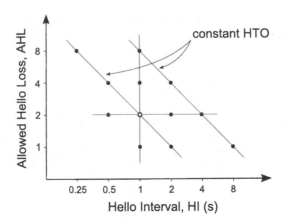

Fig. 1. The plane reporting the variations of AODV parameters. Axis are in logarithmic scale. The point (1,2) represents the default configuration.

3 Analysis of the Results

In this section we illustrate the results obtained for two configurations of our testbed (see Figure 2). The first scenario is rather common in literature, whereas the second presents a somewhat innovative approach.

The first experiment is a four node network, in which all links have been emulated with good quality (no packets are dropped by the netfilter framework); yet some fluctuations, due to the experimental nature of the test, are present. The links from the source node S to the other nodes are then dropped one by one (Figure 2(a)). In details, S is at first connected directly to the sink node D (route 1). This connection is then cut and S needs to find a two-hop path to D (route 2). Later on, this link too is broken, hence a three-hop route from S to D is established (route 3). The outcome of the tests performed in this scenario is reported in Section 3.1.

The second experiment involves a link whose quality degrades over time (path 1 in Figure 2(b)). Starting form the perfect state, we used netfilter to induce an increasing Packet Drop Rate (PDR) that reaches 100% at the end of the experiment. The other links are not affected by emulated losses. AODV parameters have been set to the default (HI = 1 s, AHL = 2). The results generated by this experiment are described in Section 3.2.

3.1 Sudden Dropping of the Links

Figure 3 reports the throughput for three configurations of the AODV parameters in the case of sudden drop of the links (refer to Figure 2(a)). With respect to the HI-AHL plane (see Figure 1), we move along the line at constant AHL, with AHL = 2. The first plot in Figure 3 refers to HI = 0.25 s and AHL = 2. Then HI is increased up to 4 s in the last plot. Note that HTO spans in the range 0.5–8 seconds, thus varying the reactivity of the routing protocol.

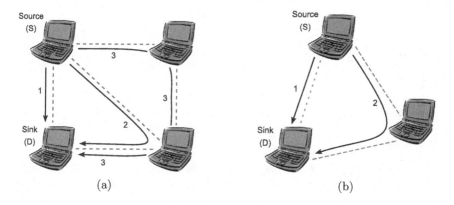

Fig. 2. The simulation scenarios. Gray dashed lines represent the radio links, black solid arrows the routes.

From the plots it can be seen that a smaller HTO makes the protocol react more quickly to topology changes, as the interval of route absence are very short (notches at roughly 60 and 120 seconds in Figure 3(a)). As a side effect, the throughput is less stable. Temporary link quality fluctuations and network congestion episodes (due to contention at the link layer) cause Hello messages to be delayed or dropped (at the MAC layer). When the HTO is short, AODV is fast to declare the route broken and to start a new route discovery (that often resolves in the same route). This temporary interruption in the data flow has a significant impact on TCP, which responds by reducing the congestion window. The result is thus an oscillating throughput.

On the contrary, increasing HI, and consequently HTO, smooths the plot, since short network congestion or broken connection episodes do not immediately trigger route failures. On the flip side, the detection of a definitely invalid route takes longer (see Figure 3(c)). In case of mostly static networks this could be a valid solution. A trade-off between the two described behaviours seems to be at HI = 1 s and AHL = 2 (Figure 3(b)), which is the default configuration of AODV. The dips are on average shorter than in Figure 3(c) and the throughput is more stable than in Figure 3(a), thus giving acceptable performance for general-purpose networks.

Let us now examine what happens when we move on a constant-HTO line, in particular with HTO = 2. The results for three possible configurations are reported in Figure 4. Note that Figure 4(b) and Figure 3(b) are two repetitions of the same test. Though slightly different, they do agree on the general behaviour.

In this case, reducing HI and increasing AHL turns out to be the best choice, as throughput is stable acros the whole test (Figure 4(a)). The default configuration of AODV, in Figure 4(b), is slightly more unstable, and reducing AHL to one (with HI = 2 s) results in even less stable connections (Figure 4(c)). Hence

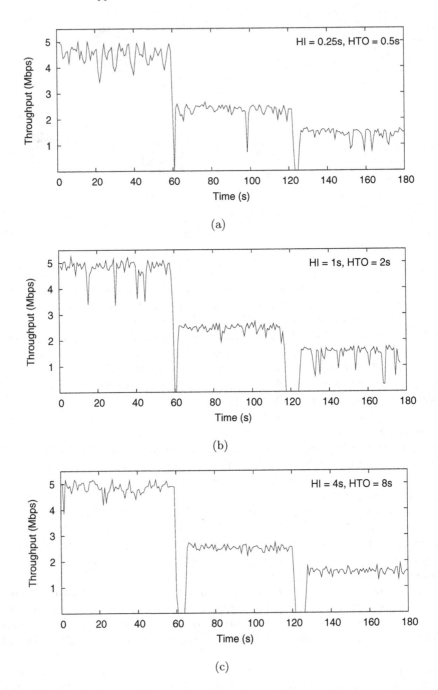

Fig. 3. Throughput for three AODV parameter configurations under the constraint
AHL = 2

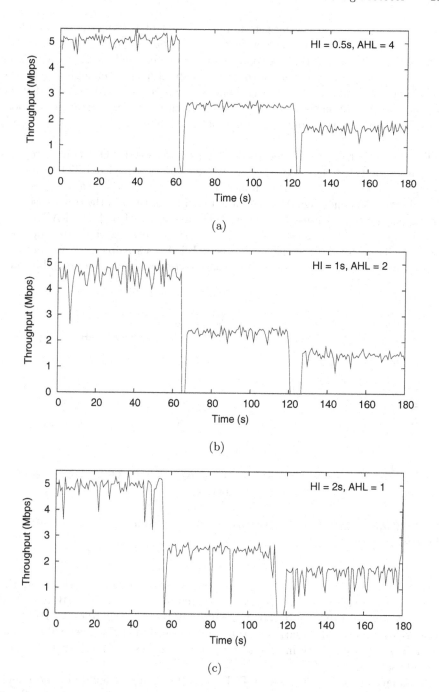

Fig. 4. Throughput for three AODV parameter configurations under the constraint HTO = 2

we can deduce that decreasing the number of control messages is not an effective solution when the links have a good, but not perfect, quality. Furthermore, using AHL = 1 implies that as soon as one expected Hello is not received, or is received with some delay (note that even a small delay is enough to pass the HTO timeout), the originating neighbour is regarded as lost. Consequently the route to that neighbour is dropped and a new route discovery is started. In most cases, however, the new route uses that same neighbour, which in fact was not lost.

This last effect can be better appreciated as we raise HTO. Figure 5 reports the throughput for the case HI = 8 s and AHL = 1, with HTO = 8. The strong oscillations in the throughput, due to frequent route failures, emerge immediately. Also, average throughput is much lower than in the other cases. As a reference consider Figure 3(c), where HTO is still 8 (HI = 4 s and AHL = 2). The differences are manifest. As a side remark, note that, since the topology does not change for most of the time, raising HTO is a sensible choice to improve performance (at the expenses of longer route reconstruction, of course), but only if AHL is raised as well.

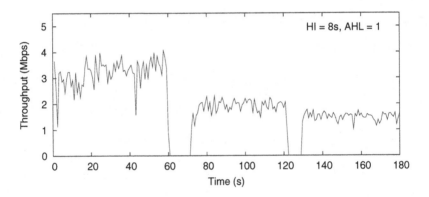

Fig. 5. Throughput for this AODV parameter configuration: HI = 8s, AHL = 1, HTO = 8

The last line to analyse should be the one at constant HI. However, this does not add much to what has been presented. Changes in the AHL and HTO have already been discussed above. In short, AHL = 1 (regardless of HI value) produces frequent false alarms of route breakage, but a too high value would produce scarce reactivity in case of true route failures. A trade-off is therefore the advisable setting.

Summarizing, the behaviour of TCP over AODV in this kind of experiments is as expected. Our tests confirm previous results (e.g. [3]), and above all add more insights to them.

3.2   Slow Degradation of One Link

The result for the second type of experiment is presented in Figure 6. From the plot we can identify several phases. At the beginning, while the loss rate is low, TCP can deliver the traffic, even if not at its maximum rate. As PDR increases, throughput rapidly degrades. Remarkably, throughput does not follow the same trend of link quality. Rather it presents a sort of knee: while PDR is below 45%, throughput diminishes gently, then it drops quickly and it may even go to zero when PDR reaches 50% (at around 120 s).

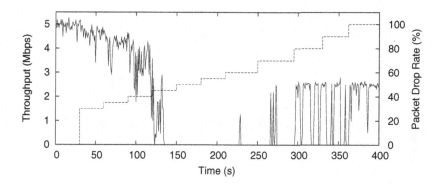

Fig. 6. Throughput (solid line) and packet drop rate (dashed line) for the second scenario

In a second part (up to 270 s), throughput is approximately zero. This is due to the different perception that TCP and AODV have of the link quality. While a loss from 50% to 70% is enough to prevent TCP from delivering data, AODV does not consider the direct route to be broken, because a fair number of Hello messages is still heard (remind that AHL is two, so with a PDR of 50% a packet every two is, on average, received). When PDR exceeds 75%, AODV starts forwarding the packets over the relayed route. Not all the traffic however is sent over that path, as the sporadic reception of some Hello messages from the sink node triggers a switch on the old route. Finally, when the link is completely broken (PDR = 100%), all the traffic is directed through the two hop route, giving stability to the throughput.

This same test has been replicated in a purely experimental way. Random dropping of the received packets has been replaced by changes in the signal to noise ratio (SNR), obtained by physically moving the terminals. Clearly, cloning the exact trend of packet losses was not possible, but we achieved a similar, and undoubtedly more realistic, trend. The results of this test are reported in Figure 7(a), with the strength of the signals coming from the source and relay stations plotted on Figure 7(b). Values of the signal strength are those reported by the driver of the network interface card (Intersil's Prism2.5).

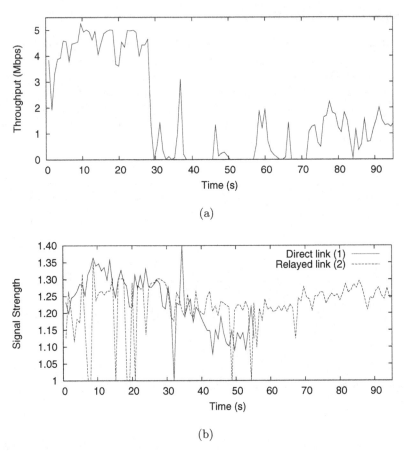

Fig. 7. Throughput and signal strength for the experimental test of the second scenario

The general trend of the throughput is very similar to what emerged from Figure 6. While the signal strengths of the direct link is high enough, data transfer is rather smooth, but as soon as the strength starts degrading, TCP is unable to deliver traffic (at around 30 s). Then, there is an interval in which the throughput is almost zero, except for some sporadic peaks, and finally, when the signal strength is so weak to force AODV to completely discard the direct route, TCP restarts to deliver data at an acceptable rate. Note however that the signal of the relayed link is always worse than the other, so a more consistent packet drop rate is present for this path, with the subsequent impossibility to get close to the theoretical upper bound.

An interesting feature that emerges in this test is the increased number of factors, beyond the pure configuration of the routing protocol, that may determine the registered behaviour. For example, different frame sizes (like data and TCP ACK) have different error probability, and link quality fluctuations easily hamper TCP. Among these, however, the role played by the MAC layer has a noteworthy impact.

The IEEE 802.11b standard provides for different transmission bit rates for the different kinds of packets. In particular, AODV Hello messages are mapped to broadcast frames, which are transmitted at a lower bit rate, whereas TCP data packets are mapped to unicast frames, which are usually transmitted at the highest bit rate (neglecting rate adaptation policies, which are subject to vendor implementations). Since lower bit rates are devised to be more robust to channel noise and interferences, the range of broadcast frames is (possibly much) longer than data frames. Hence, when the link quality is in the midway, AODV can still receive Hello messages from its neighbours, regarding the path to them as valid, but data frames can hardly be delivered. With reference to our experiment, TCP data packets are never switched over the two-hop route, or they are for very short times. So, this is why TCP throughput starves.

4   Conclusions

In this paper we have presented a set of experimental tests to evaluate the performance of TCP in an ad hoc network based on the AODV routing protocol and the IEEE 802.11b link layer. From the results, we can broadly confirm some of the findings produced by other works. Also, we have added more insights and brought to light some new findings.

TCP is quite sensitive to the behaviour of the underlying routing layer. The parameters of AODV should be carefully adjusted. For instance we have shown that for relatively static topologies, with links of good quality, decreasing the Hello Interval (HI) and increasing the Allowed Hello Loss (AHL) could be an efficient choice. However, it should be verified on a much larger test-bed whether the increased control traffic becomes too large.

The most remarkable result, however, stands in the fact that AODV and TCP perceive link quality in different ways. A link judged to be good (or acceptable) by the routing protocol, may resolve in an unserviceable path for data traffic. In our case this is also due to the IEEE 802.11b protocol implemented by the network interface cards, that makes data and control traffic perceive the links in different ways. As shown, this may lead to some detrimental performance anomalies.

In conclusion, to improve the efficiency of TCP over an ad hoc network, solutions based on a cross-layer approach and/or a routing protocol aware of the issues of the transport and MAC layer should be preferred.

Acknowledgments

The authors wish to thank Giuseppe Risi and Domenico Gallo for their help in setting up the testbed and carrying out the experiments.

One of the authors, Luca Tavanti, also wishes to thank Thales Italia SpA for sponsoring his PhD scholarship.

References

1. A. Gupta, I. Wormsbecker, C. Williamson, "Experimental Evaluation of TCP Performance in Multi-hop Wireless Ad Hoc Networks", *Proc. of MASCOTS 2004.*
2. C. K. Toh, M. Delwar, D. Allen, "Evaluating the Communication Performance of an Ad Hoc Wireless Network", *IEEE Transactions on Wireless Communications*, Vol. 1, No. 3, July 2002.
3. K. Kuladinithi, A. Udugama, N. A. Fikouras, C. Görg, "Experimental Performance Evaluation of AODV Implementations in Static Environments", available at: http://www.comnets.uni-bremen.de/~koo.
4. AODV routing protocol implementation at Uppsala University: http://core.it.uu.se/AdHoc/AodvUUImpl.
5. C. Casetti, M. Gerla, S. Mascolo, M.Y. Sansadidi, R. Wang, "TCP Westwood: End-to-End Congestion Control for Wired/Wireless Networks", *Wireless Networks Journal*, 2002.
6. The Netperf benchmark: http://www.netperf.org/netperf/NetperfPage.html.
7. The Monitoring Apparatus for General kerNel Event Tracing (MaGNET), available at: http://public.lanl.gov/radiant/research/measurement/magnet.html.
8. The Netfilter project: http://www.netfilter.org.

Stability and Dynamics of TCP-NCR(DCR) Protocol in Presence of UDP Flows

Tadeusz Czachórski[1,2], Krzysztof Grochla[1], and Ferhan Pekergin[3]

[1] IITiS PAN, 44-100 Gliwice, ul. Bałtycka 5
[2] II Politechnika Slaska, 44-100 Gliwice ul. Akademicka 16
[3] LIPN, Université Paris-Nord, 93430 Villetaneuse, France
{tadek,kgrochla}@iitis.gliwice.pl, ferhan.pekergin@lipn.univ-paris13.fr

Abstract. The fluid-flow approximation models investigate with much success the dynamics and stability of TCP/RED connections. Their main assumption is that the fluctuations of variables characterizing the behaviour of the connections are relatively small, that enables the linearization of model and the use of traditional control analysis tools to obtain such measures as Bode gain, phase margins, tracking error or delay margin. In this article, preserving linear fluid-flow model, we propose its extension to the case when a network is composed of wired and wireless part. We consider a variant of TCP algorithm (TCP-DCR or its new version TCP-NCR) and fluid-flow differential equations representing the size of congestion window, mean queue at the bottleneck router and loss probability at a RED queue are supplemented with terms representing constant loss probability due to transmission in wireless part and probability that a fraction of these errors is recovered by a link level mechanism. The decrease of congestion window due to TCP mechanism is delayed to allow the link protocol to deal with the errors. The model considers the presence of uncontrollable UDP flows.

Keywords: active queue management, RED, dynamics of TCP flows, unresponsible flows.

1 Introduction

A considerable work was done recently to capture the dynamics of TCP connections with the use of fluid flow approximation. The results include a model of a network with general topology [7], analysis of RED queue in the bottleneck router [4,9], as well as its comparison with proportional-integral control [5]. In [6,13] a mixture of TCP and UDP flows was introduced and in [11] the method is adapted to the analysis of satellite networks. In [12] an adaptation of this approach to several flavors of TCP is presented. Fluid flow approximation is relatively simple, compared to other analytical methods of queueing theory, and therefore well suited to analyze the behaviour of complex networks.

In general, the approach consists in solution of several equations. The first one concerns the dynamics of TCP congestion window W and the second refers to the changes of the mean queue at the bottleneck router:

J. García-Vidal and L. Cerdà-Alabern (Eds.): Wireless and Mobility, LNCS 4396, pp. 241–254, 2007.
© Springer-Verlag Berlin Heidelberg 2007

$$\dot{W}(t) = \frac{1}{R(t)} - \frac{W(t)}{2}\frac{W(t-R(t))}{R(t-R(t))}p(t-R(t)) \tag{1}$$

$$\dot{q}(t) = \begin{cases} -C + \dfrac{K(t)}{R(t)}W(t), & q > 0 \\[2mm] \max\{0, -C + \dfrac{K(t)}{R(t)}W(t)\}, & q = 0, \end{cases} \tag{2}$$

where $\dot{x}$ denotes time-derivative and W is the average TCP window size expressed in packets; q is the average queue length in bottleneck router [packets]; $R(t)$ is round trip time [sec]; C is link capacity [packets/sec]; p is the probability of packet dropping or marking; K is the number of TCP sessions active in the bottleneck router. The Eq. (1) may be extended to take into account the slow start procedure and time-out losses [9].

The set of equations modelling TCP flows dynamics is then linearized around the working point. The control loop may be then analyzed with standard tools appropriate to investigate the stability of a linear control system where the dynamics of its elements is represented by their transfer functions.

A way to incorporate in the model the unresponsive flows is to modify Eq. (2) in the following way [6]. Let $l(t)$ denotes the traffic of responsive flows and $u(t)$ of the unresponsive ones,

$$\dot{q}(t) = \begin{cases} -C + \dfrac{K(t)}{R(t)}W(t) + u(t), & q > 0 \\[2mm] \max\{[0, -C + \dfrac{K(t)}{R(t)}W(t) + u(t)\}, & q = 0. \end{cases} \tag{3}$$

It is supposed in [6] that $u(t)$ is a stationary process with mean u_0 and its variations are on a finer time-scale, hence it may be regarded as constant and it results in diminishing the bandwidth seen by responsive flows:

$$\dot{q}(t) = \begin{cases} -(C-u_0) + \dfrac{K(t)}{R(t)}W(t), & q > 0 \\[2mm] \max\{0, -(C-u_0) + \dfrac{K(t)}{R(t)}W(t)\}, & q = 0. \end{cases} \tag{4}$$

The linearization around working point (W_{l0}, p_0, q_0, u_0) gives transfer functions, expressed here in terms of their Laplace transforms

$$W(s) = -P_{win}(s)e^{-sR_0}p(s), \qquad l(s) = \frac{K}{R_0}W(s), \tag{5}$$

$$q(s) = P_{que}(s)\left[l(s) + u(s)\right], \qquad p(s) = q(s)C_{aqm}(s) \tag{6}$$

where

$$P_{win}(s) = \frac{\dfrac{R_0 C_{eff}^2}{2K^2}}{s + \dfrac{2K}{R_0^2 C_{eff}}}, \qquad P_{que}(s) = \frac{1}{s + \dfrac{C_{eff}}{C}\dfrac{1}{R_0}}, \qquad C_{eff} = C - u_0.$$

and $C_{aqm}(s)$ is the Laplace transform of transfer function of the AQM controller. The above equations are matched with others which define the probability of dropping or marking a packet as a function of the mean queue size. In the case of classical RED algorithm, the dropping probability is defined by a curve having three parameters: min_{th}, max_{th} and max_p,

$$p_d = \begin{cases} 0 & \text{if} \quad avg \le min_{th} \\ \dfrac{avg - min_{th}}{max_{th} - min_{th}} * max_p & \text{if} \quad min_{th} < avg \le max_{th} \\ 1 & \text{if } max_{th} < avg, \end{cases} \qquad (7)$$

where the moving average avg is calculated at the arrival of each packet and represents a low-pass filter for the actual queue length

$$avg = \begin{cases} (1-w)*avg + w*n & \text{if queue is not empty} \\ (1-w)^{\frac{\mu}{\lambda}} * avg & \text{if queue is empty,} \end{cases}$$

where w is a fixed (small) parameter and n is the instantaneous queue size.

The process of taking the moving average (denoted below by x) may be modelled as in [9]

$$\frac{dx}{dt} = \log_e(1-w)/\Delta - \log_e(1-w)/\Delta q(t) \qquad (8)$$

where Δ is the interarrival time of packets and is taken as $\Delta = 1/C$.

Hence, the transfer function of RED mechanism having changes of current queue δq at the entrance and changes of packet loss δp as the output has the form

$$C_{aqm}(s) = L_{red}\frac{k}{k+s}$$

where

$$k = -\ln(1-w)/\Delta = -C\ln(1-w) \qquad \text{and} \qquad L_{red} = \frac{max_p}{max_{th} - min_{th}}.$$

The above equation may be replaced by another if the AQM algorithm changes.

This way a control loop schema as in Fig. 1 is formulated and analysed. Below, we present some notions on the stability analysis following [10]. The stability of the system may be investigated with the use of Nyquist criterion. In general, the closer the transfer function $G(j\omega)$ representing the whole control loop transfer functions, comes to encircling the $(-1 + j0)$ point, the more oscillatory is the system response. The closeness of $G(j\omega)$ locus to the $(-1 + j0)$ point can be used as a measure of the margin of stability. It is common practice to represent the closeness in terms of *phase margin* and *gain margin*. *Phase margin* is the amount of additional phase lag at the gain crossover frequency required to bring the system to the verge of instability. The gain crossover frequency is the frequency at which $|G(j\omega)|$, the magnitude of open-loop transfer function, is unity. The phase margin γ is 180 deg plus the phase angle φ of the open-loop transfer function at the gain crossover frequency, or $\gamma = 180$ deg $+\varphi$. On the Nyquist diagram, a line may be drawn from the origin to the point at which the unit circle crosses the $|G(j\omega)|$ locus. The angle from the negative real axis to this line is the phase margin. The phase margin is positive for $\gamma > 0$. For a minimum phase system to be stable, the phase margin must be positive [10].

Gain margin is the reciprocal of the magnitude $|G(j\omega)|$ at the frequency where the phase angle is -180^{deg} Defining the phase crossover frequency ω_1 to be the frequency at which the phase angle of the open-loop transfer function equals -180^{deg} gives the gain margin $K_g = 1/|G(j\omega_1)|$. The gain margin may be expressed in decibels $K_g db = 20 \log K_g = -20 \log = |G(j\omega_1)|$. In this case it is positive if K_g is greater than unity and negative if if K_g is smaller than unity. Thus, a positive gain margin (in decibels) means the system is stable, and the negative gain margin (in decibels) means that the system is unstable.

Another stability indices are *tracking error* which informs how good systems tracks the desired steady state queue and what are oscillations around it, hence what is the transmission jitter) and *delay margin* (the amount of additional delay that can exist in the feedback without making the system unstable). Figures 3 - 5 illustrate the influence of the transmission and control parameters on the shape of Nyquist plots. In plots, similarly as in [9] the presence of transfer function $\Delta(s)$, see fig. 2 was neglected and considered as a source of noise.

In this numerical example $C = 12500$ packets/s, $K = 60$, and RED parameters are $p_{max} = 0.01$, $max_{th} = 200$, $min_{th} = 100$, $w = 0.0001$. Delay R is varied between 10 ms and 100ms, C_{eff} is equal $0.25C$, $0.5C$, and $0.75C$.

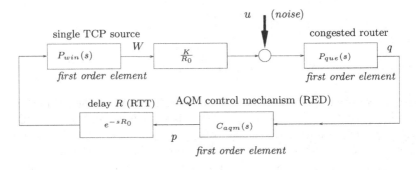

Fig. 1. Control schema 1

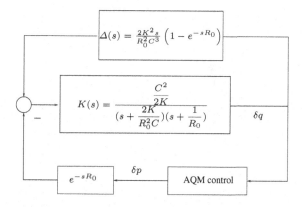

Fig. 2. Control schema of TCP Reno connections, see [9]

In section 2 we propose an extension of this model to capture the performance of TCP algorithm at wired-wireless environment.

2   TCP in Wireless Environment, TCP-DCR

In traditional TCP implementation, like New Reno, even if the wireless channel recovery mechanism is able to retransmit the packet, it is considered as a packet loss by the transport layer, due to the high delay. In wireless networks the packet loss often occur due to transmission errors, in typical cases with a ratio going up to a few percent. The classical TCP implementation does not work well in this case. That is why some modification of the classical New Reno algorithm were proposed, e.g. TCP Westwood [8]. Recently, several solutions have been proposed to improve the performance of TCP over wireless networks. In general, these solutions are classified in four categories *split connection* approaches, *link layer scheme, explicit loss notification* approaches and *receiver-based* approaches.

Here, we concentrate on TCP-Delayed Control Rate (or Delayed Congestion Response) TCP-DCR, [1]. It is a modification of the TCP protocol created to improve its robustness to channel errors in wireless network. The TCP-DCR is based on the idea of allowing the link level mechanism to recover the packets lost due to channel errors. This is done by delaying the triggering of congestion response (fast retransmission-recovery) algorithms due to reception of dupacks or due to time-out of the retransmission timer, for a small bounded period of time τ to allow the link level retransmission to recover the loss due to channel errors. The choice of τ is critical, makes a trade off between unnecessarily inferring congestion, and unnecessarily waiting for a long time before retransmitting a lost packet. Analytical considerations in [1] indicate that both upper and lower limit for τ is RTT, hence the best choice is $\tau = RTT$.

These principles then evolved in document [2] where the non-congestion robustness (NCR) is discussed and two variants of TCP-NCR are proposed:

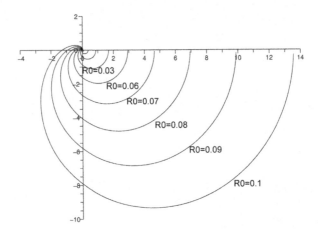

Fig. 3. Reno connections, $G(jm)$ for various values of delay R, stable and unstable cases

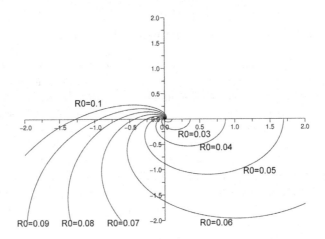

Fig. 4. Nyquist plot for various delays R_0 (fragment)

(i) *Careful Limited Transmit* which calls for reducing the sending rate at approximately the same time implementations reduce the congestion window, as defined by RFC 2581, while at the same time withholding a retransmission (and the final congestion determination) for approximately one RTT. (ii) *Aggressive Limited Transmit* that calls for maintaining the sending rate in the face of duplicate ACKs until TCP concludes that a segment is lost and needs to be retransmitted (which TCP-NCR delays by one RTT when compared with current loss recovery schemes).

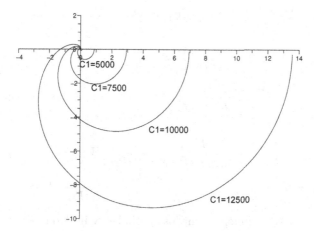

Fig. 5. Reno connections, $G(jm)$ for various values of effective band C_{eff}, stable and unstable cases

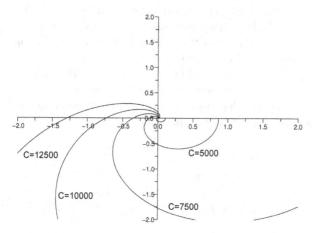

Fig. 6. Reno connections, $G(jm)$ for various values of effective band C_{eff}, stable and unstable cases (fragment)

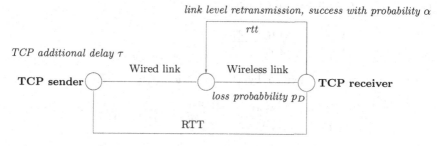

Fig. 7. DCR parameters

According to TCP-DCR philosophy, the eqs. (1,2) are modified:

$$\dot{W}(t) = \frac{1 - P_D}{R(t)} + \frac{P_D \alpha}{R(t) + rtt} - \frac{W(t)}{2} \times$$

$$\times \frac{W(t - R(t) - \tau)}{R(t - R(t) - \tau)} [p(t - R(t) - \tau) + P_D(1 - \alpha)], \qquad (9)$$

$$\dot{q}(t) = \begin{cases} -C + \dfrac{K(t)}{R(t)(1 - P_D) + (R(t) + rtt)P_D\alpha} W(t), & q > 0 \\[3mm] \max\{0, -C + \dfrac{K(t)}{R(t)(1 - P_D) + (R(t) + rtt)P_D\alpha} W(t)\}, q = 0, \end{cases} \qquad (10)$$

where P_D is congestion-independent loss probability in wireless part of the network, rtt is time after which the wireless protocol is able to recover from an error with probability α.

Fig. 11 presents the block diagram of this control. We linearized eqs. (9) and (2) in the same way as eqs. (1) and (2) were linearized in [4]. First we assume that the number of TCP sessions and link capacity are constant, i.e., $K(t) \equiv K$ and $C(t) \equiv C$. Taking (W, q) as the state and p as input, the operating point (W_0, q_0, p_0) is then defined by $\dot{W} = 0$ and $\dot{q} = 0$.

To proceed with linearization of (1), we ignore the dependence of the time-delay argument $t - R$ on queue-length q, and assume it fixed to $t - R_0$. On the other hand, we retain the dependence of round-trip time on queue length in the dynamics parameters. We have two functions:

$$\dot{W}(t) = f_1\Big(W(t), W(t - R(t) - \tau), q(t), q(t - R(t) - \tau), p(t - R(t) - \tau)\Big)$$

$$= f_1(W, W_{R+\tau}, q, q_{R+\tau}, p_{R+\tau})$$

$$= \frac{1 - P_D}{q/C + T_p} + \frac{P_D \alpha}{q/C + T_p + rtt} - \frac{W}{2} \frac{W_{R+\tau}}{q_{R+\tau}/C + T_p} [p_{R+\tau} + P_D(1 - \alpha)]$$

$$\dot{q}(t) = f_2\Big(q(t), W(t)\Big) = f_2(q, W)$$

Linearization of a function $f(x_1, x_2, \ldots, x_n)$ is done around a working point $(x_{1,0}, x_{2,0}, \ldots, x_{n,0})$ for small changes of arguments

$$\delta f = \sum_{i=1}^n \frac{\partial f(x_1, x_2, \ldots, x_n)}{\partial x_i} \bigg|_{(x_1 = x_{1,0}, x_2 = x_{2,0}, \ldots, x_n = x_{n,0})} \delta x_i$$

The working point is defined by the condition $f_1(.) = f_2(.) = 0$, hence by relations

$$\frac{1 - P_D}{R_0} + \frac{P_D \alpha}{R_0 + rtt} - \frac{W_0^2}{2R_0}[p_0 + P_D(1 - \alpha)] = 0$$

and

$$-C + \frac{KW_0}{R_0(1 - P_D) + (R_0 + rtt)P_D\alpha} = 0$$

We obtain

$$\delta \dot{W} = \frac{\partial f_1}{\partial W}\delta W + \frac{\partial f_1}{\partial W_{R+\tau}}\delta W_{R+\tau} + \frac{\partial f_1}{\partial p_{R+\tau}}\delta p_{R+\tau} + \frac{\partial f_1}{\partial q}\delta q + \frac{\partial f_1}{\partial q_{R+\tau}}\delta q_{R+\tau}$$

$$\delta \dot{q} = \frac{\partial f_2}{\partial W}\delta W + \frac{\partial f_2}{\partial q}\delta q$$

where

$$\frac{\partial f_1}{\partial W} = -\frac{W_0}{2}\frac{p_0 + P_D(1-\alpha)}{R_0},$$

$$\frac{\partial f_1}{\partial W_{R+\tau}} = \frac{\partial f_1}{\partial W},$$

$$\frac{\partial f_1}{\partial p_{R+\tau}} = -\frac{W_0^2}{2}\frac{1}{R_0},$$

$$\frac{\partial f_1}{\partial q} = -\frac{(1-P_D)}{CR_0^2} - \frac{P_D\alpha}{C(R_0+rtt)^2},$$

$$\frac{\partial f_1}{\partial q_{R+\tau}} = \frac{W_0^2}{2}\frac{p_0 + P_D(1-\alpha)}{CR_0^2},$$

$$\frac{\partial f_2}{\partial W} = \frac{K}{R_0(1-P_D)+(R_0+rtt)P_D\alpha},$$

$$\frac{\partial f_2}{\partial q} = -\frac{KW_0(1-P_D+P_D\alpha)}{C[R_0(1-P_D)+(R_0+rtt)P_D\alpha]^2}.$$

Fig. 12 displays the block diagram of the control loop resulting from this linearization. Figs 8 – 10 present an example of the influence of the changes of effective bandwidth (the presence of UDP connections taking a part of the bandwidth C) on the connection behaviour: the impact on TCP congestion window and queue length at the congested router (solution of eqs. 9, 10 before their linearization).

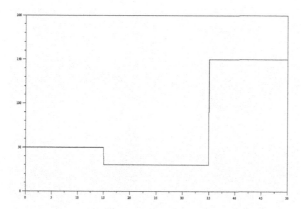

Fig. 8. Channel throughput C, changes in time

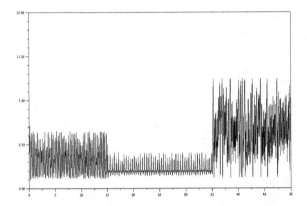

Fig. 9. Congestion window, reaction on the changes of C

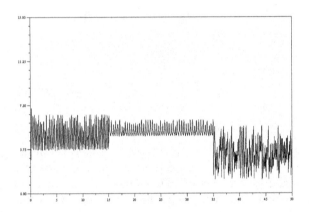

Fig. 10. Queue length at router, reaction on the changes of C

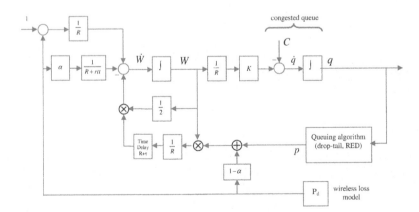

Fig. 11. Block diagram for nonlinear TCP-DCR rate control

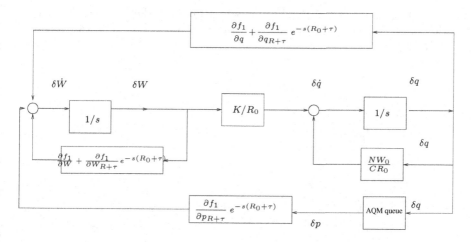

Fig. 12. Block diagram for linearized TCP-DCR control

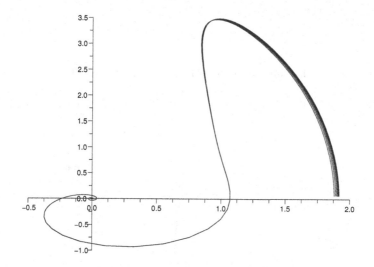

Fig. 13. $G(jm)$, the influence of the changes of $rtt = 0.1RTT, \ldots, 0.9RTT$

In numerical example below we assumed the following parameters: link capacity $C = 12500$ packets/s, number of connections $K = 60$; RED parameters $p_{max} = 0.01$, $max_{th} = 200$, $min_{th} = 100$ $w = 0.0001$ at the working point loss probability due to congestion is $p_0 = 0.05$, the size of congestion widow $W_0 = 10$, $R_0 = 0.05$; other parameters such as loss probability for wireless part P_D, , τ, rtt, probability of successful retransmission in wireless part α, are varied as indicated in figures. Figures 13 - 15 represent some exemplary curves $G(j\omega)$ as a function of mentioned above parameters. Fig. 16 compares plots for two versions od NCR protocol.

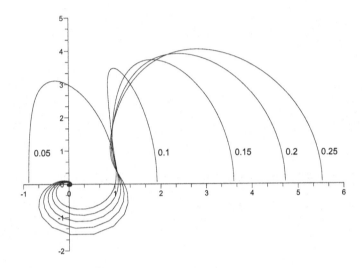

Fig. 14. $G(jm)$, the influence of losses in wireless part $P_D = 0.05, 0.10, \ldots 0.25$

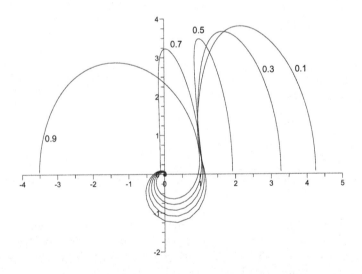

Fig. 15. $G(jm)$, the influence of the probability $\alpha = 0.1, 0.3, 0.5, 0.7, 0.9$ of successful retransmission in the wireless part

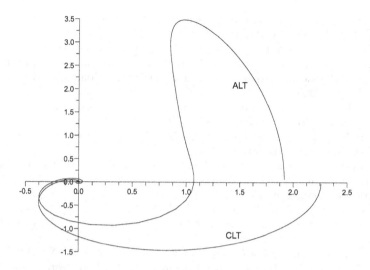

Fig. 16. $G(jm)$ The influence of multiplicative factor a to decrease the congestion window in case of a transmission ($a = 1/2$ in case of *aggressive limited transmit NCR* (ALT), and $a = 2/3$ in case of *careful limited transmit NCR* (CLT)

3 Conclusions

The presented model adapts the fluid-flow model of TCP/RED congestion control mechanism to the case when a network is composed of wired and wireless part. A DCR-TCP and its successing two variants of NCR-TCP protocol are considered. Presented numerical examples illustrate the influence of several parameters of these protocols on the stability of connections. Further systematic numerical investigations to determine stability areas are needed.

Acknowledgments

This work was partially supported by the Polish Ministry of Science and Higher Education grant no N517 025 31/2997.

References

1. S. Bhandarkar, N. Sadry, A.L.N. Reddy, N. Vaidya, *TCP-DCR: A novel protocol for tolerating wireless channel errors*, Technical Report TAMU-ECE-2003-01, February 2003.
2. S. Bhandarkar, A.L.N. Reddy, M. Allman, E. Blanton, *Improving the Robustness of TCP to Non-Congestion Events*, Network Working Group Request for Comments: RFC 4653
3. J. Chen, F. Paganini, R. Wang, M. Y. Sanadidi, M. Gerla, *Fluid-flow analysis of TCP Westwood with RED*, Computer Networks: The International Journal of Computer and Telecommunications Networking, Vol. 50, Iss. 9, June 2006.

254   T. Czachórski, K. Grochla, and F. Pekergin

4. C. V. Hollot, Vishal Misra, Don Towsley et al. *A control theoretic analysis of RED*, Proc of IEEE/INFOCOM, 2001.
5. C. V. Hollot, V. Misra, D. Towsley, W.B. Dong, *Analysis and Design of Controllers for AQM Routers Supporting TCP Flows*, IEEE Transactions on Automatic Control, special issue on Systems and Control Methods for Communication Networks, vol. 47, no. 6, 2002.
6. C. V. Hollot, Y. Liu, V. Misra, D. Towsley et al. *Unresponsive flows and AQM Performance*, Proc. of IEEE INFOCOM 2003.
7. Y. Liu, F. Lo Presti, V. Misra, Y. Gu, *Fluid Models and Solutions for Large-Scale IP Networks*, ACM/SigMetrics 2003.
8. S. Mascolo, C. Casetti, M. Gerla, M.Y. Sanadidi, R. Wang: *TCP Westwood Bandwidth Estimation for Enhanced Transport over Wireless Links*, in: Mobile Computing and Networking, pp.287-297, 2001.
9. V. Misra, W.-B. Gong, D. Towsley: *Fluidbased Analysis of a Network of AQM Routers Supporting TCP Flows with an Application to RED*, ACM SIGCOMM 2000.
10. K. Ogata, *Modern Control Engineering*, Prentice Hall of India, New Dehli 1977.
11. M. Sridharan, et al, *Tuning RED parameters in Satellite Networks Using Control Theory*, Proc. of Performance and Control of Next Generation Communication Networks, SPIE Vol. 5244, Orlando Florida, September 7-11, pp.145-153.
12. R. Srikant, *The Mathematics of Internet Congestion Control*, Springer Series: Systems and Control: Foundations and Applications, Berlin 2004.
13. Wang Li, LI Zeng-zi, Chen Yan-ping, Xue Ke, *Fluid-Based stability Analysis of Mixed TCP and UDP Traffic under RED*, Proc of the 10th Int. Conf on Engineering of Complex Computer Systems, (ICECCS), 2005.

Optimization Models for Application Migration to Support Mobile Thin Clients

Pieter Simoens*, Lien Deboosere, Davy De Winter,
Filip De Turck**, Bart Dhoedt, and Piet Demeester

IBCN-INTEC, Ghent University, IBBT
Gaston Crommenlaan 201 bus 8, B-9040 Gent, Belgium
{pieter.simoens,lien.deboosere}@intec.ugent.be
www.ibcn.intec.ugent.be

Abstract. Thin clients are lightweight devices from which all hardware, not related to input and output, is removed. Applications are executed on remote servers that render the graphical output and send it back to the client. As the reaction on user events can appear on the screen only after a two-way path delay, thin client computing can suffer from a high latency that degrades the user experience. We therefore propose that the application follows the user through the network by migrating to a server near enough to the user.

In this paper, a theoretical model and heuristics are presented to efficiently select servers for mobile users, in order to minimize the number of migrations and the corresponding application downtime. A sample scenario is presented, which clearly exposes the trade-off between the number of migrations and the average client-server latency. We then detail a theoretical model to determine the optimal allocation of applications to servers, in order to minimize the number of handovers. This model is based on the knowledge of the exact user movements and is only useful in an off-line setting. As this is impossible in real-time, several heuristics are presented. Their performance is compared and validated against the theoretical model.

1 Introduction

With thin client computing, the applications run on a server in the network instead of locally on the user's device. All functionality and hardware that is not related to user input and output is removed from the device, making it light and low-energy. Since complex calculations are performed on the servers in the network, energy consumption decreases and battery lifetime extends. Besides this weight reduction and autonomy extension, the centralization of data and software on application servers has also other advantages. Securing data is much easier when all data is present at one place. Users are released from daily software patches and virus definition updates, as this will be done by the server administrator.

---

* Research Assistant for the Fund of Scientific Research (F.W.O.-V, Belgium).
** Postdoctoral Fellow for the Fund of Scientific Research (F.W.O.-V, Belgium).

J. García-Vidal and L. Cerdà-Alabern (Eds.): Wireless and Mobility, LNCS 4396, pp. 255–270, 2007.
© Springer-Verlag Berlin Heidelberg 2007

The communication between thin client and application server is accomplished by a remote display protocol. All user events, like key strokes and mouse movements, are sent to the server. This server processes the commands, renders the corresponding graphical output and sends the results back to the client. Since reactions to user events can appear on the screen only after a two-way path delay, the thin client paradigm can inherently suffer from an increased latency. Application responsiveness decreases when the user moves further away from his server. To guarantee a high ubiquitous mobile user experience, the delay should be kept as low as possible. This can be realized when the applications make a movement parallel to the user. Applications travel through the network and migrate to an available server close to the mobile user's current location.

Ideally, the user should not notice when his application migrates from one server to another. However, each migration causes an application downtime period and places a load on the overlay network management platform that controls the migration. Application migrations are hence costly operations and should be avoided as much as possible. Only when the quality of a client-server connection drops below a predefined threshold, a migration should be initiated. An intelligent choice of the server to migrate the application to, can reduce the number of migrations and increase the user experience. It is therefore important to have well-performing algorithms for the selection of the target server. These algorithms can take the mobility of the user into account.

The remainder of this paper is structured as follows. In section 2, an overview of related work is given. Section 3 elaborates on the application migration mechanism and presents a sample scenario and the considered architecture. The trade-off between the average client-server delay and the number of migrations will be exposed. Our theoretical model for an optimal server selection is detailed in section 4, together with heuristics for real-time calculations. Simulation results for both the theoretical model and the heuristics are presented in section 4.3. Conclusions are drawn in section 5.

2   Related Work

The migration of applications is a challenging problem. Open files and network connections, inter-process communication and memory address conflicts make transparent application migration a trying task. The concept of application (or process) migration between servers was originally developed for load balancing in a server cluster. Some examples are Condor [1] and MOSIX [2]. With these techniques, only processes without inter-process communication or open network connections can be migrated successfully. Furthermore, the migration is not fully transparent, as open files are not migrated and the application at the new server relies on the open files at the original server. More recently, process migration techniques like ZAP [3] and its successor Cruz [4] have solved these drawbacks, by interposing a thin layer between applications and the OS. When an application with an open TCP connection is migrated, the tuple identifying the connection must be updated. ZAP uses a virtual-physical address mapping mechanism [5] to achieve this, while in MIGSOCK [6], messages are exchanged to inform the other (non-moving) end of the network connection about the connection migration. In [7], the performance of ZAP and MIGSOCK is compared.

A range of wide-area network server selection algorithms is developed for Content Distribution Networks (CDN). In such networks, multiple servers offer the same content. The decision of which server will handle a user request is in almost all cases done by the client. In [8], the selection is based on the Round-Trip Time and the actual number of server calls. Administrative Servers organize this information of the servers within their domain in a minimum heap structure and send it to the client. In [9], a technique is presented to transform the server selection decision into a problem of optimal routing and the redirection process is shifted from the client to the server-side. An interesting server selection algorithm that takes the user mobility into account, was described in [10]. Servers are grouped in hierarchical tiers. Higher-tier servers have a larger coverage area and hence occur fewer server hand-offs, but they give a higher end-to-end latency. The trade-off between the number of hand-offs and the latency will also be discussed in this paper. All these algorithms can however not be applied directly for thin clients. In CDN, multiple servers are offering the same content, while in thin client networks each user has his unique set of running applications.

In [11], we presented a theoretical model to find the most optimal locations to install application servers in the network. The follow-up paper [12] discussed the number of migrations and proposed three mechanisms to perform a seamless migration between application servers. In this paper, we elaborate on a minimization of the number of migrations.

3   Application Migration

3.1   Architecture

Figure 1 presents a generic view on the foreseen architecture for thin client computing and application migration. The application servers are interconnected by the routers of the core network. Users can access these global infrastructure by connecting (possibly wireless) to an access point. The traffic from several access points towards the core network is aggregated by access gateways (AGW). When a user moves around and experiences a high latency, a closer application server is selected and a migration is initiated.

Current research projects such as PlanetLab [13,14] and XenoServer [15] are envisioning the deployment of a world-wide server infrastructure for public computing. We foresee a more dense distribution of servers to enable thin-client computing than currently provisioned in these infrastructures, but the technological and research challenges for the management and allocation of the computing resources are the same. Therefore, this paper only addresses the server selection and assumes the presence of a well-managed server platform.

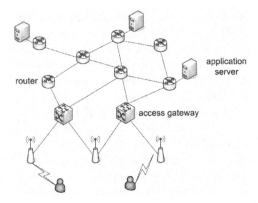

Fig. 1. Architecture for thin client computing. Users are connected to an access gateway and the applications run on servers in the core network.

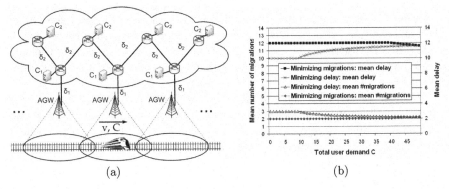

Fig. 2. Architecture for the elementary train scenario and the mean client-server delay and number of migrations for a train passing $N = 4$ AGWs, with sample values $C_1 = 10$, $C_2 = 20$, $\delta_1 = 10$ and $\delta_2 = 2$

3.2   Sample Scenario

To illustrate the concept of application migration, we consider an elementary train scenario. The topology is shown in Figure 2(a). Several access gateways (AGWs) are placed at regular distances along a railway. The core network consists of two types of server farms for the passengers' applications, with capacities C_1 and C_2 respectively, expressing e.g. the CPU capacity. The links introduce a delay of δ_1 and δ_2 and the train advances at speed v. To run all passengers' applications, a total server capacity of C is required. As the train moves forward, the passengers connect to the next AGW along the track and when necessary, the applications migrate to keep the user-server delay within the latency constraints. We assume that a client-server delay of at most $\delta_1 + \delta_2$ is acceptable.

In this elementary scenario, it is clear that the applications should reside on the upper servers (with capacity C_2) to minimize the number of migrations; and on the lower servers (with capacity C_1) to minimize the average client-server delay. Equations (1) - (4) give the average delay $\bar{\delta}$ and the mean number of migrations $\overline{M}$ for both minimizations when N AGWs are passed. Ideally, only servers on the upper or lower layer are used, depending on the minimization scenario. When the user demand increases, more and more servers are required and also servers on the other layer will host applications. We suppose that the load is uniformly distributed over all used servers of one layer. The results for different user demands C are presented in Figure 2(b) for some sample values. The curves start to converge when servers on the other layer are used. The trade-off between the number of migrations and the average user-server delay is clearly visible.

Minimizing the number of migrations

$$\bar{\delta} = \begin{cases} \delta_1 + \delta_2 & \text{if } C \le 2C_2 \\ (\delta_1 + \delta_2) \cdot \frac{2C_2}{C} + \delta_1 \cdot \frac{C - 2C_2}{C} & \text{if } 2C_2 < C \le 2C_2 + C_1 \end{cases} \quad (1)$$

$$\overline{M} = \begin{cases} \frac{N}{2} & \text{if } C \le 2C_2 \\ \frac{N}{2} \cdot \frac{2C_2}{C} + (N - 1) \cdot \frac{C - 2C_2}{C} & \text{if } 2C_2 < C \le 2C_2 + C_1 \end{cases} \quad (2)$$

Minimizing the average user-server delay

$$\bar{\delta} = \begin{cases} \delta_1 & \text{if } C \le C_1 \\ \delta_1 \cdot \frac{C_1}{C} + (\delta_1 + \delta_2) \cdot \frac{C - C_1}{C} & \text{if } C_1 < C \le 2C_2 + C_1 \end{cases} \quad (3)$$

$$\overline{M} = \begin{cases} N - 1 & \text{if } C \le C_1 \\ (N - 1) \cdot \frac{C_1}{C} + \frac{N}{2} \cdot \frac{C - C_1}{C} & \text{if } C_1 < C \le 2C_2 + C_1 \end{cases} \quad (4)$$

4   Server Selection Algorithms

For more complex situations, with non-simultaneously moving users and larger networks, efficient algorithms are needed to reduce the number of migrations as much as possible, while still guaranteeing the latency constraints of the applications. To solve this trade-off, we developed a model that can be solved by Integer Linear Programming techniques. Since the calculation time increases exponentially with the number of variables, this becomes impractical for larger networks. We therefore introduce four heuristics and compare their performance with the exact result as presented by our model.

4.1   Theoretical Model

Parameters. We assume the network topology is given and can be characterized by its set of I nodes and (unidirectional) links:

$$\begin{aligned} N &= \{n_i\} & \text{with } i = 0, 1, ..., I - 1 \\ L &= \{(n_i, n_{i'})\} & \text{with } n_i, n_{i'} \in N \end{aligned} \quad (5)$$

The set N is composed of two subsets. The first subset S contains all interior nodes, the second U the access gateways. We assume that servers can be installed at all nodes of S, but not at nodes of U. The application processing requirements are expressed as Floating Point Operations Per Second (FLOPS). The total FLOPS processing capacity of the server farm at node n_i is given by F_i. Locations with no installed servers can be modeled by assigning the corresponding F_i a value of zero. If we have X internal network nodes and $N - X$ access gateways:

$$\begin{aligned} S &= \{n_i\} \quad \text{with } i = 0, 1, ..., X - 1 \\ U &= \{n_i\} \quad \text{with } i = X, X + 1, ..., N - 1 \end{aligned} \quad (6)$$

Users can execute K types of applications. The total simulation time is T. Each of the J users is connected at every (discrete) moment t to an access gateway. We introduce the following variable to model this mobility at time t:

$$u_{ijk}(t) = \begin{cases} 1 & \text{if user } j \text{ is at } t \text{ at node } n_i, \text{ executing an application of type } k \\ 0 & \text{otherwise} \end{cases} \quad (7)$$

with $i = X, ..., N - 1$; $j = 0, ..., J - 1$ and $k = 0, ..., K - 1$. Each type of application has its own requirements, both to the network and the application server. We model the user demand by assigning each type of application a certain FLOPS demand f_k. The maximum allowable latency is different for each type of application and is modeled by d_k^{max}. We assume this delay only depends on the number of nodes between the router to which the server is connected and the AGW to which the user is connected. In future work, we could include the delay due to the server processing, which is related to the server load.

Decision Variables. We want to find the optimal distribution of the applications of all users over the available servers, in order to minimize the number of migrations. To indicate on which server an application is running at time t, we introduce the following binary variables:

$$s_{ijk}(t) = \begin{cases} 1 & \text{if a server at node } n_i \text{ executes user } j\text{'s application of type } k \\ 0 & \text{otherwise} \end{cases} \quad (8)$$

with $i = 0, ..., X - 1$; $j = 0, ..., J - 1$ and $k = 0, ..., K - 1$. Assuming that process migrations take less than one discrete timestamp, we introduce the binary variables $p_{ijk}(t)$ to denote if an application of user j has migrated between t and $t + 1$ from or towards a server at n_i.

$$p_{ijk}(t) = \begin{cases} 1 & \text{if } s_{ijk}(t) \neq s_{ijk}(t + 1) \\ 0 & \text{otherwise} \end{cases} \quad (9)$$

Finally, the following variables are introduced to express the routing of the traffic between client and server. With $(n_i, n_{i'}) \in S$ and $j = 0, ..., J - 1; k = 0, ..., K - 1$:

$$a_{ii'jk}(t) = \begin{cases} 1 & \text{if } (n_i, n_{i'}) \text{ is used for user } j\text{'s application of type } k \\ 0 & \text{otherwise} \end{cases} \quad (10)$$

Objective Function. By using the introduced decision variables, we can express the objective function. In order to minimize the number of migrations, the following minimization problem should be solved:

$$\min \sum_{t=0}^{T-1} \sum_{i=0}^{X-1} \sum_{j=0}^{J-1} \sum_{k=0}^{K-1} p_{n_i jk}(t) \tag{11}$$

Constraints. The solution space for (11) is limited by several constraints. However, to relax the problem slightly, we assume that the bandwidth of the links is sufficient to route all traffic. Hence, routing decisions are only constrained by the maximum number of hops between client and server:

$$\forall j, \forall k, \forall t : \sum_{(n_i, n_{i'}) \in L} a_{ii'jk}(t) \leq d_k^{max}. \tag{12}$$

At every timestamp, exactly one server farm has to be selected to serve the application k of user j. The maximum capacity demand for a server farm cannot exceed the installed capacity. Both constraints are imposed by the following expressions:

$$\forall j, \forall k, \forall t : \sum_{i=0}^{X-1} s_{ijk}(t) = \sum_{i=X}^{X+U-1} u_{ijk}(t). \tag{13}$$

$$\forall i : i < X, \forall t : \sum_{j=0}^{J-1} \sum_{k=0}^{K-1} f_k \times s_{ijk}(t) \leq F_i. \tag{14}$$

The last set of constraints, expresses the flow conservation constraints:

$$\forall i, j, k, t :$$
$$\begin{cases} \sum\limits_{i':(n_i, n_{i'}) \in L} a_{ii'jk}(t) - \sum\limits_{i':(n_{i'}, n_i) \in L} a_{ii'jk}(t) = -s_{ijk}(t) \text{ if } i < X, \\ \sum\limits_{i':(n_i, n_{i'}) \in L} a_{ii'jk}(t) - \sum\limits_{i':(n_{i'}, n_i) \in L} a_{ii'jk}(t) = u_{ijk}(t) \text{ if } X \leq i < N - 1, \end{cases} \tag{15}$$

The final constraint expresses the relation between the binary variables $p_{ijk}(t)$ and $s_{ijk}(t)$.

$$\forall i, j, k : \sum_{t=0}^{T-1} p_{ijk}(t) \geq s_{ijk}(t+1) - s_{ijk}(t) \tag{16}$$

4.2 Heuristics

As the number of variables increases, the calculation time to solve the optimization problem becomes too high. Furthermore, the theoretical model presented in the previous section is only able to determine the most optimal server once all information is known, in particular the mobility of the users. Since this is impossible in practice, heuristics for real-time server selection are needed. Every time the AGW changes to which a user is connected, for all the applications of the user a check of the latency between the current server and the new AGW is executed. If the latency exceeds the maximum allowable delay, heuristically a new server is selected for the application. Each of the presented heuristics starts with the composition of a list of candidate servers to host the application. Which server is finally selected, depends on the applied heuristic. The decision can be based on the previous movements, a prediction of the next movements or a combination of both. In the next section, these three heuristics are presented. First, the algorithm to compose a list of candidate servers, common for each heuristic, is detailed.

Selection of Candidate Servers. When a mobile user changes his AGW and the latency with his current server becomes too high, each heuristic calls this algorithm first to compose a list of candidate servers to which the application could migrate. Viable candidates must be near enough to the new AGW in terms of latency, and must have enough remaining processing capacity to host the application. This is summarized in Algorithm 1.

Algorithm 1. Candidate Selection Algorithm (CSA)

$C \leftarrow \{\}$ (empty list to hold candidate servers)
$U \leftarrow$ user that has just changed his AGW
$A \leftarrow$ application of the user for which latency is too high
for each application server S in the network **do**
    if delay(U.connectedAGW, S) $\leq$ A.maxDelay **then**
        if A.requiredProcessingCapacity $<$ S.remainingProcessingCapacity **then**
        add S to C
    end if
  end if
end for

Basic Server Selection Heuristic. The basic heuristic starts from the assumption that by selecting a server that can host a lot of AGWs, the application can remain for a long time on the same server, even when the user moves around. This is presented in Heuristic 1. After calling the CSA, for each of the servers in the list, the number of AGWs that can be reached within the latency constraint of the application is counted. The server with the highest count is then selected. If multiple servers can serve the same number of AGWs, the tie is broken by looking at the average delay towards each AGW. This tie-breaking mechanism is not shown.

Prediction Heuristic. The basic heuristic does not take the direction of user movement into account. By choosing a server that can serve the most AGWs, one hopes that the next AGWs to which the user will connect, are amongst them. If

Heuristic 1. Basic Heuristic (BH)

$A \leftarrow$ application to migrate
$C \leftarrow$ list of candidate servers from CSA
max_noServedAGW = 0, $k = 0$
for each Candidate Server (CS) $\in$ C **do**
  for $k <\#$ AGWs in the network **do**
    no_servedAGWs = 0
    if delay(AGW[k], CS) $\leq$ A.maxDelay) **then**
      no_servedAGWs++
    end if
    if no_servedAGWs > max_noServedAGW **then**
      max_noServedAGW = no_ServedAGW
      selectedServer = CS
    end if
  end for
  A.server $\leftarrow$ selectedServer
  k++
end for

---

the user trajectory would be known in advance, a more accurate server selection could be achieved, resulting in less migrations. Heuristic 2 tries to incorporate this idea and uses a prediction of the next access gateways to which the user will connect. After running the CSA, for each candidate server it is checked how many of the predicted next gateways are within the latency constraint of the application to migrate. The prediction algorithm itself is not detailed, as several approaches have been reported in literature [16,17]. For our simulations, we only implemented an elementary prediction module. For each AGW, it holds transition probabilities to all other AGWs. Every time a user disconnects from an AGW and connects to another, this move is tracked by the module and the transition probabilities are updated. The maximum number of predicted AGWs that is checked, is an input parameter for the heuristic. From the viewpoint of handover minimization, it is no use to select a server that can serve the second or third predicted next AGW but not the first one predicted. Therefore, an additional stop condition is added to the while-loop in Heuristic 2.

User History Heuristic. While the previous heuristic was based on a prediction of the next user movements, one could also base the server selection on the past user mobility. Heuristic 3 starts from the assumption that a user will not return on his previous steps. Just as in the BH, the server is selected that can serve the most access gateways within the latency constraint of the application. However, only access gateways are considered that were not visited by the user in one of his previous N movements. The number N of previously visited access gateways that is taken into account, is an input parameter for the algorithm.

History and Prediction Heuristic. The History and Prediction Heuristic (HPH) is a combination of the two previous heuristics and takes both user

Heuristic 2. Prediction Heuristic (PH)

$C \leftarrow$ list of candidate servers from CSA
$PAGW \leftarrow$ predicted next hops of user U
max_noServedAGW = 0
for each Candidate Server (CS) $\in$ C **do**
  no_servedAGWs = 0, m = 0
  bool stop $\leftarrow$ 0
  while stop $\neq$ 1 AND m < PAGW.length **do**
    if (delay(CS, PAGW(m)) $\leq$ A.maxDelay) **then**
      no_servedAGWs ++
    else
      stop $\leftarrow$ 1
    end if
    m ++
  end while
  if no_servedAGWs > max_noServedAGW **then**
    max_noServedAGW = no_ServedAGW
    selectedServer = CS
  end if
end for

Heuristic 3. History Heuristic (HH)

$A \leftarrow$ Application to migrate
$C \leftarrow$ list of candidate servers from CSA
$HAGW \leftarrow$ History of previous N hops of user U
$ToCheckAGW \leftarrow$ all AGWs in the network
for each AGW $\in$ HAGW **do**
  if AGW $\neq$ U.currentAGW **then**
    delete AGW from ToCheckAGW
  end if
end for
for each Candidate Server (CS) $\in$ C **do**
  k = 0
  for k < ToCheckAGW.length **do**
    no_servedAGWs = 0
    if delay(ToCheckAGW[k], CS) $\leq$ A.maxDelay) **then**
      no_servedAGWs++
    end if
    if no_servedAGWs > max_noServedAGW **then**
      max_noServedAGW = no_ServedAGW
      selectedServer = CS
    end if
    k++
  end for
  A.server $\leftarrow$ selectedServer
end for

---

mobility history and prediction into account. Starting from a list of N predicted AGWs, this list is reduced to the first M AGWs in the list to which the user was not connected in one of his previous P movements. Both N and P are input parameters of the heuristic. Then, for each candidate server, it is checked how many of the AGWs of this reduced prediction list can be served within the latency constraint of the application to migrate. The heuristic is detailed in Heuristic 4. Like in the PH, the order of the prediction is important and an additional stop condition for the while-loop is added.

Heuristic 4. History and Prediction Heuristic (HPH)

$A \leftarrow$ Application to migrate
$C \leftarrow$ list of candidate servers from CSA
$PAGW \leftarrow$ predicted N next hops of user U
$HAGW \leftarrow$ previous P hops of user U
$m = 0, M = 0$, max_noServedAGW $= 0$
bool $stop \leftarrow 0$
while stop $\neq 1$ AND m $<$ PAGW.length **do**
  if PAGW[m] $\in$ HAGW **then**
    stop $\leftarrow 1$, M $= m$
  end if
  m $++$
end while
reduce PAGW to its first M elements
for each Candidate Server (CS) $\in$ C **do**
  no_servedAGWs $= 0$, k $= 0$
  bool stop $\leftarrow 0$
  while stop $\neq 1$ AND k $<$ M **do**
    if (delay(CS, PAGW(k)) $\leq$ A.maxDelay) **then**
      no_servedAGWs $++$
    else
      stop $\leftarrow 1$
    end if
    k $++$
  end while
  if no_servedAGWs $>$ max_noServedAGW **then**
    max_noServedAGW $=$ no_ServedAGW
    selectedServer $=$ CS
  end if
end for

4.3   Experimental Results

In order to compare the performance of the heuristics with the theoretical model, we implemented a discrete event simulator, based on the Telecom Research Software library [18]. Every time a user moves around and changes his AGW, a new event is generated and the heuristic is triggered. The optimal solution for the theoretical model was determined by using a Branch and Bound Integer Linear

Programming (ILP) Solution approach [19]. The simulations were run for different network topologies and trace files with user movements to minimize random influences. As presented in equation (6), our network consists of two types of interconnected nodes: server locations and access gateways. For our simulations, we first placed 20 nodes randomly in a 100x100 plane. These nodes represent possible server locations in the core network. They are interconnected by 40 edges added to the topology by applying the Waxman-model [20]. This model takes 2 parameters. We selected 10 different parameter combinations and generated 5 networks for each, resulting in 50 networks. The latency of the added edges is uniformly distributed in the interval (5, 15). We then added 16 nodes uniformly distributed over the plane, representing the access gateways. Each node was connected to the 3 most nearby server locations by links with a fixed latency of 15. This models the observation that most of the latency is introduced in the access network, often due to the presence of wireless interfaces. The user mobility is simulated by a change of the AGW to which the user is connected. Two patterns of user movements are considered. In the first pattern, users change randomly to one of the neighboring AGWs. In the second pattern, movements of all users are correlated by fixing for each AGW transition probabilities to its neighboring AGWs. On average, a user changes his AGW every 100 discrete timestamps, with a total simulation time of 100000 discrete timestamps. For each pattern, 10 tracefiles were generated, containing the mobility information of 50 users. The maximum delay between a client and his application server is varied between 15, 25 and 35. The heuristics HH, PH and HPH take a number N of previously visited or predicted next AGWs of a user as input parameter. In the remainder of this section, this will be referred to as the hop input parameter.

The time to solve equation (11) with ILP increases exponentially when the number of variables grows. This is shown in Table 1. The test machine, an AMD Athlon64+ 2800 (1800 MHz) with 512 MB RAM, ran out of memory for simulations with 7 or more users. This table clearly emerges the need for fast and reliable heuristics. In Table 2, the average calculation time of the heuristics is presented, to select a new server for a user. The calculation time increases for larger values of the hop input parameter and the maximum delay.

In Figure 3, the solution of the ILP-problem is compared with the solutions of the heuristics BH, HH, PH and HPH. The number of users had to be reduced to only one user, in order to solve the problem in an acceptable time. The ILP-solution clearly yields the minimal number of handovers.

Due to the high calculation times, only a limited range of simulations could be performed to test the theoretical model. To fully assess the performance of the different heuristics, more elaborate simulations were carried out with 50 users,

Table 1. Solving time for a maximum delay of 25 and a hop input parameter of 3

# users	1	2	3	4	5	6	7
time (s)	17.50	39.55	66.90	137.66	662.638	7521.039	/

Table 2. Calculation times in msec for each heuristic. The BH results are indepent from the number of hops.

hops	BH			HH			PH			HPH		
	15	25	35	15	25	35	15	25	35	15	25	35
1	4	7	18	3	6	13	2	2	4	2	2	3
2	4	7	18	3	7	15	2	3	5	2	2	4
3	4	7	18	4	7	15	2	3	6	2	3	5
5	4	7	18	3	7	14	3	4	8	2	4	7
10	4	7	18	3	6	13	3	6	13	3	5	12
20	4	7	18	3	5	12	4	10	22	4	10	20

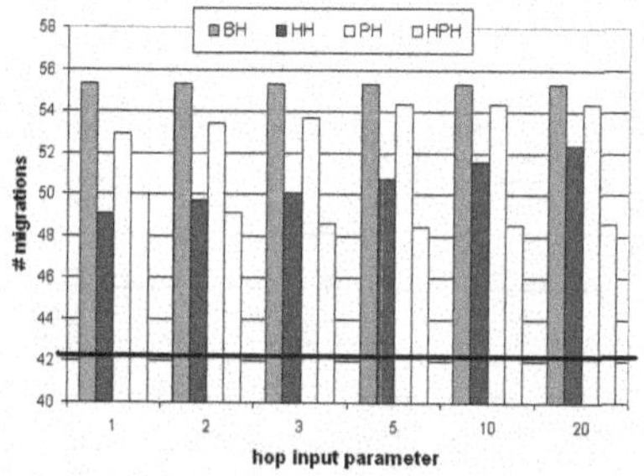

Fig. 3. The ILP yields 42.11 migrations and clearly outperforms the heuristics

each running 1 application. In Figure 4, the performance of all heuristics is compared for a hop input parameter of 3. The trade-off between the average number of migrations and the average client-server delay can be clearly distinguished. All heuristics have in common that a higher number of migrations results in a lower average delay and that the highest number of migrations is seen for a maximum allowable delay of 15. For a delay of 15, only the nearest application servers of the AGW can be selected and most likely, the application must be migrated when a user connects to another gateway. With a relaxed delay constraint, more servers can host the application and less migrations are necessary when users move around.

For all heuristics, the number of migrations decreases when the maximum allowable delay increases. By taking the user history or the prediction of movements into account, the number of migrations is decreased. The history-based heuristic HH clearly outperforms PH. This can be accounted to the fact that the HH takes all neighboring AGWs into account (except for the one previously visited), while the PH looks for only one path leading away from the current AGW. As a result, the HH will probably select a server more close to the connected AGW, which can almost certainly serve all neighboring AGWs. In contrast, the PH will select a server somewhere along the path at a greater distance from the the current AGW. If the prediction hampers, this will result in an increase of the number of migrations. Finally, by combining both approaches (HPH), the greatest reduction is achieved.

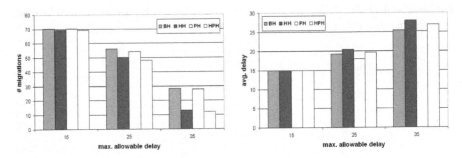

Fig. 4. Trade-off between the average number of migrations and the average delay, for a hop input parameter of 3

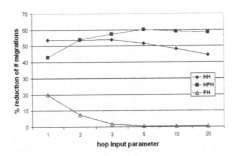

Fig. 5. Influence of the hop input parameter on the number of migrations, in terms of percentage compared to the BH

In order to assess the influence of the input hop parameter, Figure 5 shows the reduction in terms of percentage of the number of migrations, compared to the Basic Heuristic, for a hop input parameter of 3 and correlated user movements. The gain decreases for heuristics HH and PH when more hops are taken into account for the server selection. For PH, this can be explained by the fact that it is more difficult to predict the next few steps than to predict only the first next movement. Wrong predictions will result in a sub-optimal server selection and more migrations. For larger values of the hop input parameter, the PH-curve remains steady. This is explained by the order in which the predicted AGWs are checked. When one AGW cannot be reached within the latency constraint, the remainder of the AGWs in the prediction list is not checked anymore. The influence of the hop input parameter will diminish for larger values, as e.g. most servers will be within the latency constraint for the next 5 predicted AGWs, but not for the next 10, so the range of checked AGWs will be the same for both input parameter values. A similar explanation holds for the decrease of the HH-curve. Stating that a user won't visit his previous N hops is actually a negative prediction, which becomes less accurate for larger values of N. Again, we see that combining both approaches yields the best results, except for a hop input parameter of 1: at most a reduction of 60% can be obtained relative to the BH.

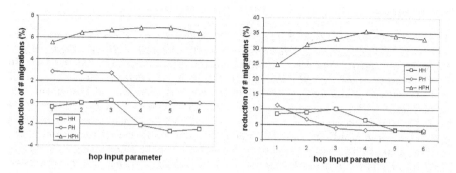

Fig. 6. Reduction in terms of percentage of the number of migrations for correlated user movements compared to randomly moving users. The left figure is for a maximum delay of 25, the right for a delay of 35.

Finally, Figure 6 shows the reduction in terms of percentage of the number of migrations when the user movements are correlated, compared to random user movements. In almost all cases, the heuristics perform better for correlated user movements. Only for the HH with a maximum latency of 25, less migrations are needed for randomly moving users. For a maximum latency of 15, the server selection is too constrained and there is no noticeable difference between both user movement patterns.

5   Conclusion and Future Work

With thin clients, applications are executed on remote servers instead of locally on the user's device. Reactions to user events can appear on the screen not before a client-server roundtrip delay. This latency, which highly influences the user experience, can be kept low if the application migrates to the server nearest to the client. In this paper, a general architecture for thin client computing was proposed. A sample train scenario revealed the trade-off between the client-server latency and the number of migrations. We detailed a theoretical model that yields the optimal distribution of the applications amongst the servers in order to minimize the number of migrations. As this model is based on the knowledge of the user movements and the calculation time increases exponentially with the number of variables, several heuristics were proposed to do the server selection in real-time. These heuristics are based on the past and predicted next user movements. For the given simulation set-up, it was shown that by taking into account user mobility information the number of migrations can be reduced by up to 60%. If prediction accuracy could be improved, an even greater reduction can be achieved. One could also adapt the value of the hop input parameter to the prediction accuracy. For highly reliable predictions, a larger value can be taken. This will be the focus of our future work.

References

1. M. Litzkow and M. Livny. Supporting Checkpointing and Process Migration Outside the UNIX Kernel. In *Proceedings of the Winter 1992 USENIX Conference.*
2. A. Barak and R. Wheeler. "MOSIX: An Integrated Multiprocessor UNIX". In *Proceedings of the USENIX Winter 1989 Technical Conference,* 1989.
3. S. Osman, D. Subhraveti, G. Su, and J. Nieh. "the Design and Implementation of Zap: A System for Migrating Computing Environment". In *Proceedings of the Fifth Symposium on Operating Systems Design and Implementation (OSDI 2002).*
4. G. Janakirama, J.R. Santos, D. Subrahveti, and Y. Turner. Cruz: Application-Transparent Distributed Checkpoint-Restart on Standard Operating Systems. In *Proc. of The International Conference on Dependable Systems & Networks,* 2005.
5. G. Su. *"MOVE: Mobility with Persistent Network Connections".* PhD thesis, Department of Computer Science, Columbia University, October 2004.
6. B. Kuntz and KL. Rajan. "MIGSOCK: Migratable TCP socket in Linux", 2002. Master's thesis, Information Networking Institutie, Carnegie Mellon University.
7. K. Lee. "Migsock vs Zap". Carnegie Mellon University, Pittsburgh, USA.
8. S.-H. Han, S.-S. Kim, and S.-H. Kim. A Framework for Selecting Appropriate Content Delivery Server Considering Round-Trip Time and Actual Serving Calls. In *10th Asia-Pacific Conference on Communications and 5th International Symposium on Multi-Dimensional Mobile Communications,* September 2004.
9. S. Bakiras. Approximate Server Selection Algorithms in Content Distribution Networks. In *IEEE International Conference on Communications,* 2005.
10. M. Tariq, R. Jain, and Kawahara T. Mobility Aware Server Selection for Mobile Streaming Multimedia Content Distribution Networks. In *Web Content Caching and Distribution: the Proceedings of the 8th International Workshop,* 2003.
11. L. Deboosere, P. Simoens, D. De Winter, F. De Turck, B. Dhoedt, and P. Demeester. Dimensioning a Wide-Area Thin-Client Computing Network Supporting Mobile Users. In *the Proceedings of The International Conference on Networking and Services,* San Jose, California, USA, July 17-19 2006.
12. P. Simoens, L. Deboosere, D. De Winter, F. De Turck, B. Dhoedt, and P. Demeester. Modelling Application Handovers for Thin-Client Mobility. In *the Proceedings of The 2006 International Conference on Pervasive Systems and Computing,* Las Vegas, Nevada, USA, June 26-29 2006.
13. L. Peterson, D. Culler, T. Anderson, and T. Roscoe. A Blueprint for Introducing Disruptive Technology into the Internet. In *Proceedings of the 1st Workshop on Hot Topics in Networks (HotNets-I),* Princeton, New Jersey, USA, October 2002.
14. D. Thain et al. Distributed Computing in Practice: the Condor Experience, 2004.
15. K. A. Fraser et al. The Xenoserver Computing Infrastructure. Technical Report UCAM-CL-TR-552, University of Cambridge, Computer Laboratory, 2003.
16. J. Chan et al. Integrating Mobility Prediction and Resource Pre-allocation into a Home-Proxy Based Wireless Internet Framework. In *Proceedings of ICON 2000.*
17. J. Chan and A. Seneviratne. A Practical User Mobility Prediction Algorithm for Supporting Adaptive QoS in Wireless Networks. In *Proceedings of ICON 1999.*
18. K. Casier et al. "Using aspect-oriented programming for event-handling in a telecom research software library". In *Poster presentation at the 8th International Conference on Software Reuse,* Spain, 2004.
19. G. L. Newhauser and L. A. Wolsey. *"Integer and Combinatorial Optimalization".* Wiley, New York, 1988.
20. B. Waxman. Routing of Multipoint Connections. In *IEEE Journal on Selected Areas in Communication,* 1988.

Author Index

Lecture Notes in Computer Science

For information about Vols. 1–4295

please contact your bookseller or Springer

Vol. 4347: J. Lopez (Ed.), Critical Information Infrastructures Security. X, 286 pages. 2006.

Vol. 4345: N. Maglaveras, I. Chouvarda, V. Koutkias, R. Brause (Eds.), Biological and Medical Data Analysis. XIII, 496 pages. 2006. (Sublibrary LNBI).

Vol. 4344: V. Gruhn, F. Oquendo (Eds.), Software Architecture. X, 245 pages. 2006.

Vol. 4342: H. de Swart, E. Orłowska, G. Schmidt, M. Roubens (Eds.), Theory and Applications of Relational Structures as Knowledge Instruments II. X, 373 pages. 2006. (Sublibrary LNAI).

Vol. 4341: P.Q. Nguyen (Ed.), Progress in Cryptology - VIETCRYPT 2006. XI, 385 pages. 2006.

Vol. 4340: R. Prodan, T. Fahringer, Grid Computing. XXIII, 317 pages. 2007.

Vol. 4339: E. Ayguadé, G. Baumgartner, J. Ramanujam, P. Sadayappan (Eds.), Languages and Compilers for Parallel Computing. XI, 476 pages. 2006.

Vol. 4338: P. Kalra, S. Peleg (Eds.), Computer Vision, Graphics and Image Processing. XV, 965 pages. 2006.

Vol. 4337: S. Arun-Kumar, N. Garg (Eds.), FSTTCS 2006: Foundations of Software Technology and Theoretical Computer Science. XIII, 430 pages. 2006.

Vol. 4335: S.A. Brueckner, S. Hassas, M. Jelasity, D. Yamins (Eds.), Engineering Self-Organising Systems. XII, 212 pages. 2007. (Sublibrary LNAI).

Vol. 4334: B. Beckert, R. Hähnle, P.H. Schmitt (Eds.), Verification of Object-Oriented Software. XXIX, 658 pages. 2007. (Sublibrary LNAI).

Vol. 4333: U. Reimer, D. Karagiannis (Eds.), Practical Aspects of Knowledge Management. XII, 338 pages. 2006. (Sublibrary LNAI).

Vol. 4332: A. Bagchi, V. Atluri (Eds.), Information Systems Security. XV, 382 pages. 2006.

Vol. 4331: G. Min, B. Di Martino, L.T. Yang, M. Guo, G. Ruenger (Eds.), Frontiers of High Performance Computing and Networking – ISPA 2006 Workshops. XXXVII, 1141 pages. 2006.

Vol. 4330: M. Guo, L.T. Yang, B. Di Martino, H.P. Zima, J. Dongarra, F. Tang (Eds.), Parallel and Distributed Processing and Applications. XVIII, 953 pages. 2006.

Vol. 4329: R. Barua, T. Lange (Eds.), Progress in Cryptology - INDOCRYPT 2006. X, 454 pages. 2006.

Vol. 4328: D. Penkler, M. Reitenspiess, F. Tam (Eds.), Service Availability. X, 289 pages. 2006.

Vol. 4327: M. Baldoni, U. Endriss (Eds.), Declarative Agent Languages and Technologies IV. VIII, 257 pages. 2006. (Sublibrary LNAI).

Vol. 4326: S. Göbel, R. Malkewitz, I. Iurgel (Eds.), Technologies for Interactive Digital Storytelling and Entertainment. X, 384 pages. 2006.

Vol. 4325: J. Cao, I. Stojmenovic, X. Jia, S.K. Das (Eds.), Mobile Ad-hoc and Sensor Networks. XIX, 887 pages. 2006.

Vol. 4323: G. Doherty, A. Blandford (Eds.), Interactive Systems. XI, 269 pages. 2007.

Vol. 4320: R. Gotzhein, R. Reed (Eds.), System Analysis and Modeling: Language Profiles. X, 229 pages. 2006.

Vol. 4319: L.-W. Chang, W.-N. Lie (Eds.), Advances in Image and Video Technology. XXVI, 1347 pages. 2006.

Vol. 4318: H. Lipmaa, M. Yung, D. Lin (Eds.), Information Security and Cryptology. XI, 305 pages. 2006.

Vol. 4317: S.K. Madria, K.T. Claypool, R. Kannan, P. Uppuluri, M.M. Gore (Eds.), Distributed Computing and Internet Technology. XIX, 466 pages. 2006.

Vol. 4316: M.M. Dalkilic, S. Kim, J. Yang (Eds.), Data Mining and Bioinformatics. VIII, 197 pages. 2006. (Sublibrary LNBI).

Vol. 4314: C. Freksa, M. Kohlhase, K. Schill (Eds.), KI 2006: Advances in Artificial Intelligence. XII, 458 pages. 2007. (Sublibrary LNAI).

Vol. 4313: T. Margaria, B. Steffen (Eds.), Leveraging Applications of Formal Methods. IX, 197 pages. 2006.

Vol. 4312: S. Sugimoto, J. Hunter, A. Rauber, A. Morishima (Eds.), Digital Libraries: Achievements, Challenges and Opportunities. XVIII, 571 pages. 2006.

Vol. 4311: K. Cho, P. Jacquet (Eds.), Technologies for Advanced Heterogeneous Networks II. XI, 253 pages. 2006.

Vol. 4310: T. Boyanov, S. Dimova, K. Georgiev, G. Nikolov (Eds.), Numerical Methods and Applications. XIII, 715 pages. 2007.

Vol. 4309: P. Inverardi, M. Jazayeri (Eds.), Software Engineering Education in the Modern Age. VIII, 207 pages. 2006.

Vol. 4308: S. Chaudhuri, S.R. Das, H.S. Paul, S. Tirthapura (Eds.), Distributed Computing and Networking. XIX, 608 pages. 2006.

Vol. 4307: P. Ning, S. Qing, N. Li (Eds.), Information and Communications Security. XIV, 558 pages. 2006.

Vol. 4306: Y. Avrithis, Y. Kompatsiaris, S. Staab, N.E. O'Connor (Eds.), Semantic Multimedia. XII, 241 pages. 2006.

Vol. 4305: A.A. Shvartsman (Ed.), Principles of Distributed Systems. XIII, 441 pages. 2006.

Vol. 4304: A. Sattar, B.-H. Kang (Eds.), AI 2006: Advances in Artificial Intelligence. XXVII, 1303 pages. 2006. (Sublibrary LNAI).

Vol. 4303: A. Hoffmann, B.-H. Kang, D. Richards, S. Tsumoto (Eds.), Advances in Knowledge Acquisition and Management. XI, 259 pages. 2006. (Sublibrary LNAI).

Vol. 4302: J. Domingo-Ferrer, L. Franconi (Eds.), Privacy in Statistical Databases. XI, 383 pages. 2006.

Vol. 4301: D. Pointcheval, Y. Mu, K. Chen (Eds.), Cryptology and Network Security. XIII, 381 pages. 2006.

Vol. 4300: Y.Q. Shi (Ed.), Transactions on Data Hiding and Multimedia Security I. IX, 139 pages. 2006.

Vol. 4299: S. Renals, S. Bengio, J.G. Fiscus (Eds.), Machine Learning for Multimodal Interaction. XII, 470 pages. 2006.

Vol. 4297: Y. Robert, M. Parashar, R. Badrinath, V.K. Prasanna (Eds.), High Performance Computing - HiPC 2006. XXIV, 642 pages. 2006.

Vol. 4296: M.S. Rhee, B. Lee (Eds.), Information Security and Cryptology – ICISC 2006. XIII, 358 pages. 2006.